THE STEP IN PARENTING

RALPH PITTMAN JR.

13TH & JOAN

For permission requests, write to the publisher, addressed "Attention: Permissions Coordinator," 205 N. Michigan Avenue, Suite #810, Chicago, IL 60601. 13th & Joan books may be purchased for educational, business or sales promotional use. For information, please email the Sales Department at sales@13thandjoan.com.

Printed in the U. S. A.

First Printing, June 2022.

Library of Congress Cataloging-in-Publication Data has been applied for.

ISBN: 978-1-7322479-7-0

THE STEP IN PARENTING

RALPH PITTMAN JR.

The Beginning

WHILE DREW AND I were dating, she was very intentional not to allow me to play the dad role. She didn't want to scare me off or put responsibility on me before we had a chance to know if our relationship would last. Her family also assisted in our dating process. Their goal was to help Drew find the man of her dreams and would take JoJo so she could go out on dates. Well, that strategy worked! Drew and I went on a date that lasted 12hrs. Her family wasn't very happy when I brought her home at 4am. To no despair, we stayed in contact and she became my wife. I would ask Drew if I could take JoJo for ice cream or take him to the park while she was working if I felt she needed a helping hand so I could build a stronger bond with him. I knew if I married Drew, he would become my son. JoJo's biological father currently wasn't around and I knew JoJo needed a male influence to help him navigate the world, instill moral and values and grow into the man he would become. I had great expectations however I didn't know what a son or father figure meant from my wifes's eyes. My thought was once we were married, I would automatically take on the father role.

In our scenario, we got married extremely fast and Drew was pregnant 2mo after. We had a huge decision to make, where do we stay to raise the kids. At the time we were in LA and didn't feel like we had much support. We could either go to NJ to my family or Chicago with her family. I spoke with Drew's mom and she said I really can't help you if you stay in LA. Drew has a big family, her mom and dad and 4 sisters. It was a no brainer and we relocated to Chicago before Machai was born. I didn't have a chance to fully assume the "Dad" role as everything was moving fast. We were living under the same roof however Drew was making moves the way she programmed and without much involvement or opinion from my side. There were a few things that I didn't like entirely too much such as JoJo staying up until any time he wanted as if he was a little rockstar in a diaper and him sleeping in the same bed. Drew wasn't receptive to him staying up late and defended by saying she's an actress and her hours flucturate. To combat, I provided studies and reports on best practices for sleeping. I also provided a guidance for the tv staying on all night and she said her parents did it with them and everyone is okay so it's not that bad. I tried developing the "My House, My Rules" concept but it quickly fell on death ears as my concerns weren't enforced. Opposed to supporting, JoJo would cry and mom would come to the rescue. I began to see a common thread, where JoJo was also learning how to get his way and It then became an issue where it was Me vs. Them.

Boiling Point where I felt I couldn't parent

Due to JoJo not receiving adequate sleep, he struggled to get up for school in the morning. Being a man, I had my way of getting you to follow directions which was to place the fear of God in you because at the end of the day, I'm the parent. JoJo stood by the sink and didn't want to brush his teeth so I "acted" as if I was going to give him a pinch and he started crying, not because of pain but because of the act. His mother ran upstairs and grabbed JoJo, asking what happened. JoJo responded, daddy pinched me. Drew grabbed JoJo and repremanded me saying I told you not to do that to him. I asked JoJo to demonstrate on his mother exactly how hard I pinched him and he barely touched his mother. I walked out the room as I felt emasculated and minimized below a child. I thought to myself if I wanted to stay in a relationship where I didn't have a parenting voice. Besides all that I've done and contributed, I should feel more respected. We ended up seeking out a marriage counselor that told us we're doing things all wrong. We didn't have a plan and it shows.

but she did ask for my thoughts to correct him sleeping in the bed.

Introduce Drew's mom, millinial

Support we had and lacked

Realistic / Unrealistic Expectations

It's either him or me

Village mindset, when JoJo's dad came home, Respect. Territorial. No this is my house.

Drew received a call from JoJo's biological dad that he came home from jail and wanted to see his son if possible. At the time Drew was still hurt by the lack of support and effort. Her perspective was, if you haven't been around or made an effort all this time, why now. JoJo doesn't need you. Besides she had me in her life which "filled" the void of JoJo's lack of a father figure. Once Drew brought the conversation and intention to my attention, I had a lot of thinking to do also. As a man or the other man in the situation, I had several thoughts run through my mind. As men, we can rightfully be territorial and protective of their castle. After I let my pride down, put myself in his shoes and think big picture, there were a few things I had to evaluate. Did JoJo's father approach the situation respectfully for my wife and also for me? Did he do anything to neglect the wellbeing and safety of JoJo? What is the intention? Is this relationship in the best interest for JoJo? I immediately thought of my father and our circumstances.

As a child, no one couldn't tell me that my father wasn't the best in the world and guess what, that's my perspective. If you measured or quantified the value of our relationship, there would be large gaps in his presence, missed games and events, missed birthdays, missed growth and bonding opportunities. Yet, my father was still the best thing that could have ever happened to me. How could this be, the heart doesn't measure value in the way our minds do. Love is blind and that's what makes love beautiful, innocent and cherished. Without love, we would be robots, incapable of forgiving or giving someone an opportunity to succeed. If we were robotic in our heart, we would leave a baby that didn't learn to walk fast enough or talk. Sometimes the greatest lessons on earth is experiencing life.

Interesting enough, Initially I didn't speak with JoJo's biological father as Drew had to feel comfortable with the interaction first however I was always by her side supporting the process. Change is very hard especially on a child therefore she wanted to make sure he wanted to really be part of his life before introducing his Father and he deciding he didn't want that role. Consistency is important to know if you're in this for the long run or if it's a nice experience because you think you should do it. Drew put JoJo's father on a call schedule to slowly introduce JoJo to his Father. JoJo visited with him as a baby but it's been years since they spoke and as a child, they don't know what a father means. The first few interactions was awkward just as any person that walks into a child's life that doesn't have kids, there is a learning process.

Adoption Because JoJo's father wasn't around, people would ask if I would adopt him, which is a great question. These are my rules on adopting in a blended family:

The Father doesn't want to be in the child's life therefore the child is fatherless

The Father is deceased.

The child is in harm or danger, therefore it's an unfit home.

The child doesn't have parents

In the event the child's mother dies, custody can be established through court order.....Find out the process. I really don't know.

If I would have adopted Josiah.

JoJo will get to a point where he seeks information and understanding for himself and he would approach his father asking, why didn't he make an effort to be in his life. His Father would more than likely respond, your parents didn't allow me to be a part of your life and pushed me out. JoJo can possibly develop resentment due to our actions, even if we felt it was in his best interest.

This is a great segway into the definition of "Dad." Dads come in all different forms, types, relationships and can be interchangeable for almost anyone providing support that uplifts positive change and growth. When my father wasn't around, coaches became father figures to me including men in the community that taught me fundamentals of manhood. When my father wasn't around, men in the community would hire me and my brother to pickup leaves. It probably was one of the worst jobs I've ever experienced but it built character and work ethic that I wouldn't trade for the world. There is a village that becomes available to instill the lessons children need to learn and the role of "dad" can often be spread throughout the village to ensure children learn fundamentals of life. This concept also applies when the dad is around. Everyone is limited on the amount of information we know. If someone excels in a certain area, send the child to exceed your own understanding as the future depends on our children being smarter and more skilled than us.

Confidence I'm a firm believer that what's for me is for me and no one can take it away. If something isn't for me, then it was only supposed to be in my life for a season and I'm fine.

Being okay with JoJo's biological dad coming into the picture Studies show, 85% of blended familes are dysfunctional.

While Drew and I were dating, she was very intentional not to allow me to play the dad role. She didn't want to scare me off or put responsibility on me before we had a chance to know if our relationship would last. Her family also assisted in our dating process. Their goal was to help Drew find the man of her dreams and would take JoJo so she could go out on dates. Well, that strategy worked! Drew and I went on a date that lasted 12hrs. Her family wasn't very happy when I brought her home at 4am. To no despair, we stayed in contact and she became my wife. I would ask Drew if I could take JoJo for ice cream or take him to the park while she was working if I felt she needed a helping hand so I could build a stronger bond with him. I knew if I married Drew, he would become my son. JoJo's biological father currently wasn't around and I knew JoJo needed a male influence to help him navigate the world, instill moral and values and grow into the man he would become. I had great expectations however I didn't know what a son or father figure meant from my wifes's eyes. My thought was once we were married, I would automatically take on the father role.

In our scenario, we got married extremely fast and Drew was pregnant 2mo after. We had a huge decision to make, where do we stay to raise the kids. At the time we were in LA and didn't feel like we had much support. We could either go to NJ to my family or Chicago with her family. I spoke with Drew's mom and she said I really can't help you if you stay in LA. Drew has a big family, her mom and dad and 4 sisters. It was a no brainer and we relocated to Chicago before Machai was born. I didn't have a chance to fully assume the "Dad" role as everything was moving fast. We were living under the same roof however Drew was making moves the way she programmed and without much involvement or opinion from my side. There were a few things that I didn't like entirely too much such as JoJo staying up until any time he wanted as if he was a little rockstar in a diaper and him sleeping in the same bed. Drew wasn't receptive to him staying up late and defended by saying she's an actress and her hours flucturate. To combat, I provided studies and reports on best practices for sleeping. I also provided a guidance for the tv staying on all night and she said her parents did it with them and everyone is okay so it's not that bad. I tried developing the "My House, My Rules" concept but it quickly fell on death ears as my concerns weren't enforced. Opposed to supporting, JoJo would cry and mom would come to the rescue. I began to see a common thread, where JoJo was also learning how to get his way and It then became an issue where it was Me vs. Them.

Boiling Point where I felt I couldn't parent

Due to JoJo not receiving adequate sleep, he struggled to get up for school in the morning. Being a man, I had my way of getting you to follow directions which was to place the fear of God in you because at the end of the day, I'm the parent. JoJo stood by the sink and didn't want to brush his teeth so I "acted" as if I was going to give him a pinch and he started crying, not because of pain but because of the act. His mother ran upstairs and grabbed JoJo, asking what happened. JoJo responded, daddy pinched me. Drew grabbed JoJo and repremanded me saying I told you not to do that to him. I asked JoJo to demonstrate on his mother exactly how hard I pinched him and he barely touched his mother. I walked out the room as I felt emasculated and minimized below a child. I thought to myself if I wanted to stay in a relationship where I didn't have a parenting voice. Besides all that I've done and contributed, I should feel more respected. We ended up seeking out a marriage counselor that told us we're doing things all wrong. We didn't have a plan and it shows.

but she did ask for my thoughts to correct him sleeping in the bed.

Introduce Drew's mom, millinial

Support we had and lacked

Realistic / Unrealistic Expectations

It's either him or me

Village mindset, when JoJo's dad came home, Respect. Territorial. No this is my house.

Drew received a call from JoJo's biological dad that he came home from jail and wanted to see his son if possible. At the time Drew was still hurt by the lack of support and effort. Her perspective was, if you haven't been around or made an effort all this time, why now. JoJo doesn't need you. Besides she had me in her life which "filled" the void of JoJo's lack of a father figure. Once Drew brought the conversation and intention to my attention, I had a lot of thinking to do also. As a man or the other man in the situation, I had several thoughts run through my mind. As men, we can rightfully be territorial and protective of their castle. After I let my pride down, put myself in his shoes and think big picture, there were a few things I had to evaluate. Did JoJo's father approach the situation respectfully for my wife and also for me? Did he do anything to neglect the wellbeing and safety of JoJo? What is the intention? Is this relationship in the best interest for JoJo? I immediately thought of my father and our circumstances.

As a child, no one couldn't tell me that my father wasn't the best in the world and guess what, that's my perspective. If you measured or quantified the value of our relationship, there would be large gaps in his presence, missed games and events, missed birthdays, missed growth and bonding opportunities. Yet, my father was still the best thing that could have ever happened to me. How could this be, the heart doesn't measure value in the way our minds do. Love is blind and that's what makes love beautiful, innocent and cherished. Without love, we would be robots, incapable of forgiving or giving someone an opportunity to succeed. If we were robotic in our heart, we would leave a baby that didn't learn to walk fast enough or talk. Sometimes the greatest lessons on earth is experiencing life.

Interesting enough, Initially I didn't speak with JoJo's biological father as Drew had to feel comfortable with the interaction first however I was always by her side supporting the process. Change is very hard especially on a child therefore she wanted to make sure he wanted to really be part of his life before introducing his Father and he deciding he didn't want that role. Consistency is important to know if you're in this for the long run or if it's a nice experience because you think you should do it. Drew put JoJo's father on a call schedule to slowly introduce JoJo to his Father. JoJo visited with him as a baby but it's been years since they spoke and as a child, they don't know what a father means. The first few interactions was awkward just as any person that walks into a child's life that doesn't have kids, there is a learning process.

Adoption Because JoJo's father wasn't around, people would ask if I would adopt him, which is a great question. These are my rules on adopting in a blended family:

The Father doesn't want to be in the child's life therefore the child is fatherless

The Father is deceased.

The child is in harm or danger, therefore it's an unfit home.

The child doesn't have parents

In the event the child's mother dies, custody can be established through court order.....Find out the process. I really don't know.

If I would have adopted Josiah.

JoJo will get to a point where he seeks information and understanding for himself and he would approach his father asking, why didn't he make an effort to be in his life. His Father would more than likely respond, your parents didn't allow me to be a part of your life and pushed me out. JoJo can possibly develop resentment due to our actions, even if we felt it was in his best interest.

This is a great segway into the definition of "Dad." Dads come in all different forms, types, relationships and can be interchangeable for almost anyone providing support that uplifts positive change and growth. When my father wasn't around, coaches became father figures to me including men in the community that taught me fundamentals of manhood. When my father wasn't around, men in the community would hire me and my brother to pickup leaves. It probably was one of the worst jobs I've ever experienced but it built character and work ethic that I wouldn't trade for the world. There is a village that becomes available to instill the lessons children need to learn and the role of "dad" can often be spread throughout the village to ensure children learn fundamentals of life. This concept also applies when the dad is around. Everyone is limited on the amount of information we know. If someone excels in a certain area, send the child to exceed your own understanding as the future depends on our children being smarter and more skilled than us.

Confidence I'm a firm believer that what's for me is for me and no one can take it away. If something isn't for me, then it was only supposed to be in my life for a season and I'm fine.

Being okay with JoJo's biological dad coming into the picture Studies show, 85% of blended familes are dysfunctional.

While Drew and I were dating, she was very intentional not to allow me to play the dad role. She didn't want to scare me off or put responsibility on me before we had a chance to know if our relationship would last. Her family also assisted in our dating process. Their goal was to help Drew find the man of her dreams and would take JoJo so she could go out on dates. Well, that strategy worked! Drew and I went on a date that lasted 12hrs. Her family wasn't very happy when I brought her home at 4am. To no despair, we stayed in contact and she became my wife. I would ask Drew if I could take JoJo for ice cream or take him to the park while she was working if I felt she needed a helping hand so I could build a stronger bond with him. I knew if I married Drew, he would become my son. JoJo's biological father currently wasn't around and I knew JoJo needed a male influence to help him navigate the world, instill moral and values and grow into the man he would become. I had great expectations however I didn't know what a son or father figure meant from my wifes's eyes. My thought was once we were married, I would automatically take on the father role.

In our scenario, we got married extremely fast and Drew was pregnant 2mo after. We had a huge decision to make, where do we stay to raise the kids. At the time we were in LA and didn't feel like we had much support. We could either go to NJ to my family or Chicago with her family. I spoke with Drew's mom and she said I really can't help you if you stay in LA. Drew has a big family, her mom and dad and 4 sisters. It was a no brainer and we relocated to Chicago before Machai was born. I didn't have a chance to fully assume the "Dad" role as everything was moving fast. We were living under the same roof however Drew was making moves the way she programmed and without much involvement or opinion from my side. There were a few things that I didn't like entirely too much such as JoJo staying up until any time he wanted as if he was a little rockstar in a diaper and him sleeping in the same bed. Drew wasn't receptive to him staying up late and defended by saying she's an actress and her hours fluctuate. To combat, I provided studies and reports on best practices for sleeping. I also provided a guidance for the tv staying on all night and she said her parents did it with them and everyone is okay so it's not that bad. I tried developing the "My House, My Rules" concept but it quickly fell on death ears as my concerns weren't enforced. Opposed to supporting, JoJo would cry and mom would come to the rescue. I began to see a common thread, where JoJo was also learning how to get his way and It then became an issue where it was Me vs. Them.

Boiling Point where I felt I couldn't parent

Due to JoJo not receiving adequate sleep, he struggled to get up for school in the morning. Being a man, I had my way of getting you to follow directions which was to place the fear of God in you because at the end of the day, I'm the parent. JoJo stood by the sink and didn't want to brush his teeth so I "acted" as if I was going to give him a pinch and he started crying, not because of pain but because of the act. His mother ran upstairs and grabbed JoJo, asking what happened. JoJo responded, daddy pinched me. Drew grabbed JoJo and reprimanded me saying I told you not to do that to him. I asked JoJo to demonstrate on his mother exactly how hard I pinched him and he barely touched his mother. I walked out the room as I felt emasculated and minimized below a child. I thought to myself if I wanted to stay in a relationship where I didn't have a parenting voice. Besides all that I've done and contributed, I should feel more respected. We ended up seeking out a marriage counselor that told us we're doing things all wrong. We didn't have a plan and it shows.

but she did ask for my thoughts to correct him sleeping in the bed.

Introduce Drew's mom, millinial

Support we had and lacked

Realistic / Unrealistic Expectations

It's either him or me

Village mindset, when JoJo's dad came home, Respect. Territorial. No this is my house.

Drew received a call from JoJo's biological dad that he came home from jail and wanted to see his son if possible. At the time Drew was still hurt by the lack of support and effort. Her perspective was, if you haven't been around or made an effort all this time, why now. JoJo doesn't need you. Besides she had me in her life which "filled" the void of JoJo's lack of a father figure. Once Drew brought the conversation and intention to my attention, I had a lot of thinking to do also. As a man or the other man in the situation, I had several thoughts run through my mind. As men, we can rightfully be territorial and protective of their castle. After I let my pride down, put myself in his shoes and think big picture, there were a few things I had to evaluate. Did JoJo's father approach the situation respectfully for my wife and also for me? Did he do anything to neglect the wellbeing and safety of JoJo? What is the intention? Is this relationship in the best interest for JoJo? I immediately thought of my father and our circumstances.

As a child, no one couldn't tell me that my father wasn't the best in the world and guess what, that's my perspective. If you measured or quantified the value of our relationship, there would be large gaps in his presence, missed games and events, missed birthdays, missed growth and bonding opportunities. Yet, my father was still the best thing that could have ever happened to me. How could this be, the heart doesn't measure value in the way our minds do. Love is blind and that's what makes love beautiful, innocent and cherished. Without love, we would be robots, incapable of forgiving or giving someone an opportunity to succeed.

If we were robotic in our heart, we would leave a baby that didn't learn to walk fast enough or talk. Sometimes the greatest lessons on earth is experiencing life.

Interesting enough, Initially I didn't speak with JoJo's biological father as Drew had to feel comfortable with the interaction first however I was always by her side supporting the process. Change is very hard especially on a child therefore she wanted to make sure he wanted to really be part of his life before introducing his Father and he deciding he didn't want that role. Consistency is important to know if you're in this for the long run or if it's a nice experience because you think you should do it. Drew put JoJo's father on a call schedule to slowly introduce JoJo to his Father. JoJo visited with him as a baby but it's been years since they spoke and as a child, they don't know what a father means. The first few interactions was awkward just as any person that walks into a child's life that doesn't have kids, there is a learning process.

Adoption Because JoJo's father wasn't around, people would ask if I would adopt him, which is a great question. These are my rules on adopting in a blended family:

The Father doesn't want to be in the child's life therefore the child is fatherless

The Father is deceased.

The child is in harm or danger, therefore it's an unfit home.

The child doesn't have parents

In the event the child's mother dies, custody can be established through court order.....Find out the process. I really don't know.

If I would have adopted Josiah.

JoJo will get to a point where he seeks information and understanding for himself and he would approach his father asking, why didn't he make an effort to be in his life. His Father would more than likely respond, your parents didn't allow me to be a part of your life and pushed me out. JoJo can possibly develop resentment due to our actions, even if we felt it was in his best interest.

13

This is a great segway into the definition of "Dad." Dads come in all different forms, types, relationships and can be interchangeable for almost anyone providing support that uplifts positive change and growth. When my father wasn't around, coaches became father figures to me including men in the community that taught me fundamentals of manhood. When my father wasn't around, men in the community would hire me and my brother to pickup leaves. It probably was one of the worst jobs I've ever experienced but it built character and work ethic that I wouldn't trade for the world. There is a village that becomes available to instill the lessons children need to learn and the role of "dad" can often be spread throughout the village to ensure children learn fundamentals of life. This concept also applies when the dad is around. Everyone is limited on the amount of information we know. If someone excels in a certain area, send the child to exceed your own understanding as the future depends on our children being smarter and more skilled than us.

Confidence I'm a firm believer that what's for me is for me and no one can take it away. If something isn't for me, then it was only supposed to be in my life for a season and I'm fine.

Being okay with JoJo's biological dad coming into the picture

Studies show, 85% of blended familes are dysfunctional. While Drew and I were dating, she was very intentional not to allow me to play the dad role. She didn't want to scare me off or put responsibility on me before we had a chance to know if our relationship would last. Her family also assisted in our dating process. Their goal was to help Drew find the man of her dreams and would take JoJo so she could go out on dates. Well, that strategy worked! Drew and I went on a date that lasted 12hrs. Her family wasn't very happy when I brought her home at 4am. To no despair, we stayed in contact and she became my wife. I would ask Drew if I could take JoJo for ice cream or take him to the park while she was working if I felt she needed a helping hand so I could build a stronger bond with him. I knew if I married Drew, he would become my son. JoJo's biological father currently

wasn't around and I knew JoJo needed a male influence to help him navigate the world, instill moral and values and grow into the man he would become. I had great expectations however I didn't know what a son or father figure meant from my wifes's eyes. My thought was once we were married, I would automatically take on the father role.

In our scenario, we got married extremely fast and Drew was pregnant 2mo after. We had a huge decision to make, where do we stay to raise the kids. At the time we were in LA and didn't feel like we had much support. We could either go to NJ to my family or Chicago with her family. I spoke with Drew's mom and she said I really can't help you if you stay in LA. Drew has a big family, her mom and dad and 4 sisters. It was a no brainer and we relocated to Chicago before Machai was born. I didn't have a chance to fully assume the "Dad" role as everything was moving fast. We were living under the same roof however Drew was making moves the way she programmed and without much involvement or opinion from my side. There were a few things that I didn't like entirely too much such as JoJo staying up until any time he wanted as if he was a little rockstar in a diaper and him sleeping in the same bed. Drew wasn't receptive to him staying up late and defended by saying she's an actress and her hours flucturate. To combat, I provided studies and reports on best practices for sleeping. I also provided a guidance for the tv staying on all night and she said her parents did it with them and everyone is okay so it's not that bad. I tried developing the "My House, My Rules" concept but it quickly fell on death ears as my concerns weren't enforced. Opposed to supporting, JoJo would cry and mom would come to the rescue. I began to see a common thread, where JoJo was also learning how to get his way and It then became an issue where it was Me vs. Them.

Boiling Point where I felt I couldn't parent

Due to JoJo not receiving adequate sleep, he struggled to get up for school in the morning. Being a man, I had my way of getting you to follow directions which was to place the fear of God

in you because at the end of the day, I'm the parent. JoJo stood by the sink and didn't want to brush his teeth so I "acted" as if I was going to give him a pinch and he started crying, not because of pain but because of the act. His mother ran upstairs and grabbed JoJo, asking what happened. JoJo responded, daddy pinched me. Drew grabbed JoJo and reprimanded me saying I told you not to do that to him. I asked JoJo to demonstrate on his mother exactly how hard I pinched him and he barely touched his mother. I walked out the room as I felt emasculated and minimized below a child. I thought to myself if I wanted to stay in a relationship where I didn't have a parenting voice. Besides all that I've done and contributed, I should feel more respected. We ended up seeking out a marriage counselor that told us we're doing things all wrong. We didn't have a plan and it shows.

but she did ask for my thoughts to correct him sleeping in the bed.

Introduce Drew's mom, millinial

Support we had and lacked

Realistic / Unrealistic Expectations

It's either him or me

Village mindset, when JoJo's dad came home, Respect. Territorial. No this is my house.

Drew received a call from JoJo's biological dad that he came home from jail and wanted to see his son if possible. At the time Drew was still hurt by the lack of support and effort. Her perspective was, if you haven't been around or made an effort all this time, why now. JoJo doesn't need you. Besides she had me in her life which "filled" the void of JoJo's lack of a father figure. Once Drew brought the conversation and intention to my attention, I had a lot of thinking to do also. As a man or the other man in the situation, I had several thoughts run through my mind. As men, we can rightfully be territorial and protective of their castle. After I let my pride down, put myself in his shoes and think big picture, there were a few things I had to evaluate. Did JoJo's father approach the situation respectfully for my wife and

also for me? Did he do anything to neglect the wellbeing and safety of JoJo? What is the intention? Is this relationship in the best interest for JoJo? I immediately thought of my father and our circumstances.

As a child, no one couldn't tell me that my father wasn't the best in the world and guess what, that's my perspective. If you measured or quantified the value of our relationship, there would be large gaps in his presence, missed games and events, missed birthdays, missed growth and bonding opportunities. Yet, my father was still the best thing that could have ever happened to me. How could this be, the heart doesn't measure value in the way our minds do. Love is blind and that's what makes love beautiful, innocent and cherished. Without love, we would be robots, incapable of forgiving or giving someone an opportunity to succeed. If we were robotic in our heart, we would leave a baby that didn't learn to walk fast enough or talk. Sometimes the greatest lessons on earth is experiencing life.

Interesting enough, Initially I didn't speak with JoJo's biological father as Drew had to feel comfortable with the interaction first however I was always by her side supporting the process. Change is very hard especially on a child therefore she wanted to make sure he wanted to really be part of his life before introducing his Father and he deciding he didn't want that role. Consistency is important to know if you're in this for the long run or if it's a nice experience because you think you should do it. Drew put JoJo's father on a call schedule to slowly introduce JoJo to his Father. JoJo visited with him as a baby but it's been years since they spoke and as a child, they don't know what a father means. The first few interactions was awkward just as any person that walks into a child's life that doesn't have kids, there is a learning process.

Adoption Because JoJo's father wasn't around, people would ask if I would adopt him, which is a great question. These are my rules on adopting in a blended family:

The Father doesn't want to be in the child's life therefore the child is fatherless

The Father is deceased.

The child is in harm or danger, therefore it's an unfit home.

The child doesn't have parents

In the event the child's mother dies, custody can be established through court order......Find out the process. I really don't know.

If I would have adopted Josiah.

JoJo will get to a point where he seeks information and understanding for himself and he would approach his father asking, why didn't he make an effort to be in his life. His Father would more than likely respond, your parents didn't allow me to be a part of your life and pushed me out. JoJo can possibly develop resentment due to our actions, even if we felt it was in his best interest.

This is a great segway into the definition of "Dad." Dads come in all different forms, types, relationships and can be interchangeable for almost anyone providing support that uplifts positive change and growth. When my father wasn't around, coaches became father figures to me including men in the community that taught me fundamentals of manhood. When my father wasn't around, men in the community would hire me and my brother to pickup leaves. It probably was one of the worst jobs I've ever experienced but it built character and work ethic that I wouldn't trade for the world. There is a village that becomes available to instill the lessons children need to learn and the role of "dad" can often be spread throughout the village to ensure children learn fundamentals of life. This concept also applies when the dad is around. Everyone is limited on the amount of information we know. If someone excels in a certain area, send the child to exceed your own understanding as the future depends on our children being smarter and more skilled than us.

Confidence I'm a firm believer that what's for me is for me and no one can take it away. If something isn't for me, then it was only supposed to be in my life for a season and I'm fine.

Being okay with JoJo's biological dad coming into the picture Studies show, 85% of blended familes are dysfunctional. While Drew and I were dating, she was very intentional not to allow me to play the dad role. She didn't want to scare me off or put responsibility on me before we had a chance to know if our relationship would last. Her family also assisted in our dating process. Their goal was to help Drew find the man of her dreams and would take JoJo so she could go out on dates. Well, that strategy worked! Drew and I went on a date that lasted 12hrs. Her family wasn't very happy when I brought her home at 4am. To no despair, we stayed in contact and she became my wife. I would ask Drew if I could take JoJo for ice cream or take him to the park while she was working if I felt she needed a helping hand so I could build a stronger bond with him. I knew if I married Drew, he would become my son. JoJo's biological father currently wasn't around and I knew JoJo needed a male influence to help him navigate the world, instill moral and values and grow into the man he would become. I had great expectations however I didn't know what a son or father figure meant from my wifes's eyes. My thought was once we were married, I would automatically take on the father role.

In our scenario, we got married extremely fast and Drew was pregnant 2mo after. We had a huge decision to make, where do we stay to raise the kids. At the time we were in LA and didn't feel like we had much support. We could either go to NJ to my family or Chicago with her family. I spoke with Drew's mom and she said I really can't help you if you stay in LA. Drew has a big family, her mom and dad and 4 sisters. It was a no brainer and we relocated to Chicago before Machai was born. I didn't have a chance to fully assume the "Dad" role as everything was moving fast. We were living under the same roof however Drew was making moves the way she programmed and without much involvement or opinion from my side. There were a few things that I didn't like entirely too much such as JoJo staying up until any time he wanted as if he was a little rockstar in a diaper and

him sleeping in the same bed. Drew wasn't receptive to him staying up late and defended by saying she's an actress and her hours flucturate. To combat, I provided studies and reports on best practices for sleeping. I also provided a guidance for the tv staying on all night and she said her parents did it with them and everyone is okay so it's not that bad. I tried developing the "My House, My Rules" concept but it quickly fell on death ears as my concerns weren't enforced. Opposed to supporting, JoJo would cry and mom would come to the rescue. I began to see a common thread, where JoJo was also learning how to get his way and It then became an issue where it was Me vs. Them.

Boiling Point where I felt I couldn't parent

Due to JoJo not receiving adequate sleep, he struggled to get up for school in the morning. Being a man, I had my way of getting you to follow directions which was to place the fear of God in you because at the end of the day, I'm the parent. JoJo stood by the sink and didn't want to brush his teeth so I "acted" as if I was going to give him a pinch and he started crying, not because of pain but because of the act. His mother ran upstairs and grabbed JoJo, asking what happened. JoJo responded, daddy pinched me. Drew grabbed JoJo and reprimanded me saying I told you not to do that to him. I asked JoJo to demonstrate on his mother exactly how hard I pinched him and he barely touched his mother. I walked out the room as I felt emasculated and minimized below a child. I thought to myself if I wanted to stay in a relationship where I didn't have a parenting voice. Besides all that I've done and contributed, I should feel more respected. We ended up seeking out a marriage counselor that told us we're doing things all wrong. We didn't have a plan and it shows.

but she did ask for my thoughts to correct him sleeping in the bed.

Introduce Drew's mom, millinial

Support we had and lacked

Realistic / Unrealistic Expectations

It's either him or me

Village mindset, when JoJo's dad came home, Respect. Territorial. No this is my house.

Drew received a call from JoJo's biological dad that he came home from jail and wanted to see his son if possible. At the time Drew was still hurt by the lack of support and effort. Her perspective was, if you haven't been around or made an effort all this time, why now. JoJo doesn't need you. Besides she had me in her life which "filled" the void of JoJo's lack of a father figure. Once Drew brought the conversation and intention to my attention, I had a lot of thinking to do also. As a man or the other man in the situation, I had several thoughts run through my mind. As men, we can rightfully be territorial and protective of their castle. After I let my pride down, put myself in his shoes and think big picture, there were a few things I had to evaluate. Did JoJo's father approach the situation respectfully for my wife and also for me? Did he do anything to neglect the wellbeing and safety of JoJo? What is the intention? Is this relationship in the best interest for JoJo? I immediately thought of my father and our circumstances.

As a child, no one couldn't tell me that my father wasn't the best in the world and guess what, that's my perspective. If you measured or quantified the value of our relationship, there would be large gaps in his presence, missed games and events, missed birthdays, missed growth and bonding opportunities. Yet, my father was still the best thing that could have ever happened to me. How could this be, the heart doesn't measure value in the way our minds do. Love is blind and that's what makes love beautiful, innocent and cherished. Without love, we would be robots, incapable of forgiving or giving someone an opportunity to succeed. If we were robotic in our heart, we would leave a baby that didn't learn to walk fast enough or talk. Sometimes the greatest lessons on earth is experiencing life.

Interesting enough, Initially I didn't speak with JoJo's biological father as Drew had to feel comfortable with the interaction first however I was always by her side supporting the process.

Change is very hard especially on a child therefore she wanted to make sure he wanted to really be part of his life before introducing his Father and he deciding he didn't want that role. Consistency is important to know if you're in this for the long run or if it's a nice experience because you think you should do it. Drew put JoJo's father on a call schedule to slowly introduce JoJo to his Father. JoJo visited with him as a baby but it's been years since they spoke and as a child, they don't know what a father means. The first few interactions was awkward just as any person that walks into a child's life that doesn't have kids, there is a learning process.

Adoption Because JoJo's father wasn't around, people would ask if I would adopt him, which is a great question. These are my rules on adopting in a blended family:

The Father doesn't want to be in the child's life therefore the child is fatherless

The Father is deceased.

The child is in harm or danger, therefore it's an unfit home.

The child doesn't have parents

In the event the child's mother dies, custody can be established through court order.....Find out the process. I really don't know.

If I would have adopted Josiah.

JoJo will get to a point where he seeks information and understanding for himself and he would approach his father asking, why didn't he make an effort to be in his life. His Father would more than likely respond, your parents didn't allow me to be a part of your life and pushed me out. JoJo can possibly develop resentment due to our actions, even if we felt it was in his best interest.

This is a great segway into the definition of "Dad." Dads come in all different forms, types, relationships and can be interchangeable for almost anyone providing support that uplifts positive change and growth. When my father wasn't around, coaches became father figures to me including men in the community that taught me fundamentals of manhood. When my father wasn't

around, men in the community would hire me and my brother to pickup leaves. It probably was one of the worst jobs I've ever experienced but it built character and work ethic that I wouldn't trade for the world. There is a village that becomes available to instill the lessons children need to learn and the role of "dad" can often be spread throughout the village to ensure children learn fundamentals of life. This concept also applies when the dad is around. Everyone is limited on the amount of information we know. If someone excels in a certain area, send the child to exceed your own understanding as the future depends on our children being smarter and more skilled than us.

Confidence I'm a firm believer that what's for me is for me and no one can take it away. If something isn't for me, then it was only supposed to be in my life for a season and I'm fine.

Being okay with JoJo's biological dad coming into the picture Studies show, 85% of blended familes are dysfunctional. While Drew and I were dating, she was very intentional not to allow me to play the dad role. She didn't want to scare me off or put responsibility on me before we had a chance to know if our relationship would last. Her family also assisted in our dating process. Their goal was to help Drew find the man of her dreams and would take JoJo so she could go out on dates. Well, that strategy worked! Drew and I went on a date that lasted 12hrs. Her family wasn't very happy when I brought her home at 4am. To no despair, we stayed in contact and she became my wife. I would ask Drew if I could take JoJo for ice cream or take him to the park while she was working if I felt she needed a helping hand so I could build a stronger bond with him. I knew if I married Drew, he would become my son. JoJo's biological father currently wasn't around and I knew JoJo needed a male influence to help him navigate the world, instill moral and values and grow into the man he would become. I had great expectations however I didn't know what a son or father figure meant from my wifes's eyes. My thought was once we were married, I would automatically take on the father role.

In our scenario, we got married extremely fast and Drew was pregnant 2mo after. We had a huge decision to make, where do we stay to raise the kids. At the time we were in LA and didn't feel like we had much support. We could either go to NJ to my family or Chicago with her family. I spoke with Drew's mom and she said I really can't help you if you stay in LA. Drew has a big family, her mom and dad and 4 sisters. It was a no brainer and we relocated to Chicago before Machai was born. I didn't have a chance to fully assume the "Dad" role as everything was moving fast. We were living under the same roof however Drew was making moves the way she programmed and without much involvement or opinion from my side. There were a few things that I didn't like entirely too much such as JoJo staying up until any time he wanted as if he was a little rockstar in a diaper and him sleeping in the same bed. Drew wasn't receptive to him staying up late and defended by saying she's an actress and her hours flucturate. To combat, I provided studies and reports on best practices for sleeping. I also provided a guidance for the tv staying on all night and she said her parents did it with them and everyone is okay so it's not that bad. I tried developing the "My House, My Rules" concept but it quickly fell on death ears as my concerns weren't enforced. Opposed to supporting, JoJo would cry and mom would come to the rescue. I began to see a common thread, where JoJo was also learning how to get his way and It then became an issue where it was Me vs. Them.

Boiling Point where I felt I couldn't parent

Due to JoJo not receiving adequate sleep, he struggled to get up for school in the morning. Being a man, I had my way of getting you to follow directions which was to place the fear of God in you because at the end of the day, I'm the parent. JoJo stood by the sink and didn't want to brush his teeth so I "acted" as if I was going to give him a pinch and he started crying, not because of pain but because of the act. His mother ran upstairs and grabbed JoJo, asking what happened. JoJo responded, daddy pinched me. Drew grabbed JoJo and repremanded me saying I

told you not to do that to him. I asked JoJo to demonstrate on his mother exactly how hard I pinched him and he barely touched his mother. I walked out the room as I felt emasculated and minimized below a child. I thought to myself if I wanted to stay in a relationship where I didn't have a parenting voice. Besides all that I've done and contributed, I should feel more respected. We ended up seeking out a marriage counselor that told us we're doing things all wrong. We didn't have a plan and it shows.

but she did ask for my thoughts to correct him sleeping in the bed.

Introduce Drew's mom, millinial

Support We Had and Lacked

DREW RECEIVED A call from JoJo's biological dad that he came home from jail and wanted to see his son if possible. At the time Drew was still hurt by the lack of support and effort. Her perspective was, if you haven't been around or made an effort all this time, why now. JoJo doesn't need you. Besides she had me in her life which "filled" the void of JoJo's lack of a father figure. Once Drew brought the conversation and intention to my attention, I had a lot of thinking to do also. As a man or the other man in the situation, I had several thoughts run through my mind. As men, we can rightfully be territorial and protective of their castle. After I let my pride down, put myself in his shoes and think big picture, there were a few things I had to evaluate. Did JoJo's father approach the situation respectfully for my wife and also for me? Did he do anything to neglect the wellbeing and safety of JoJo? What is the intention? Is this relationship in the best interest for JoJo? I immediately thought of my father and our circumstances.

As a child, no one couldn't tell me that my father wasn't the best in the world and guess what, that's my perspective. If you measured or quantified the value of our relationship, there would be large gaps in his presence, missed games and events, missed birthdays, missed growth and bonding opportunities.

Yet, my father was still the best thing that could have ever happened to me. How could this be, the heart doesn't measure value in the way our minds do. Love is blind and that's what makes love beautiful, innocent and cherished. Without love, we would be robots, incapable of forgiving or giving someone an opportunity to succeed. If we were robotic in our heart, we would leave a baby that didn't learn to walk fast enough or talk. Sometimes the greatest lessons on earth is experiencing life.

Interesting enough, Initially I didn't speak with JoJo's biological father as Drew had to feel comfortable with the interaction first however I was always by her side supporting the process. Change is very hard especially on a child therefore she wanted to make sure he wanted to really be part of his life before introducing his Father and he deciding he didn't want that role. Consistency is important to know if you're in this for the long run or if it's a nice experience because you think you should do it. Drew put JoJo's father on a call schedule to slowly introduce JoJo to his Father. JoJo visited with him as a baby but it's been years since they spoke and as a child, they don't know what a father means. The first few interactions was awkward just as any person that walks into a child's life that doesn't have kids, there is a learning process.

Adoption Because JoJo's father wasn't around, people would ask if I would adopt him, which is a great question. These are my rules on adopting in a blended family:

The Father doesn't want to be in the child's life therefore the child is fatherless

The Father is deceased.

The child is in harm or danger, therefore it's an unfit home.

The child doesn't have parents

In the event the child's mother dies, custody can be established through court order.....Find out the process. I really don't know.

If I would have adopted Josiah.

JoJo will get to a point where he seeks information and understanding for himself and he would approach his father asking, why didn't he make an effort to be in his life. His Father would more than likely respond, your parents didn't allow me to be a part of your life and pushed me out. JoJo can possibly develop resentment due to our actions, even if we felt it was in his best interest.

This is a great segway into the definition of "Dad." Dads come in all different forms, types, relationships and can be interchangeable for almost anyone providing support that uplifts positive change and growth. When my father wasn't around, coaches became father figures to me including men in the community that taught me fundamentals of manhood. When my father wasn't around, men in the community would hire me and my brother to pickup leaves. It probably was one of the worst jobs I've ever experienced but it built character and work ethic that I wouldn't trade for the world. There is a village that becomes available to instill the lessons children need to learn and the role of "dad" can often be spread throughout the village to ensure children learn fundamentals of life. This concept also applies when the dad is around. Everyone is limited on the amount of information we know. If someone excels in a certain area, send the child to exceed your own understanding as the future depends on our children being smarter and more skilled than us.

Being okay with JoJo's biological dad coming into the picture Studies show, 85% of blended familes are dysfunctional. While Drew and I were dating, she was very intentional not to allow me to play the dad role. She didn't want to scare me off or put responsibility on me before we had a chance to know if our relationship would last. Her family also assisted in our dating process. Their goal was to help Drew find the man of her dreams and would take JoJo so she could go out on dates. Well, that strategy worked! Drew and I went on a date that lasted 12hrs. Her family wasn't very happy when I brought her home at 4am. To no despair, we stayed in contact and she became my wife. I would ask Drew if I could take JoJo for ice cream or take him to the park while she was working if I felt she needed a helping hand

so I could build a stronger bond with him. I knew if I married Drew, he would become my son. JoJo's biological father currently wasn't around and I knew JoJo needed a male influence to help him navigate the world, instill moral and values and grow into the man he would become. I had great expectations however I didn't know what a son or father figure meant from my wifes's eyes. My thought was once we were married, I would automatically take on the father role.

In our scenario, we got married extremely fast and Drew was pregnant 2mo after. We had a huge decision to make, where do we stay to raise the kids. At the time we were in LA and didn't feel like we had much support. We could either go to NJ to my family or Chicago with her family. I spoke with Drew's mom and she said I really can't help you if you stay in LA. Drew has a big family, her mom and dad and 4 sisters. It was a no brainer and we relocated to Chicago before Machai was born. I didn't have a chance to fully assume the "Dad" role as everything was moving fast. We were living under the same roof however Drew was making moves the way she programmed and without much involvement or opinion from my side. There were a few things that I didn't like entirely too much such as JoJo staying up until any time he wanted as if he was a little rockstar in a diaper and him sleeping in the same bed. Drew wasn't receptive to him staying up late and defended by saying she's an actress and her hours flucturate. To combat, I provided studies and reports on best practices for sleeping. I also provided a guidance for the tv staying on all night and she said her parents did it with them and everyone is okay so it's not that bad. I tried developing the "My House, My Rules" concept but it quickly fell on death ears as my concerns weren't enforced. Opposed to supporting, JoJo would cry and mom would come to the rescue. I began to see a common thread, where JoJo was also learning how to get his way and It then became an issue where it was Me vs. Them.

Due to JoJo not receiving adequate sleep, he struggled to get up for school in the morning. Being a man, I had my way of getting you to follow directions which was to place the fear of God in you because at the end of the day, I'm the parent. JoJo stood by the sink and didn't want to brush his teeth so I "acted" as if I was going to give him a pinch and he started crying, not because of pain but because of the act. His mother ran upstairs and grabbed JoJo, asking what happened. JoJo responded, daddy pinched me. Drew grabbed JoJo and repremanded me saying I told you not to do that to him. I asked JoJo to demonstrate on his mother exactly how hard I pinched him and he barely touched his mother. I walked out the room as I felt emasculated and minimized below a child. I thought to myself if I wanted to stay in a relationship where I didn't have a parenting voice. Besides all that I've done and contributed, I should feel more respected. We ended up seeking out a marriage counselor that told us we're doing things all wrong. We didn't have a plan and it shows.

but she did ask for my thoughts to correct him sleeping in the bed.

Introduce Drew's mom, millinial

Support we had and lacked

Realistic / Unrealistic Expectations

It's either him or me

Village mindset, when JoJo's dad came home, Respect. Territorial. No this is my house.

Drew received a call from JoJo's biological dad that he came home from jail and wanted to see his son if possible. At the time Drew was still hurt by the lack of support and effort. Her perspective was, if you haven't been around or made an effort all this time, why now. JoJo doesn't need you. Besides she had me in her life which "filled" the void of JoJo's lack of a father figure. Once Drew brought the conversation and intention to my attention, I had a lot of thinking to do also. As a man or the other man in the situation, I had several thoughts run through my mind. As men, we can rightfully be territorial and protective of their castle. After I let my pride down, put myself in his shoes and think big picture, there were a few things I had to evaluate. Did

JoJo's father approach the situation respectfully for my wife and also for me? Did he do anything to neglect the wellbeing and safety of JoJo? What is the intention? Is this relationship in the best interest for JoJo? I immediately thought of my father and our circumstances.

As a child, no one couldn't tell me that my father wasn't the best in the world and guess what, that's my perspective. If you measured or quantified the value of our relationship, there would be large gaps in his presence, missed games and events, missed birthdays, missed growth and bonding opportunities. Yet, my father was still the best thing that could have ever happened to me. How could this be, the heart doesn't measure value in the way our minds do. Love is blind and that's what makes love beautiful, innocent and cherished. Without love, we would be robots, incapable of forgiving or giving someone an opportunity to succeed. If we were robotic in our heart, we would leave a baby that didn't learn to walk fast enough or talk. Sometimes the greatest lessons on earth is experiencing life.

Interesting enough, Initially I didn't speak with JoJo's biological father as Drew had to feel comfortable with the interaction first however I was always by her side supporting the process. Change is very hard especially on a child therefore she wanted to make sure he wanted to really be part of his life before introducing his Father and he deciding he didn't want that role. Consistency is important to know if you're in this for the long run or if it's a nice experience because you think you should do it. Drew put JoJo's father on a call schedule to slowly introduce JoJo to his Father. JoJo visited with him as a baby but it's been years since they spoke and as a child, they don't know what a father means. The first few interactions was awkward just as any person that walks into a child's life that doesn't have kids, there is a learning process.

Adoption Because JoJo's father wasn't around, people would ask if I would adopt him, which is a great question. These are my rules on adopting in a blended family:

The Father doesn't want to be in the child's life therefore the child is fatherless

The Father is deceased.

The child is in harm or danger, therefore it's an unfit home.

The child doesn't have parents

In the event the child's mother dies, custody can be established through court order.....Find out the process. I really don't know.

If I would have adopted Josiah.

JoJo will get to a point where he seeks information and understanding for himself and he would approach his father asking, why didn't he make an effort to be in his life. His Father would more than likely respond, your parents didn't allow me to be a part of your life and pushed me out. JoJo can possibly develop resentment due to our actions, even if we felt it was in his best interest.

This is a great segway into the definition of "Dad." Dads come in all different forms, types, relationships and can be interchangeable for almost anyone providing support that uplifts positive change and growth. When my father wasn't around, coaches became father figures to me including men in the community that taught me fundamentals of manhood. When my father wasn't around, men in the community would hire me and my brother to pickup leaves. It probably was one of the worst jobs I've ever experienced but it built character and work ethic that I wouldn't trade for the world. There is a village that becomes available to instill the lessons children need to learn and the role of "dad" can often be spread throughout the village to ensure children learn fundamentals of life. This concept also applies when the dad is around. Everyone is limited on the amount of information we know. If someone excels in a certain area, send the child to exceed your own understanding as the future depends on our children being smarter and more skilled than us.

Confidence I'm a firm believer that what's for me is for me and no one can take it away. If something isn't for me, then it was only supposed to be in my life for a season and I'm fine.

Being okay with JoJo's biological dad coming into the picture
Studies show, 85% of blended familes are dysfunctional.
While Drew and I were dating, she was very intentional not to
allow me to play the dad role. She didn't want to scare me off
or put responsibility on me before we had a chance to know if
our relationship would last. Her family also assisted in our dating
process. Their goal was to help Drew find the man of her dreams
and would take JoJo so she could go out on dates. Well, that strategy worked! Drew and I went on a date that lasted 12hrs. Her
family wasn't very happy when I brought her home at 4am. To
no despair, we stayed in contact and she became my wife. I would
ask Drew if I could take JoJo for ice cream or take him to the
park while she was working if I felt she needed a helping hand
so I could build a stronger bond with him. I knew if I married
Drew, he would become my son. JoJo's biological father currently wasn't around and I knew JoJo needed a male influence to
help him navigate the world, instill moral and values and grow
into the man he would become. I had great expectations however
I didn't know what a son or father figure meant from my wifes's
eyes. My thought was once we were married, I would automatically take on the father role.

In our scenario, we got married extremely fast and Drew was
pregnant 2mo after. We had a huge decision to make, where do
we stay to raise the kids. At the time we were in LA and didn't
feel like we had much support. We could either go to NJ to my
family or Chicago with her family. I spoke with Drew's mom
and she said I really can't help you if you stay in LA. Drew has
a big family, her mom and dad and 4 sisters. It was a no brainer
and we relocated to Chicago before Machai was born. I didn't
have a chance to fully assume the "Dad" role as everything was
moving fast. We were living under the same roof however Drew
was making moves the way she programmed and without much
involvement or opinion from my side. There were a few things
that I didn't like entirely too much such as JoJo staying up until
any time he wanted as if he was a little rockstar in a diaper and

him sleeping in the same bed. Drew wasn't receptive to him staying up late and defended by saying she's an actress and her hours flucturate. To combat, I provided studies and reports on best practices for sleeping. I also provided a guidance for the tv staying on all night and she said her parents did it with them and everyone is okay so it's not that bad. I tried developing the "My House, My Rules" concept but it quickly fell on death ears as my concerns weren't enforced. Opposed to supporting, JoJo would cry and mom would come to the rescue. I began to see a common thread, where JoJo was also learning how to get his way and It then became an issue where it was Me vs. Them.

Boiling Point where I felt I couldn't parent

Due to JoJo not receiving adequate sleep, he struggled to get up for school in the morning. Being a man, I had my way of getting you to follow directions which was to place the fear of God in you because at the end of the day, I'm the parent. JoJo stood by the sink and didn't want to brush his teeth so I "acted" as if I was going to give him a pinch and he started crying, not because of pain but because of the act. His mother ran upstairs and grabbed JoJo, asking what happened. JoJo responded, daddy pinched me. Drew grabbed JoJo and repremanded me saying I told you not to do that to him. I asked JoJo to demonstrate on his mother exactly how hard I pinched him and he barely touched his mother. I walked out the room as I felt emasculated and minimized below a child. I thought to myself if I wanted to stay in a relationship where I didn't have a parenting voice. Besides all that I've done and contributed, I should feel more respected. We ended up seeking out a marriage counselor that told us we're doing things all wrong. We didn't have a plan and it shows.

but she did ask for my thoughts to correct him sleeping in the bed.

Introduce Drew's mom, millinial

Support we had and lacked

Realistic / Unrealistic Expectations

It's either him or me

Village mindset, when JoJo's dad came home, Respect. Territorial. No this is my house.

Drew received a call from JoJo's biological dad that he came home from jail and wanted to see his son if possible. At the time Drew was still hurt by the lack of support and effort. Her perspective was, if you haven't been around or made an effort all this time, why now. JoJo doesn't need you. Besides she had me in her life which "filled" the void of JoJo's lack of a father figure. Once Drew brought the conversation and intention to my attention, I had a lot of thinking to do also. As a man or the other man in the situation, I had several thoughts run through my mind. As men, we can rightfully be territorial and protective of their castle. After I let my pride down, put myself in his shoes and think big picture, there were a few things I had to evaluate. Did JoJo's father approach the situation respectfully for my wife and also for me? Did he do anything to neglect the wellbeing and safety of JoJo? What is the intention? Is this relationship in the best interest for JoJo? I immediately thought of my father and our circumstances.

As a child, no one couldn't tell me that my father wasn't the best in the world and guess what, that's my perspective. If you measured or quantified the value of our relationship, there would be large gaps in his presence, missed games and events, missed birthdays, missed growth and bonding opportunities. Yet, my father was still the best thing that could have ever happened to me. How could this be, the heart doesn't measure value in the way our minds do. Love is blind and that's what makes love beautiful, innocent and cherished. Without love, we would be robots, incapable of forgiving or giving someone an opportunity to succeed. If we were robotic in our heart, we would leave a baby that didn't learn to walk fast enough or talk. Sometimes the greatest lessons on earth is experiencing life.

Interesting enough, Initially I didn't speak with JoJo's biological father as Drew had to feel comfortable with the interaction first however I was always by her side supporting the process.

Change is very hard especially on a child therefore she wanted to make sure he wanted to really be part of his life before introducing his Father and he deciding he didn't want that role. Consistency is important to know if you're in this for the long run or if it's a nice experience because you think you should do it. Drew put JoJo's father on a call schedule to slowly introduce JoJo to his Father. JoJo visited with him as a baby but it's been years since they spoke and as a child, they don't know what a father means. The first few interactions was awkward just as any person that walks into a child's life that doesn't have kids, there is a learning process.

Adoption Because JoJo's father wasn't around, people would ask if I would adopt him, which is a great question. These are my rules on adopting in a blended family:

The Father doesn't want to be in the child's life therefore the child is fatherless

The Father is deceased.

The child is in harm or danger, therefore it's an unfit home.

The child doesn't have parents

In the event the child's mother dies, custody can be established through court order.....Find out the process. I really don't know.

If I would have adopted Josiah.

JoJo will get to a point where he seeks information and understanding for himself and he would approach his father asking, why didn't he make an effort to be in his life. His Father would more than likely respond, your parents didn't allow me to be a part of your life and pushed me out. JoJo can possibly develop resentment due to our actions, even if we felt it was in his best interest.

This is a great segway into the definition of "Dad." Dads come in all different forms, types, relationships and can be interchangeable for almost anyone providing support that uplifts positive change and growth. When my father wasn't around, coaches became father figures to me including men in the community that taught me fundamentals of manhood. When my father wasn't

around, men in the community would hire me and my brother to pickup leaves. It probably was one of the worst jobs I've ever experienced but it built character and work ethic that I wouldn't trade for the world. There is a village that becomes available to instill the lessons children need to learn and the role of "dad" can often be spread throughout the village to ensure children learn fundamentals of life. This concept also applies when the dad is around. Everyone is limited on the amount of information we know. If someone excels in a certain area, send the child to exceed your own understanding as the future depends on our children being smarter and more skilled than us.

Confidence I'm a firm believer that what's for me is for me and no one can take it away. If something isn't for me, then it was only supposed to be in my life for a season and I'm fine.

Being okay with JoJo's biological dad coming into the picture Studies show, 85% of blended familes are dysfunctional. While Drew and I were dating, she was very intentional not to allow me to play the dad role. She didn't want to scare me off or put responsibility on me before we had a chance to know if our relationship would last. Her family also assisted in our dating process. Their goal was to help Drew find the man of her dreams and would take JoJo so she could go out on dates. Well, that strategy worked! Drew and I went on a date that lasted 12hrs. Her family wasn't very happy when I brought her home at 4am. To no despair, we stayed in contact and she became my wife. I would ask Drew if I could take JoJo for ice cream or take him to the park while she was working if I felt she needed a helping hand so I could build a stronger bond with him. I knew if I married Drew, he would become my son. JoJo's biological father currently wasn't around and I knew JoJo needed a male influence to help him navigate the world, instill moral and values and grow into the man he would become. I had great expectations however I didn't know what a son or father figure meant from my wifes's eyes. My thought was once we were married, I would automatically take on the father role.

In our scenario, we got married extremely fast and Drew was pregnant 2mo after. We had a huge decision to make, where do we stay to raise the kids. At the time we were in LA and didn't feel like we had much support. We could either go to NJ to my family or Chicago with her family. I spoke with Drew's mom and she said I really can't help you if you stay in LA. Drew has a big family, her mom and dad and 4 sisters. It was a no brainer and we relocated to Chicago before Machai was born. I didn't have a chance to fully assume the "Dad" role as everything was moving fast. We were living under the same roof however Drew was making moves the way she programmed and without much involvement or opinion from my side. There were a few things that I didn't like entirely too much such as JoJo staying up until any time he wanted as if he was a little rockstar in a diaper and him sleeping in the same bed. Drew wasn't receptive to him staying up late and defended by saying she's an actress and her hours flucturate. To combat, I provided studies and reports on best practices for sleeping. I also provided a guidance for the tv staying on all night and she said her parents did it with them and everyone is okay so it's not that bad. I tried developing the "My House, My Rules" concept but it quickly fell on death ears as my concerns weren't enforced. Opposed to supporting, JoJo would cry and mom would come to the rescue. I began to see a common thread, where JoJo was also learning how to get his way and It then became an issue where it was Me vs. Them.

Boiling Point where I felt I couldn't parent

Due to JoJo not receiving adequate sleep, he struggled to get up for school in the morning. Being a man, I had my way of getting you to follow directions which was to place the fear of God in you because at the end of the day, I'm the parent. JoJo stood by the sink and didn't want to brush his teeth so I "acted" as if I was going to give him a pinch and he started crying, not because of pain but because of the act. His mother ran upstairs and grabbed JoJo, asking what happened. JoJo responded, daddy pinched me. Drew grabbed JoJo and repremanded me saying I

told you not to do that to him. I asked JoJo to demonstrate on his mother exactly how hard I pinched him and he barely touched his mother. I walked out the room as I felt emasculated and minimized below a child. I thought to myself if I wanted to stay in a relationship where I didn't have a parenting voice. Besides all that I've done and contributed, I should feel more respected. We ended up seeking out a marriage counselor that told us we're doing things all wrong. We didn't have a plan and it shows.

but she did ask for my thoughts to correct him sleeping in the bed.

Introduce Drew's mom, millinial

Support we had and lacked

Realistic / Unrealistic Expectations

It's either him or me

Village mindset, when JoJo's dad came home, Respect. Territorial. No this is my house.

Drew received a call from JoJo's biological dad that he came home from jail and wanted to see his son if possible. At the time Drew was still hurt by the lack of support and effort. Her perspective was, if you haven't been around or made an effort all this time, why now. JoJo doesn't need you. Besides she had me in her life which "filled" the void of JoJo's lack of a father figure. Once Drew brought the conversation and intention to my attention, I had a lot of thinking to do also. As a man or the other man in the situation, I had several thoughts run through my mind. As men, we can rightfully be territorial and protective of their castle. After I let my pride down, put myself in his shoes and think big picture, there were a few things I had to evaluate. Did JoJo's father approach the situation respectfully for my wife and also for me? Did he do anything to neglect the wellbeing and safety of JoJo? What is the intention? Is this relationship in the best interest for JoJo? I immediately thought of my father and our circumstances.

As a child, no one couldn't tell me that my father wasn't the best in the world and guess what, that's my perspective. If you

measured or quantified the value of our relationship, there would be large gaps in his presence, missed games and events, missed birthdays, missed growth and bonding opportunities. Yet, my father was still the best thing that could have ever happened to me. How could this be, the heart doesn't measure value in the way our minds do. Love is blind and that's what makes love beautiful, innocent and cherished. Without love, we would be robots, incapable of forgiving or giving someone an opportunity to succeed. If we were robotic in our heart, we would leave a baby that didn't learn to walk fast enough or talk. Sometimes the greatest lessons on earth is experiencing life.

Interesting enough, Initially I didn't speak with JoJo's biological father as Drew had to feel comfortable with the interaction first however I was always by her side supporting the process. Change is very hard especially on a child therefore she wanted to make sure he wanted to really be part of his life before introducing his Father and he deciding he didn't want that role. Consistency is important to know if you're in this for the long run or if it's a nice experience because you think you should do it. Drew put JoJo's father on a call schedule to slowly introduce JoJo to his Father. JoJo visited with him as a baby but it's been years since they spoke and as a child, they don't know what a father means. The first few interactions was awkward just as any person that walks into a child's life that doesn't have kids, there is a learning process.

Adoption Because JoJo's father wasn't around, people would ask if I would adopt him, which is a great question. These are my rules on adopting in a blended family:

The Father doesn't want to be in the child's life therefore the child is fatherless

The Father is deceased.

The child is in harm or danger, therefore it's an unfit home.

The child doesn't have parents

In the event the child's mother dies, custody can be established through court order.....Find out the process. I really don't know.

If I would have adopted Josiah.

JoJo will get to a point where he seeks information and understanding for himself and he would approach his father asking, why didn't he make an effort to be in his life. His Father would more than likely respond, your parents didn't allow me to be a part of your life and pushed me out. JoJo can possibly develop resentment due to our actions, even if we felt it was in his best interest.

This is a great segway into the definition of "Dad." Dads come in all different forms, types, relationships and can be interchangeable for almost anyone providing support that uplifts positive change and growth. When my father wasn't around, coaches became father figures to me including men in the community that taught me fundamentals of manhood. When my father wasn't around, men in the community would hire me and my brother to pickup leaves. It probably was one of the worst jobs I've ever experienced but it built character and work ethic that I wouldn't trade for the world. There is a village that becomes available to instill the lessons children need to learn and the role of "dad" can often be spread throughout the village to ensure children learn fundamentals of life. This concept also applies when the dad is around. Everyone is limited on the amount of information we know. If someone excels in a certain area, send the child to exceed your own understanding as the future depends on our children being smarter and more skilled than us.

Confidence I'm a firm believer that what's for me is for me and no one can take it away. If something isn't for me, then it was only supposed to be in my life for a season and I'm fine.

Being okay with JoJo's biological dad coming into the picture Studies show, 85% of blended familes are dysfunctional. While Drew and I were dating, she was very intentional not to allow me to play the dad role. She didn't want to scare me off or put responsibility on me before we had a chance to know if our relationship would last. Her family also assisted in our dating process. Their goal was to help Drew find the man of her dreams

and would take JoJo so she could go out on dates. Well, that strategy worked! Drew and I went on a date that lasted 12hrs. Her family wasn't very happy when I brought her home at 4am. To no despair, we stayed in contact and she became my wife. I would ask Drew if I could take JoJo for ice cream or take him to the park while she was working if I felt she needed a helping hand so I could build a stronger bond with him. I knew if I married Drew, he would become my son. JoJo's biological father currently wasn't around and I knew JoJo needed a male influence to help him navigate the world, instill moral and values and grow into the man he would become. I had great expectations however I didn't know what a son or father figure meant from my wifes's eyes. My thought was once we were married, I would automatically take on the father role.

In our scenario, we got married extremely fast and Drew was pregnant 2mo after. We had a huge decision to make, where do we stay to raise the kids. At the time we were in LA and didn't feel like we had much support. We could either go to NJ to my family or Chicago with her family. I spoke with Drew's mom and she said I really can't help you if you stay in LA. Drew has a big family, her mom and dad and 4 sisters. It was a no brainer and we relocated to Chicago before Machai was born. I didn't have a chance to fully assume the "Dad" role as everything was moving fast. We were living under the same roof however Drew was making moves the way she programmed and without much involvement or opinion from my side. There were a few things that I didn't like entirely too much such as JoJo staying up until any time he wanted as if he was a little rockstar in a diaper and him sleeping in the same bed. Drew wasn't receptive to him staying up late and defended by saying she's an actress and her hours flucturate. To combat, I provided studies and reports on best practices for sleeping. I also provided a guidance for the tv staying on all night and she said her parents did it with them and everyone is okay so it's not that bad. I tried developing the "My House, My Rules" concept but it quickly fell on death ears as my

concerns weren't enforced. Opposed to supporting, JoJo would cry and mom would come to the rescue. I began to see a common thread, where JoJo was also learning how to get his way and It then became an issue where it was Me vs. Them.

Boiling Point where I felt I couldn't parent

Due to JoJo not receiving adequate sleep, he struggled to get up for school in the morning. Being a man, I had my way of getting you to follow directions which was to place the fear of God in you because at the end of the day, I'm the parent. JoJo stood by the sink and didn't want to brush his teeth so I "acted" as if I was going to give him a pinch and he started crying, not because of pain but because of the act. His mother ran upstairs and grabbed JoJo, asking what happened. JoJo responded, daddy pinched me. Drew grabbed JoJo and repremanded me saying I told you not to do that to him. I asked JoJo to demonstrate on his mother exactly how hard I pinched him and he barely touched his mother. I walked out the room as I felt emasculated and minimized below a child. I thought to myself if I wanted to stay in a relationship where I didn't have a parenting voice. Besides all that I've done and contributed, I should feel more respected. We ended up seeking out a marriage counselor that told us we're doing things all wrong. We didn't have a plan and it shows.

but she did ask for my thoughts to correct him sleeping in the bed.

Introduce Drew's mom, millinial

Support we had and lacked

Realistic / Unrealistic Expectations

It's either him or me

Village mindset, when JoJo's dad came home, Respect. Territorial. No this is my house.

Drew received a call from JoJo's biological dad that he came home from jail and wanted to see his son if possible. At the time Drew was still hurt by the lack of support and effort. Her perspective was, if you haven't been around or made an effort all this time, why now. JoJo doesn't need you. Besides she had me

in her life which "filled" the void of JoJo's lack of a father figure. Once Drew brought the conversation and intention to my attention, I had a lot of thinking to do also. As a man or the other man in the situation, I had several thoughts run through my mind. As men, we can rightfully be territorial and protective of their castle. After I let my pride down, put myself in his shoes and think big picture, there were a few things I had to evaluate. Did JoJo's father approach the situation respectfully for my wife and also for me? Did he do anything to neglect the wellbeing and safety of JoJo? What is the intention? Is this relationship in the best interest for JoJo? I immediately thought of my father and our circumstances.

As a child, no one couldn't tell me that my father wasn't the best in the world and guess what, that's my perspective. If you measured or quantified the value of our relationship, there would be large gaps in his presence, missed games and events, missed birthdays, missed growth and bonding opportunities. Yet, my father was still the best thing that could have ever happened to me. How could this be, the heart doesn't measure value in the way our minds do. Love is blind and that's what makes love beautiful, innocent and cherished. Without love, we would be robots, incapable of forgiving or giving someone an opportunity to succeed. If we were robotic in our heart, we would leave a baby that didn't learn to walk fast enough or talk. Sometimes the greatest lessons on earth is experiencing life.

Interesting enough, Initially I didn't speak with JoJo's biological father as Drew had to feel comfortable with the interaction first however I was always by her side supporting the process. Change is very hard especially on a child therefore she wanted to make sure he wanted to really be part of his life before introducing his Father and he deciding he didn't want that role. Consistency is important to know if you're in this for the long run or if it's a nice experience because you think you should do it. Drew put JoJo's father on a call schedule to slowly introduce JoJo to his Father. JoJo visited with him as a baby but it's been

years since they spoke and as a child, they don't know what a father means. The first few interactions was awkward just as any person that walks into a child's life that doesn't have kids, there is a learning process.

Adoption Because JoJo's father wasn't around, people would ask if I would adopt him, which is a great question. These are my rules on adopting in a blended family:

The Father doesn't want to be in the child's life therefore the child is fatherless

The Father is deceased.

The child is in harm or danger, therefore it's an unfit home.

The child doesn't have parents

In the event the child's mother dies, custody can be established through court order.....Find out the process. I really don't know.

If I would have adopted Josiah.

JoJo will get to a point where he seeks information and understanding for himself and he would approach his father asking, why didn't he make an effort to be in his life. His Father would more than likely respond, your parents didn't allow me to be a part of your life and pushed me out. JoJo can possibly develop resentment due to our actions, even if we felt it was in his best interest.

This is a great segway into the definition of "Dad." Dads come in all different forms, types, relationships and can be interchangeable for almost anyone providing support that uplifts positive change and growth. When my father wasn't around, coaches became father figures to me including men in the community that taught me fundamentals of manhood. When my father wasn't around, men in the community would hire me and my brother to pickup leaves. It probably was one of the worst jobs I've ever experienced but it built character and work ethic that I wouldn't trade for the world. There is a village that becomes available to instill the lessons children need to learn and the role of "dad" can often be spread throughout the village to ensure children learn fundamentals of life. This concept also applies when the

dad is around. Everyone is limited on the amount of information we know. If someone excels in a certain area, send the child to exceed your own understanding as the future depends on our children being smarter and more skilled than us.

Confidence I'm a firm believer that what's for me is for me and no one can take it away. If something isn't for me, then it was only supposed to be in my life for a season and I'm fine.

Being okay with JoJo's biological dad coming into the picture Studies show, 85% of blended familes are dysfunctional. While Drew and I were dating, she was very intentional not to allow me to play the dad role. She didn't want to scare me off or put responsibility on me before we had a chance to know if our relationship would last. Her family also assisted in our dating process. Their goal was to help Drew find the man of her dreams and would take JoJo so she could go out on dates. Well, that strategy worked! Drew and I went on a date that lasted 12hrs. Her family wasn't very happy when I brought her home at 4am. To no despair, we stayed in contact and she became my wife. I would ask Drew if I could take JoJo for ice cream or take him to the park while she was working if I felt she needed a helping hand so I could build a stronger bond with him. I knew if I married Drew, he would become my son. JoJo's biological father currently wasn't around and I knew JoJo needed a male influence to help him navigate the world, instill moral and values and grow into the man he would become. I had great expectations however I didn't know what a son or father figure meant from my wifes's eyes. My thought was once we were married, I would automatically take on the father role.

In our scenario, we got married extremely fast and Drew was pregnant 2mo after. We had a huge decision to make, where do we stay to raise the kids. At the time we were in LA and didn't feel like we had much support. We could either go to NJ to my family or Chicago with her family. I spoke with Drew's mom and she said I really can't help you if you stay in LA. Drew has a big family, her mom and dad and 4 sisters. It was a no brainer and we relocated to Chicago before Machai was born. I didn't have a chance to fully assume the "Dad" role as everything was moving fast. We were living under the same roof however Drew was making moves the way she programmed and without much involvement or opinion from my side. There were a few things that I didn't like entirely too much such as JoJo staying up until any time he wanted as if he was a little rockstar in a diaper and him sleeping in the same bed. Drew wasn't receptive to him staying up late and defended by saying she's an actress and her hours flucturate. To combat, I provided studies and reports on best practices for sleeping. I also provided a guidance for the tv staying on all night and she said her parents did it with them and everyone is okay so it's not that bad. I tried developing the "My House, My Rules" concept but it quickly fell on death ears as my concerns weren't enforced. Opposed to supporting, JoJo would cry and mom would come to the rescue. I began to see a common thread, where JoJo was also learning how to get his way and It then became an issue where it was Me vs. Them.

Boiling Point where I felt I couldn't parent

Due to JoJo not receiving adequate sleep, he struggled to get up for school in the morning. Being a man, I had my way of getting you to follow directions which was to place the fear of God in you because at the end of the day, I'm the parent. JoJo stood by the sink and didn't want to brush his teeth so I "acted" as if I was going to give him a pinch and he started crying, not because of pain but because of the act. His mother ran upstairs and grabbed JoJo, asking what happened. JoJo responded, daddy pinched me. Drew grabbed JoJo and repremanded me saying I told you not to do that to him. I asked JoJo to demonstrate on his mother exactly how hard I pinched him and he barely touched his mother. I walked out the room as I felt emasculated and minimized below a child. I thought to myself if I wanted to stay in a relationship where I didn't have a parenting voice. Besides all that I've done and contributed, I should feel more respected. We

ended up seeking out a marriage counselor that told us we're doing things all wrong. We didn't have a plan and it shows.

but she did ask for my thoughts to correct him sleeping in the bed.

Introduce Drew's mom, millinial

Support we had and lacked

Realistic / Unrealistic Expectations

It's either him or me

Village mindset, when JoJo's dad came home, Respect. Territorial. No this is my house.

Drew received a call from JoJo's biological dad that he came home from jail and wanted to see his son if possible. At the time Drew was still hurt by the lack of support and effort. Her perspective was, if you haven't been around or made an effort all this time, why now. JoJo doesn't need you. Besides she had me in her life which "filled" the void of JoJo's lack of a father figure. Once Drew brought the conversation and intention to my attention, I had a lot of thinking to do also. As a man or the other man in the situation, I had several thoughts run through my mind. As men, we can rightfully be territorial and protective of their castle. After I let my pride down, put myself in his shoes and think big picture, there were a few things I had to evaluate. Did JoJo's father approach the situation respectfully for my wife and also for me? Did he do anything to neglect the wellbeing and safety of JoJo? What is the intention? Is this relationship in the best interest for JoJo? I immediately thought of my father and our circumstances.

As a child, no one couldn't tell me that my father wasn't the best in the world and guess what, that's my perspective. If you measured or quantified the value of our relationship, there would be large gaps in his presence, missed games and events, missed birthdays, missed growth and bonding opportunities. Yet, my father was still the best thing that could have ever happened to me. How could this be, the heart doesn't measure value in the way our minds do. Love is blind and that's what makes

love beautiful, innocent and cherished. Without love, we would be robots, incapable of forgiving or giving someone an opportunity to succeed. If we were robotic in our heart, we would leave a baby that didn't learn to walk fast enough or talk. Sometimes the greatest lessons on earth is experiencing life.

Interesting enough, Initially I didn't speak with JoJo's biological father as Drew had to feel comfortable with the interaction first however I was always by her side supporting the process. Change is very hard especially on a child therefore she wanted to make sure he wanted to really be part of his life before introducing his Father and he deciding he didn't want that role. Consistency is important to know if you're in this for the long run or if it's a nice experience because you think you should do it. Drew put JoJo's father on a call schedule to slowly introduce JoJo to his Father. JoJo visited with him as a baby but it's been years since they spoke and as a child, they don't know what a father means. The first few interactions was awkward just as any person that walks into a child's life that doesn't have kids, there is a learning process.

Adoption Because JoJo's father wasn't around, people would ask if I would adopt him, which is a great question. These are my rules on adopting in a blended family:

The Father doesn't want to be in the child's life therefore the child is fatherless

The Father is deceased.

The child is in harm or danger, therefore it's an unfit home.

The child doesn't have parents

In the event the child's mother dies, custody can be established through court order.....Find out the process. I really don't know.

If I would have adopted Josiah.

JoJo will get to a point where he seeks information and understanding for himself and he would approach his father asking, why didn't he make an effort to be in his life. His Father would more than likely respond, your parents didn't allow me to be a part of your life and pushed me out. JoJo can possibly develop

resentment due to our actions, even if we felt it was in his best interest.

This is a great segway into the definition of "Dad." Dads come in all different forms, types, relationships and can be interchangeable for almost anyone providing support that uplifts positive change and growth. When my father wasn't around, coaches became father figures to me including men in the community that taught me fundamentals of manhood. When my father wasn't around, men in the community would hire me and my brother to pickup leaves. It probably was one of the worst jobs I've ever experienced but it built character and work ethic that I wouldn't trade for the world. There is a village that becomes available to instill the lessons children need to learn and the role of "dad" can often be spread throughout the village to ensure children learn fundamentals of life. This concept also applies when the dad is around. Everyone is limited on the amount of information we know. If someone excels in a certain area, send the child to exceed your own understanding as the future depends on our children being smarter and more skilled than us.

Confidence I'm a firm believer that what's for me is for me and no one can take it away. If something isn't for me, then it was only supposed to be in my life for a season and I'm fine.

Being okay with JoJo's biological dad coming into the picture Studies show, 85% of blended familes are dysfunctional. While Drew and I were dating, she was very intentional not to allow me to play the dad role. She didn't want to scare me off or put responsibility on me before we had a chance to know if our relationship would last. Her family also assisted in our dating process. Their goal was to help Drew find the man of her dreams and would take JoJo so she could go out on dates. Well, that strategy worked! Drew and I went on a date that lasted 12hrs. Her family wasn't very happy when I brought her home at 4am. To no despair, we stayed in contact and she became my wife. I would ask Drew if I could take JoJo for ice cream or take him to the park while she was working if I felt she needed a helping hand

so I could build a stronger bond with him. I knew if I married Drew, he would become my son. JoJo's biological father currently wasn't around and I knew JoJo needed a male influence to help him navigate the world, instill moral and values and grow into the man he would become. I had great expectations however I didn't know what a son or father figure meant from my wifes's eyes. My thought was once we were married, I would automatically take on the father role.

In our scenario, we got married extremely fast and Drew was pregnant 2mo after. We had a huge decision to make, where do we stay to raise the kids. At the time we were in LA and didn't feel like we had much support. We could either go to NJ to my family or Chicago with her family. I spoke with Drew's mom and she said I really can't help you if you stay in LA. Drew has a big family, her mom and dad and 4 sisters. It was a no brainer and we relocated to Chicago before Machai was born. I didn't have a chance to fully assume the "Dad" role as everything was moving fast. We were living under the same roof however Drew was making moves the way she programmed and without much involvement or opinion from my side. There were a few things that I didn't like entirely too much such as JoJo staying up until any time he wanted as if he was a little rockstar in a diaper and him sleeping in the same bed. Drew wasn't receptive to him staying up late and defended by saying she's an actress and her hours flucturate. To combat, I provided studies and reports on best practices for sleeping. I also provided a guidance for the tv staying on all night and she said her parents did it with them and everyone is okay so it's not that bad. I tried developing the "My House, My Rules" concept but it quickly fell on death ears as my concerns weren't enforced. Opposed to supporting, JoJo would cry and mom would come to the rescue. I began to see a common thread, where JoJo was also learning how to get his way and It then became an issue where it was Me vs. Them.

Boiling Point

DUE TO JOJO not receiving adequate sleep, he struggled to get up for school in the morning. Being a man, I had my way of getting you to follow directions which was to place the fear of God in you because at the end of the day, I'm the parent. JoJo stood by the sink and didn't want to brush his teeth so I "acted" as if I was going to give him a pinch and he started crying, not because of pain but because of the act. His mother ran upstairs and grabbed JoJo, asking what happened. JoJo responded, daddy pinched me. Drew grabbed JoJo and reprimanded me saying I told you not to do that to him. I asked JoJo to demonstrate on his mother exactly how hard I pinched him and he barely touched his mother. I walked out the room as I felt emasculated and minimized below a child. I thought to myself if I wanted to stay in a relationship where I didn't have a parenting voice. Besides all that I've done and contributed, I should feel more respected. We ended up seeking out a marriage counselor that told us we're doing things all wrong. We didn't have a plan and it shows.

but she did ask for my thoughts to correct him sleeping in the bed.

Introduce Drew's mom, millinial

Support we had and lacked

Realistic / Unrealistic Expectations

Village mindset, when JoJo's dad came home, Respect. Territorial. No this is my house.

Drew received a call from JoJo's biological dad that he came home from jail and wanted to see his son if possible. At the time Drew was still hurt by the lack of support and effort. Her perspective was, if you haven't been around or made an effort all this time, why now. JoJo doesn't need you. Besides she had me in her life which "filled" the void of JoJo's lack of a father figure. Once Drew brought the conversation and intention to my attention, I had a lot of thinking to do also. As a man or the other man in the situation, I had several thoughts run through my mind. As men, we can rightfully be territorial and protective of their castle. After I let my pride down, put myself in his shoes and think big picture, there were a few things I had to evaluate. Did JoJo's father approach the situation respectfully for my wife and also for me? Did he do anything to neglect the wellbeing and safety of JoJo? What is the intention? Is this relationship in the best interest for JoJo? I immediately thought of my father and our circumstances.

As a child, no one couldn't tell me that my father wasn't the best in the world and guess what, that's my perspective. If you measured or quantified the value of our relationship, there would be large gaps in his presence, missed games and events, missed birthdays, missed growth and bonding opportunities. Yet, my father was still the best thing that could have ever happened to me. How could this be, the heart doesn't measure value in the way our minds do. Love is blind and that's what makes love beautiful, innocent and cherished. Without love, we would be robots, incapable of forgiving or giving someone an opportunity to succeed. If we were robotic in our heart, we would leave a baby that didn't learn to walk fast enough or talk. Sometimes the greatest lessons on earth is experiencing life.

Interesting enough, Initially I didn't speak with JoJo's biological father as Drew had to feel comfortable with the interaction first however I was always by her side supporting the process. Change is very hard especially on a child therefore she wanted to make sure he wanted to really be part of his life before introducing his Father and he deciding he didn't want that role. Consistency is important to know if you're in this for the long run or if it's a nice experience because you think you should do it. Drew put JoJo's father on a call schedule to slowly introduce JoJo to his Father. JoJo visited with him as a baby but it's been years since they spoke and as a child, they don't know what a father means. The first few interactions was awkward just as any person that walks into a child's life that doesn't have kids, there is a learning process.

Adoption Because JoJo's father wasn't around, people would ask if I would adopt him, which is a great question. These are my rules on adopting in a blended family:

The Father doesn't want to be in the child's life therefore the child is fatherless

The Father is deceased.

The child is in harm or danger, therefore it's an unfit home.

The child doesn't have parents

In the event the child's mother dies, custody can be established through court order.....Find out the process. I really don't know.

If I would have adopted Josiah.

JoJo will get to a point where he seeks information and understanding for himself and he would approach his father asking, why didn't he make an effort to be in his life. His Father would more than likely respond, your parents didn't allow me to be a part of your life and pushed me out. JoJo can possibly develop resentment due to our actions, even if we felt it was in his best interest.

This is a great segway into the definition of "Dad." Dads come in all different forms, types, relationships and can be interchangeable for almost anyone providing support that uplifts positive change and growth. When my father wasn't around, coaches became father figures to me including men in the community that taught me fundamentals of manhood. When my father wasn't around, men in the community would hire me and my brother to pickup leaves. It probably was one of the worst jobs I've ever experienced but it built character and work ethic that I wouldn't trade for the world. There is a village that becomes available to instill the lessons children need to learn and the role of "dad" can often be spread throughout the village to ensure children learn fundamentals of life. This concept also applies when the dad is around. Everyone is limited on the amount of information we know. If someone excels in a certain area, send the child to exceed your own understanding as the future depends on our children being smarter and more skilled than us.

Confidence I'm a firm believer that what's for me is for me and no one can take it away. If something isn't for me, then it was only supposed to be in my life for a season and I'm fine.

Being okay with JoJo's biological dad coming into the picture Studies show, 85% of blended familes are dysfunctional. While Drew and I were dating, she was very intentional not to allow me to play the dad role. She didn't want to scare me off or put responsibility on me before we had a chance to know if our relationship would last. Her family also assisted in our dating process. Their goal was to help Drew find the man of her dreams and would take JoJo so she could go out on dates. Well, that strategy worked! Drew and I went on a date that lasted 12hrs. Her family wasn't very happy when I brought her home at 4am. To no despair, we stayed in contact and she became my wife. I would ask Drew if I could take JoJo for ice cream or take him to the park while she was working if I felt she needed a helping hand so I could build a stronger bond with him. I knew if I married Drew, he would become my son. JoJo's biological father currently wasn't around and I knew JoJo needed a male influence to help him navigate the world, instill moral and values and grow into the man he would become. I had great expectations however I didn't know what a son or father figure meant from my wifes's eyes. My thought was once we were married, I would automatically take on the father role.

In our scenario, we got married extremely fast and Drew was pregnant 2mo after. We had a huge decision to make, where do we stay to raise the kids. At the time we were in LA and didn't feel like we had much support. We could either go to NJ to my family or Chicago with her family. I spoke with Drew's mom and she said I really can't help you if you stay in LA. Drew has a big family, her mom and dad and 4 sisters. It was a no brainer and we relocated to Chicago before Machai was born. I didn't have a chance to fully assume the "Dad" role as everything was moving fast. We were living under the same roof however Drew was making moves the way she programmed and without much involvement or opinion from my side. There were a few things that I didn't like entirely too much such as JoJo staying up until any time he wanted as if he was a little rockstar in a diaper and him sleeping in the same bed. Drew wasn't receptive to him staying up late and defended by saying she's an actress and her hours flucturate. To combat, I provided studies and reports on best practices for sleeping. I also provided a guidance for the tv staying on all night and she said her parents did it with them and everyone is okay so it's not that bad. I tried developing the "My House, My Rules" concept but it quickly fell on death ears as my concerns weren't enforced. Opposed to supporting, JoJo would cry and mom would come to the rescue. I began to see a common thread, where JoJo was also learning how to get his way and It then became an issue where it was Me vs. Them.

Boiling Point where I felt I couldn't parent

Due to JoJo not receiving adequate sleep, he struggled to get up for school in the morning. Being a man, I had my way of getting you to follow directions which was to place the fear of God in you because at the end of the day, I'm the parent. JoJo stood by the sink and didn't want to brush his teeth so I "acted" as if I was going to give him a pinch and he started crying, not because of pain but because of the act. His mother ran upstairs and grabbed JoJo, asking what happened. JoJo responded, daddy pinched me. Drew grabbed JoJo and repremanded me saying I told you not to do that to him. I asked JoJo to demonstrate on his mother exactly how hard I pinched him and he barely touched his mother. I walked out the room as I felt emasculated and minimized below a child. I thought to myself if I wanted to stay in a relationship where I didn't have a parenting voice. Besides all that I've done and contributed, I should feel more respected. We ended up seeking out a marriage counselor that told us we're doing things all wrong. We didn't have a plan and it shows.

but she did ask for my thoughts to correct him sleeping in the bed.

Introduce Drew's mom, millinial

Support we had and lacked

Realistic / Unrealistic Expectations

It's either him or me

Village mindset, when JoJo's dad came home, Respect. Territorial. No this is my house.

Drew received a call from JoJo's biological dad that he came home from jail and wanted to see his son if possible. At the time Drew was still hurt by the lack of support and effort. Her perspective was, if you haven't been around or made an effort all this time, why now. JoJo doesn't need you. Besides she had me in her life which "filled" the void of JoJo's lack of a father figure. Once Drew brought the conversation and intention to my attention, I had a lot of thinking to do also. As a man or the other man in the situation, I had several thoughts run through my mind. As men, we can rightfully be territorial and protective of their castle. After I let my pride down, put myself in his shoes and think big picture, there were a few things I had to evaluate. Did JoJo's father approach the situation respectfully for my wife and also for me? Did he do anything to neglect the wellbeing and safety of JoJo? What is the intention? Is this relationship in the best interest for JoJo? I immediately thought of my father and our circumstances.

As a child, no one couldn't tell me that my father wasn't the best in the world and guess what, that's my perspective. If you measured or quantified the value of our relationship, there would be large gaps in his presence, missed games and events, missed birthdays, missed growth and bonding opportunities. Yet, my father was still the best thing that could have ever happened to me. How could this be, the heart doesn't measure value in the way our minds do. Love is blind and that's what makes love beautiful, innocent and cherished. Without love, we would be robots, incapable of forgiving or giving someone an opportunity to succeed. If we were robotic in our heart, we would leave a baby that didn't learn to walk fast enough or talk. Sometimes the greatest lessons on earth is experiencing life.

Interesting enough, Initially I didn't speak with JoJo's biological father as Drew had to feel comfortable with the interaction first however I was always by her side supporting the process. Change is very hard especially on a child therefore she wanted to make sure he wanted to really be part of his life before introducing his Father and he deciding he didn't want that role. Consistency is important to know if you're in this for the long run or if it's a nice experience because you think you should do it. Drew put JoJo's father on a call schedule to slowly introduce JoJo to his Father. JoJo visited with him as a baby but it's been years since they spoke and as a child, they don't know what a father means. The first few interactions was awkward just as any person that walks into a child's life that doesn't have kids, there is a learning process.

Adoption Because JoJo's father wasn't around, people would ask if I would adopt him, which is a great question. These are my rules on adopting in a blended family:

The Father doesn't want to be in the child's life therefore the child is fatherless

The Father is deceased.

The child is in harm or danger, therefore it's an unfit home.

The child doesn't have parents

In the event the child's mother dies, custody can be established through court order.....Find out the process. I really don't know.

If I would have adopted Josiah.

JoJo will get to a point where he seeks information and understanding for himself and he would approach his father asking, why didn't he make an effort to be in his life. His Father would more than likely respond, your parents didn't allow me to be a part of your life and pushed me out. JoJo can possibly develop resentment due to our actions, even if we felt it was in his best interest.

This is a great segway into the definition of "Dad." Dads come in all different forms, types, relationships and can be interchangeable for almost anyone providing support that uplifts positive change and growth. When my father wasn't around, coaches became father figures to me including men in the community that taught me fundamentals of manhood. When my father wasn't around, men in the community would hire me and my brother to pickup leaves. It probably was one of the worst jobs I've ever experienced but it built character and work ethic that I wouldn't trade for the world. There is a village that becomes available to instill the lessons children need to learn and the role of "dad" can often be spread throughout the village to ensure children learn fundamentals of life. This concept also applies when the dad is around. Everyone is limited on the amount of information we know. If someone excels in a certain area, send the child to exceed your own understanding as the future depends on our children being smarter and more skilled than us.

Confidence I'm a firm believer that what's for me is for me and no one can take it away. If something isn't for me, then it was only supposed to be in my life for a season and I'm fine.

Being okay with JoJo's biological dad coming into the picture

Studies show, 85% of blended familes are dysfunctional. While Drew and I were dating, she was very intentional not to allow me to play the dad role. She didn't want to scare me off or put responsibility on me before we had a chance to know if

our relationship would last. Her family also assisted in our dating process. Their goal was to help Drew find the man of her dreams and would take JoJo so she could go out on dates. Well, that strategy worked! Drew and I went on a date that lasted 12hrs. Her family wasn't very happy when I brought her home at 4am. To no despair, we stayed in contact and she became my wife. I would ask Drew if I could take JoJo for ice cream or take him to the park while she was working if I felt she needed a helping hand so I could build a stronger bond with him. I knew if I married Drew, he would become my son. JoJo's biological father currently wasn't around and I knew JoJo needed a male influence to help him navigate the world, instill moral and values and grow into the man he would become. I had great expectations however I didn't know what a son or father figure meant from my wifes's eyes. My thought was once we were married, I would automatically take on the father role.

In our scenario, we got married extremely fast and Drew was pregnant 2mo after. We had a huge decision to make, where do we stay to raise the kids. At the time we were in LA and didn't feel like we had much support. We could either go to NJ to my family or Chicago with her family. I spoke with Drew's mom and she said I really can't help you if you stay in LA. Drew has a big family, her mom and dad and 4 sisters. It was a no brainer and we relocated to Chicago before Machai was born. I didn't have a chance to fully assume the "Dad" role as everything was moving fast. We were living under the same roof however Drew was making moves the way she programmed and without much involvement or opinion from my side. There were a few things that I didn't like entirely too much such as JoJo staying up until any time he wanted as if he was a little rockstar in a diaper and him sleeping in the same bed. Drew wasn't receptive to him staying up late and defended by saying she's an actress and her hours fluctuate. To combat, I provided studies and reports on best practices for sleeping. I also provided a guidance for the tv staying on all night and she said her parents did it with them and

everyone is okay so it's not that bad. I tried developing the "My House, My Rules" concept but it quickly fell on death ears as my concerns weren't enforced. Opposed to supporting, JoJo would cry and mom would come to the rescue. I began to see a common thread, where JoJo was also learning how to get his way and It then became an issue where it was Me vs. Them.

Boiling Point where I felt I couldn't parent

Due to JoJo not receiving adequate sleep, he struggled to get up for school in the morning. Being a man, I had my way of getting you to follow directions which was to place the fear of God in you because at the end of the day, I'm the parent. JoJo stood by the sink and didn't want to brush his teeth so I "acted" as if I was going to give him a pinch and he started crying, not because of pain but because of the act. His mother ran upstairs and grabbed JoJo, asking what happened. JoJo responded, daddy pinched me. Drew grabbed JoJo and repremanded me saying I told you not to do that to him. I asked JoJo to demonstrate on his mother exactly how hard I pinched him and he barely touched his mother. I walked out the room as I felt emasculated and minimized below a child. I thought to myself if I wanted to stay in a relationship where I didn't have a parenting voice. Besides all that I've done and contributed, I should feel more respected. We ended up seeking out a marriage counselor that told us we're doing things all wrong. We didn't have a plan and it shows.

but she did ask for my thoughts to correct him sleeping in the bed.

Introduce Drew's mom, millinial

Support we had and lacked

Realistic / Unrealistic Expectations

It's either him or me

Village mindset, when JoJo's dad came home, Respect. Territorial. No this is my house.

Drew received a call from JoJo's biological dad that he came home from jail and wanted to see his son if possible. At the time Drew was still hurt by the lack of support and effort. Her

perspective was, if you haven't been around or made an effort all this time, why now. JoJo doesn't need you. Besides she had me in her life which "filled" the void of JoJo's lack of a father figure. Once Drew brought the conversation and intention to my attention, I had a lot of thinking to do also. As a man or the other man in the situation, I had several thoughts run through my mind. As men, we can rightfully be territorial and protective of their castle. After I let my pride down, put myself in his shoes and think big picture, there were a few things I had to evaluate. Did JoJo's father approach the situation respectfully for my wife and also for me? Did he do anything to neglect the wellbeing and safety of JoJo? What is the intention? Is this relationship in the best interest for JoJo? I immediately thought of my father and our circumstances.

As a child, no one couldn't tell me that my father wasn't the best in the world and guess what, that's my perspective. If you measured or quantified the value of our relationship, there would be large gaps in his presence, missed games and events, missed birthdays, missed growth and bonding opportunities. Yet, my father was still the best thing that could have ever happened to me. How could this be, the heart doesn't measure value in the way our minds do. Love is blind and that's what makes love beautiful, innocent and cherished. Without love, we would be robots, incapable of forgiving or giving someone an opportunity to succeed. If we were robotic in our heart, we would leave a baby that didn't learn to walk fast enough or talk. Sometimes the greatest lessons on earth is experiencing life.

Interesting enough, Initially I didn't speak with JoJo's biological father as Drew had to feel comfortable with the interaction first however I was always by her side supporting the process. Change is very hard especially on a child therefore she wanted to make sure he wanted to really be part of his life before introducing his Father and he deciding he didn't want that role. Consistency is important to know if you're in this for the long run or if it's a nice experience because you think you should do

it. Drew put JoJo's father on a call schedule to slowly introduce JoJo to his Father. JoJo visited with him as a baby but it's been years since they spoke and as a child, they don't know what a father means. The first few interactions was awkward just as any person that walks into a child's life that doesn't have kids, there is a learning process.

Adoption Because JoJo's father wasn't around, people would ask if I would adopt him, which is a great question. These are my rules on adopting in a blended family:

The Father doesn't want to be in the child's life therefore the child is fatherless

The Father is deceased.

The child is in harm or danger, therefore it's an unfit home.

The child doesn't have parents

In the event the child's mother dies, custody can be established through court order.....Find out the process. I really don't know.

If I would have adopted Josiah.

JoJo will get to a point where he seeks information and understanding for himself and he would approach his father asking, why didn't he make an effort to be in his life. His Father would more than likely respond, your parents didn't allow me to be a part of your life and pushed me out. JoJo can possibly develop resentment due to our actions, even if we felt it was in his best interest.

This is a great segway into the definition of "Dad." Dads come in all different forms, types, relationships and can be interchangeable for almost anyone providing support that uplifts positive change and growth. When my father wasn't around, coaches became father figures to me including men in the community that taught me fundamentals of manhood. When my father wasn't around, men in the community would hire me and my brother to pickup leaves. It probably was one of the worst jobs I've ever experienced but it built character and work ethic that I wouldn't trade for the world. There is a village that becomes available to instill the lessons children need to learn and the role of "dad"

can often be spread throughout the village to ensure children learn fundamentals of life. This concept also applies when the dad is around. Everyone is limited on the amount of information we know. If someone excels in a certain area, send the child to exceed your own understanding as the future depends on our children being smarter and more skilled than us.

Confidence I'm a firm believer that what's for me is for me and no one can take it away. If something isn't for me, then it was only supposed to be in my life for a season and I'm fine.

Being okay with JoJo's biological dad coming into the picture Studies show, 85% of blended familes are dysfunctional. While Drew and I were dating, she was very intentional not to allow me to play the dad role. She didn't want to scare me off or put responsibility on me before we had a chance to know if our relationship would last. Her family also assisted in our dating process. Their goal was to help Drew find the man of her dreams and would take JoJo so she could go out on dates. Well, that strategy worked! Drew and I went on a date that lasted 12hrs. Her family wasn't very happy when I brought her home at 4am. To no despair, we stayed in contact and she became my wife. I would ask Drew if I could take JoJo for ice cream or take him to the park while she was working if I felt she needed a helping hand so I could build a stronger bond with him. I knew if I married Drew, he would become my son. JoJo's biological father currently wasn't around and I knew JoJo needed a male influence to help him navigate the world, instill moral and values and grow into the man he would become. I had great expectations however I didn't know what a son or father figure meant from my wifes's eyes. My thought was once we were married, I would automatically take on the father role.

In our scenario, we got married extremely fast and Drew was pregnant 2mo after. We had a huge decision to make, where do we stay to raise the kids. At the time we were in LA and didn't feel like we had much support. We could either go to NJ to my family or Chicago with her family. I spoke with Drew's mom

and she said I really can't help you if you stay in LA. Drew has a big family, her mom and dad and 4 sisters. It was a no brainer and we relocated to Chicago before Machai was born. I didn't have a chance to fully assume the "Dad" role as everything was moving fast. We were living under the same roof however Drew was making moves the way she programmed and without much involvement or opinion from my side. There were a few things that I didn't like entirely too much such as JoJo staying up until any time he wanted as if he was a little rockstar in a diaper and him sleeping in the same bed. Drew wasn't receptive to him staying up late and defended by saying she's an actress and her hours flucturate. To combat, I provided studies and reports on best practices for sleeping. I also provided a guidance for the tv staying on all night and she said her parents did it with them and everyone is okay so it's not that bad. I tried developing the "My House, My Rules" concept but it quickly fell on death ears as my concerns weren't enforced. Opposed to supporting, JoJo would cry and mom would come to the rescue. I began to see a common thread, where JoJo was also learning how to get his way and It then became an issue where it was Me vs. Them.

Boiling Point where I felt I couldn't parent

Due to JoJo not receiving adequate sleep, he struggled to get up for school in the morning. Being a man, I had my way of getting you to follow directions which was to place the fear of God in you because at the end of the day, I'm the parent. JoJo stood by the sink and didn't want to brush his teeth so I "acted" as if I was going to give him a pinch and he started crying, not because of pain but because of the act. His mother ran upstairs and grabbed JoJo, asking what happened. JoJo responded, daddy pinched me. Drew grabbed JoJo and reprimanded me saying I told you not to do that to him. I asked JoJo to demonstrate on his mother exactly how hard I pinched him and he barely touched his mother. I walked out the room as I felt emasculated and minimized below a child. I thought to myself if I wanted to stay in a relationship where I didn't have a parenting voice. Besides all

65

that I've done and contributed, I should feel more respected. We ended up seeking out a marriage counselor that told us we're doing things all wrong. We didn't have a plan and it shows.

but she did ask for my thoughts to correct him sleeping in the bed.

Introduce Drew's mom, millinial

Support we had and lacked

Realistic / Unrealistic Expectations

It's either him or me

Village mindset, when JoJo's dad came home, Respect. Territorial. No this is my house.

Drew received a call from JoJo's biological dad that he came home from jail and wanted to see his son if possible. At the time Drew was still hurt by the lack of support and effort. Her perspective was, if you haven't been around or made an effort all this time, why now. JoJo doesn't need you. Besides she had me in her life which "filled" the void of JoJo's lack of a father figure. Once Drew brought the conversation and intention to my attention, I had a lot of thinking to do also. As a man or the other man in the situation, I had several thoughts run through my mind. As men, we can rightfully be territorial and protective of their castle. After I let my pride down, put myself in his shoes and think big picture, there were a few things I had to evaluate. Did JoJo's father approach the situation respectfully for my wife and also for me? Did he do anything to neglect the wellbeing and safety of JoJo? What is the intention? Is this relationship in the best interest for JoJo? I immediately thought of my father and our circumstances.

As a child, no one couldn't tell me that my father wasn't the best in the world and guess what, that's my perspective. If you measured or quantified the value of our relationship, there would be large gaps in his presence, missed games and events, missed birthdays, missed growth and bonding opportunities. Yet, my father was still the best thing that could have ever happened to me. How could this be, the heart doesn't measure value

in the way our minds do. Love is blind and that's what makes love beautiful, innocent and cherished. Without love, we would be robots, incapable of forgiving or giving someone an opportunity to succeed. If we were robotic in our heart, we would leave a baby that didn't learn to walk fast enough or talk. Sometimes the greatest lessons on earth is experiencing life.

Interesting enough, Initially I didn't speak with JoJo's biological father as Drew had to feel comfortable with the interaction first however I was always by her side supporting the process. Change is very hard especially on a child therefore she wanted to make sure he wanted to really be part of his life before introducing his Father and he deciding he didn't want that role. Consistency is important to know if you're in this for the long run or if it's a nice experience because you think you should do it. Drew put JoJo's father on a call schedule to slowly introduce JoJo to his Father. JoJo visited with him as a baby but it's been years since they spoke and as a child, they don't know what a father means. The first few interactions was awkward just as any person that walks into a child's life that doesn't have kids, there is a learning process.

Adoption Because JoJo's father wasn't around, people would ask if I would adopt him, which is a great question. These are my rules on adopting in a blended family:

The Father doesn't want to be in the child's life therefore the child is fatherless

The Father is deceased.

The child is in harm or danger, therefore it's an unfit home.

The child doesn't have parents

In the event the child's mother dies, custody can be established through court order.....Find out the process. I really don't know.

If I would have adopted Josiah.

JoJo will get to a point where he seeks information and understanding for himself and he would approach his father asking, why didn't he make an effort to be in his life. His Father would more than likely respond, your parents didn't allow me to be a

part of your life and pushed me out. JoJo can possibly develop resentment due to our actions, even if we felt it was in his best interest.

This is a great segway into the definition of "Dad." Dads come in all different forms, types, relationships and can be interchangeable for almost anyone providing support that uplifts positive change and growth. When my father wasn't around, coaches became father figures to me including men in the community that taught me fundamentals of manhood. When my father wasn't around, men in the community would hire me and my brother to pickup leaves. It probably was one of the worst jobs I've ever experienced but it built character and work ethic that I wouldn't trade for the world. There is a village that becomes available to instill the lessons children need to learn and the role of "dad" can often be spread throughout the village to ensure children learn fundamentals of life. This concept also applies when the dad is around. Everyone is limited on the amount of information we know. If someone excels in a certain area, send the child to exceed your own understanding as the future depends on our children being smarter and more skilled than us.

Confidence I'm a firm believer that what's for me is for me and no one can take it away. If something isn't for me, then it was only supposed to be in my life for a season and I'm fine.

Being okay with JoJo's biological dad coming into the picture

Studies show, 85% of blended familes are dysfunctional. While Drew and I were dating, she was very intentional not to allow me to play the dad role. She didn't want to scare me off or put responsibility on me before we had a chance to know if our relationship would last. Her family also assisted in our dating process. Their goal was to help Drew find the man of her dreams and would take JoJo so she could go out on dates. Well, that strategy worked! Drew and I went on a date that lasted 12hrs. Her family wasn't very happy when I brought her home at 4am. To no despair, we stayed in contact and she became my wife. I would ask Drew if I could take JoJo for ice cream or take him to the

park while she was working if I felt she needed a helping hand so I could build a stronger bond with him. I knew if I married Drew, he would become my son. JoJo's biological father currently wasn't around and I knew JoJo needed a male influence to help him navigate the world, instill moral and values and grow into the man he would become. I had great expectations however I didn't know what a son or father figure meant from my wifes's eyes. My thought was once we were married, I would automatically take on the father role.

In our scenario, we got married extremely fast and Drew was pregnant 2mo after. We had a huge decision to make, where do we stay to raise the kids. At the time we were in LA and didn't feel like we had much support. We could either go to NJ to my family or Chicago with her family. I spoke with Drew's mom and she said I really can't help you if you stay in LA. Drew has a big family, her mom and dad and 4 sisters. It was a no brainer and we relocated to Chicago before Machai was born. I didn't have a chance to fully assume the "Dad" role as everything was moving fast. We were living under the same roof however Drew was making moves the way she programmed and without much involvement or opinion from my side. There were a few things that I didn't like entirely too much such as JoJo staying up until any time he wanted as if he was a little rockstar in a diaper and him sleeping in the same bed. Drew wasn't receptive to him staying up late and defended by saying she's an actress and her hours flucturate. To combat, I provided studies and reports on best practices for sleeping. I also provided a guidance for the tv staying on all night and she said her parents did it with them and everyone is okay so it's not that bad. I tried developing the "My House, My Rules" concept but it quickly fell on death ears as my concerns weren't enforced. Opposed to supporting, JoJo would cry and mom would come to the rescue. I began to see a common thread, where JoJo was also learning how to get his way and It then became an issue where it was Me vs. Them.

Boiling Point where I felt I couldn't parent

Due to JoJo not receiving adequate sleep, he struggled to get up for school in the morning. Being a man, I had my way of getting you to follow directions which was to place the fear of God in you because at the end of the day, I'm the parent. JoJo stood by the sink and didn't want to brush his teeth so I "acted" as if I was going to give him a pinch and he started crying, not because of pain but because of the act. His mother ran upstairs and grabbed JoJo, asking what happened. JoJo responded, daddy pinched me. Drew grabbed JoJo and repremanded me saying I told you not to do that to him. I asked JoJo to demonstrate on his mother exactly how hard I pinched him and he barely touched his mother. I walked out the room as I felt emasculated and minimized below a child. I thought to myself if I wanted to stay in a relationship where I didn't have a parenting voice. Besides all that I've done and contributed, I should feel more respected. We ended up seeking out a marriage counselor that told us we're doing things all wrong. We didn't have a plan and it shows.

but she did ask for my thoughts to correct him sleeping in the bed.

Introduce Drew's mom, millinial

Support we had and lacked

Realistic / Unrealistic Expectations

It's either him or me

Village mindset, when JoJo's dad came home, Respect. Territorial. No this is my house.

Drew received a call from JoJo's biological dad that he came home from jail and wanted to see his son if possible. At the time Drew was still hurt by the lack of support and effort. Her perspective was, if you haven't been around or made an effort all this time, why now. JoJo doesn't need you. Besides she had me in her life which "filled" the void of JoJo's lack of a father figure. Once Drew brought the conversation and intention to my attention, I had a lot of thinking to do also. As a man or the other man in the situation, I had several thoughts run through my mind. As men, we can rightfully be territorial and protective of their

castle. After I let my pride down, put myself in his shoes and think big picture, there were a few things I had to evaluate. Did JoJo's father approach the situation respectfully for my wife and also for me? Did he do anything to neglect the wellbeing and safety of JoJo? What is the intention? Is this relationship in the best interest for JoJo? I immediately thought of my father and our circumstances.

As a child, no one couldn't tell me that my father wasn't the best in the world and guess what, that's my perspective. If you measured or quantified the value of our relationship, there would be large gaps in his presence, missed games and events, missed birthdays, missed growth and bonding opportunities. Yet, my father was still the best thing that could have ever happened to me. How could this be, the heart doesn't measure value in the way our minds do. Love is blind and that's what makes love beautiful, innocent and cherished. Without love, we would be robots, incapable of forgiving or giving someone an opportunity to succeed. If we were robotic in our heart, we would leave a baby that didn't learn to walk fast enough or talk. Sometimes the greatest lessons on earth is experiencing life.

Interesting enough, Initially I didn't speak with JoJo's biological father as Drew had to feel comfortable with the interaction first however I was always by her side supporting the process. Change is very hard especially on a child therefore she wanted to make sure he wanted to really be part of his life before introducing his Father and he deciding he didn't want that role. Consistency is important to know if you're in this for the long run or if it's a nice experience because you think you should do it. Drew put JoJo's father on a call schedule to slowly introduce JoJo to his Father. JoJo visited with him as a baby but it's been years since they spoke and as a child, they don't know what a father means. The first few interactions was awkward just as any person that walks into a child's life that doesn't have kids, there is a learning process.

Adoption Because JoJo's father wasn't around, people would ask if I would adopt him, which is a great question. These are my rules on adopting in a blended family:

The Father doesn't want to be in the child's life therefore the child is fatherless

The Father is deceased.

The child is in harm or danger, therefore it's an unfit home.

The child doesn't have parents

In the event the child's mother dies, custody can be established through court order.....Find out the process. I really don't know.

If I would have adopted Josiah.

JoJo will get to a point where he seeks information and understanding for himself and he would approach his father asking, why didn't he make an effort to be in his life. His Father would more than likely respond, your parents didn't allow me to be a part of your life and pushed me out. JoJo can possibly develop resentment due to our actions, even if we felt it was in his best interest.

This is a great segway into the definition of "Dad." Dads come in all different forms, types, relationships and can be interchangeable for almost anyone providing support that uplifts positive change and growth. When my father wasn't around, coaches became father figures to me including men in the community that taught me fundamentals of manhood. When my father wasn't around, men in the community would hire me and my brother to pickup leaves. It probably was one of the worst jobs I've ever experienced but it built character and work ethic that I wouldn't trade for the world. There is a village that becomes available to instill the lessons children need to learn and the role of "dad" can often be spread throughout the village to ensure children learn fundamentals of life. This concept also applies when the dad is around. Everyone is limited on the amount of information we know. If someone excels in a certain area, send the child to exceed your own understanding as the future depends on our children being smarter and more skilled than us.

Confidence I'm a firm believer that what's for me is for me and no one can take it away. If something isn't for me, then it was only supposed to be in my life for a season and I'm fine.

Being okay with JoJo's biological dad coming into the picture

Studies show, 85% of blended familes are dysfunctional. While Drew and I were dating, she was very intentional not to allow me to play the dad role. She didn't want to scare me off or put responsibility on me before we had a chance to know if our relationship would last. Her family also assisted in our dating process. Their goal was to help Drew find the man of her dreams and would take JoJo so she could go out on dates. Well, that strategy worked! Drew and I went on a date that lasted 12hrs. Her family wasn't very happy when I brought her home at 4am. To no despair, we stayed in contact and she became my wife. I would ask Drew if I could take JoJo for ice cream or take him to the park while she was working if I felt she needed a helping hand so I could build a stronger bond with him. I knew if I married Drew, he would become my son. JoJo's biological father currently wasn't around and I knew JoJo needed a male influence to help him navigate the world, instill moral and values and grow into the man he would become. I had great expectations however I didn't know what a son or father figure meant from my wifes's eyes. My thought was once we were married, I would automatically take on the father role.

In our scenario, we got married extremely fast and Drew was pregnant 2mo after. We had a huge decision to make, where do we stay to raise the kids. At the time we were in LA and didn't feel like we had much support. We could either go to NJ to my family or Chicago with her family. I spoke with Drew's mom and she said I really can't help you if you stay in LA. Drew has a big family, her mom and dad and 4 sisters. It was a no brainer and we relocated to Chicago before Machai was born. I didn't have a chance to fully assume the "Dad" role as everything was moving fast. We were living under the same roof however Drew was making moves the way she programmed and without much

involvement or opinion from my side. There were a few things that I didn't like entirely too much such as JoJo staying up until any time he wanted as if he was a little rockstar in a diaper and him sleeping in the same bed. Drew wasn't receptive to him staying up late and defended by saying she's an actress and her hours flucturate. To combat, I provided studies and reports on best practices for sleeping. I also provided a guidance for the tv staying on all night and she said her parents did it with them and everyone is okay so it's not that bad. I tried developing the "My House, My Rules" concept but it quickly fell on death ears as my concerns weren't enforced. Opposed to supporting, JoJo would cry and mom would come to the rescue. I began to see a common thread, where JoJo was also learning how to get his way and It then became an issue where it was Me vs. Them.

Realistic / Unrealistic Expectations

IT'S EITHER HIM or me

Drew received a call from JoJo's biological dad that he came home from jail and wanted to see his son if possible. At the time Drew was still hurt by the lack of support and effort. Her perspective was, if you haven't been around or made an effort all this time, why now. JoJo doesn't need you. Besides she had me in her life which "filled" the void of JoJo's lack of a father figure. Once Drew brought the conversation and intention to my attention, I had a lot of thinking to do also. As a man or the other man in the situation, I had several thoughts run through my mind. Did he do anything to neglect the wellbeing and safety of JoJo? What is the intention? Is this relationship in the best interest for JoJo? I immediately thought of my father and our circumstances.

As a child, no one couldn't tell me that my father wasn't the best in the world and guess what, that's my perspective. If you measured or quantified the value of our relationship, there would be large gaps in his presence, missed games and events, missed birthdays, missed growth and bonding opportunities. Yet, my father was still the best thing that could have ever happened to

75

me. How could this be, the heart doesn't measure value in the way our minds do. Love is blind and that's what makes love beautiful, innocent and cherished. Without love, we would be robots, incapable of forgiving or giving someone an opportunity to succeed. If we were robotic in our heart, we would leave a baby that didn't learn to walk fast enough or talk. Sometimes the greatest lessons on earth is experiencing life.

Interesting enough, Initially I didn't speak with JoJo's biological father as Drew had to feel comfortable with the interaction first however I was always by her side supporting the process. Change is very hard especially on a child therefore she wanted to make sure he wanted to really be part of his life before introducing his Father and he deciding he didn't want that role. Consistency is important to know if you're in this for the long run or if it's a nice experience because you think you should do it. Drew put JoJo's father on a call schedule to slowly introduce JoJo to his Father. JoJo visited with him as a baby but it's been years since they spoke and as a child, they don't know what a father means. The first few interactions was awkward just as any person that walks into a child's life that doesn't have kids, there is a learning process.

Adoption Because JoJo's father wasn't around, people would ask if I would adopt him, which is a great question. These are my rules on adopting in a blended family:

The Father doesn't want to be in the child's life therefore the child is fatherless

The Father is deceased.

The child is in harm or danger, therefore it's an unfit home.

The child doesn't have parents

In the event the child's mother dies, custody can be established through court order.....Find out the process. I really don't know.

If I would have adopted Josiah.

JoJo will get to a point where he seeks information and understanding for himself and he would approach his father asking, why didn't he make an effort to be in his life. His Father would more than likely respond, your parents didn't allow me to be a part of your life and pushed me out. JoJo can possibly develop resentment due to our actions, even if we felt it was in his best interest.

This is a great segway into the definition of "Dad." Dads come in all different forms, types, relationships and can be interchangeable for almost anyone providing support that uplifts positive change and growth. When my father wasn't around, coaches became father figures to me including men in the community that taught me fundamentals of manhood. When my father wasn't around, men in the community would hire me and my brother to pickup leaves. It probably was one of the worst jobs I've ever experienced but it built character and work ethic that I wouldn't trade for the world. There is a village that becomes available to instill the lessons children need to learn and the role of "dad" can often be spread throughout the village to ensure children learn fundamentals of life. This concept also applies when the dad is around. Everyone is limited on the amount of information we know. If someone excels in a certain area, send the child to exceed your own understanding as the future depends on our children being smarter and more skilled than us.

Confidence I'm a firm believer that what's for me is for me and no one can take it away. If something isn't for me, then it was only supposed to be in my life for a season and I'm fine.

Being okay with JoJo's biological dad coming into the picture Studies show, 85% of blended familes are dysfunctional. While Drew and I were dating, she was very intentional not to allow me to play the dad role. She didn't want to scare me off or put responsibility on me before we had a chance to know if our relationship would last. Her family also assisted in our dating process. Their goal was to help Drew find the man of her dreams and would take JoJo so she could go out on dates. Well, that strategy worked! Drew and I went on a date that lasted 12hrs. Her family wasn't very happy when I brought her home at 4am. To no despair, we stayed in contact and she became my wife. I would ask Drew if I could take JoJo for ice cream or take him to the park while she was working if I felt she needed a helping hand so I could build a stronger bond with him. I knew if I married Drew, he would become my son. JoJo's biological father currently wasn't around and I knew JoJo needed a male influence to help him navigate the world, instill moral and values and grow into the man he would become. I had great expectations however I didn't know what a son or father figure meant from my wifes's eyes. My thought was once we were married, I would automatically take on the father role.

In our scenario, we got married extremely fast and Drew was pregnant 2mo after. We had a huge decision to make, where do we stay to raise the kids. At the time we were in LA and didn't feel like we had much support. We could either go to NJ to my family or Chicago with her family. I spoke with Drew's mom and she said I really can't help you if you stay in LA. Drew has a big family, her mom and dad and 4 sisters. It was a no brainer and we relocated to Chicago before Machai was born. I didn't have a chance to fully assume the "Dad" role as everything was moving fast. We were living under the same roof however Drew was making moves the way she programmed and without much involvement or opinion from my side. There were a few things that I didn't like entirely too much such as JoJo staying up until any time he wanted as if he was a little rockstar in a diaper and him sleeping in the same bed. Drew wasn't receptive to him staying up late and defended by saying she's an actress and her hours flucturate. To combat, I provided studies and reports on best practices for sleeping. I also provided a guidance for the tv staying on all night and she said her parents did it with them and everyone is okay so it's not that bad. I tried developing the "My House, My Rules" concept but it quickly fell on death ears as my concerns weren't enforced. Opposed to supporting, JoJo would cry and mom would come to the rescue. I began to see a common thread, where JoJo was also learning how to get his way and It then became an issue where it was Me vs. Them.

Boiling Point where I felt I couldn't parent

Due to JoJo not receiving adequate sleep, he struggled to get up for school in the morning. Being a man, I had my way of getting you to follow directions which was to place the fear of God in you because at the end of the day, I'm the parent. JoJo stood by the sink and didn't want to brush his teeth so I "acted" as if I was going to give him a pinch and he started crying, not because of pain but because of the act. His mother ran upstairs and grabbed JoJo, asking what happened. JoJo responded, daddy pinched me. Drew grabbed JoJo and repremanded me saying I told you not to do that to him. I asked JoJo to demonstrate on his mother exactly how hard I pinched him and he barely touched his mother. I walked out the room as I felt emasculated and minimized below a child. I thought to myself if I wanted to stay in a relationship where I didn't have a parenting voice. Besides all that I've done and contributed, I should feel more respected. We ended up seeking out a marriage counselor that told us we're doing things all wrong. We didn't have a plan and it shows.

but she did ask for my thoughts to correct him sleeping in the bed.

Introduce Drew's mom, millinial

Support we had and lacked

Realistic / Unrealistic Expectations

It's either him or me

Village mindset, when JoJo's dad came home, Respect. Territorial. No this is my house.

Drew received a call from JoJo's biological dad that he came home from jail and wanted to see his son if possible. At the time Drew was still hurt by the lack of support and effort. Her perspective was, if you haven't been around or made an effort all this time, why now. JoJo doesn't need you. Besides she had me in her life which "filled" the void of JoJo's lack of a father figure. Once Drew brought the conversation and intention to my attention, I had a lot of thinking to do also. As a man or the other man in the situation, I had several thoughts run through my mind.

As men, we can rightfully be territorial and protective of their castle. After I let my pride down, put myself in his shoes and think big picture, there were a few things I had to evaluate. Did JoJo's father approach the situation respectfully for my wife and also for me? Did he do anything to neglect the wellbeing and safety of JoJo? What is the intention? Is this relationship in the best interest for JoJo? I immediately thought of my father and our circumstances.

As a child, no one couldn't tell me that my father wasn't the best in the world and guess what, that's my perspective. If you measured or quantified the value of our relationship, there would be large gaps in his presence, missed games and events, missed birthdays, missed growth and bonding opportunities. Yet, my father was still the best thing that could have ever happened to me. How could this be, the heart doesn't measure value in the way our minds do. Love is blind and that's what makes love beautiful, innocent and cherished. Without love, we would be robots, incapable of forgiving or giving someone an opportunity to succeed. If we were robotic in our heart, we would leave a baby that didn't learn to walk fast enough or talk. Sometimes the greatest lessons on earth is experiencing life.

Interesting enough, Initially I didn't speak with JoJo's biological father as Drew had to feel comfortable with the interaction first however I was always by her side supporting the process. Change is very hard especially on a child therefore she wanted to make sure he wanted to really be part of his life before introducing his Father and he deciding he didn't want that role. Consistency is important to know if you're in this for the long run or if it's a nice experience because you think you should do it. Drew put JoJo's father on a call schedule to slowly introduce JoJo to his Father. JoJo visited with him as a baby but it's been years since they spoke and as a child, they don't know what a father means. The first few interactions was awkward just as any person that walks into a child's life that doesn't have kids, there is a learning process.

Adoption Because JoJo's father wasn't around, people would ask if I would adopt him, which is a great question. These are my rules on adopting in a blended family:

The Father doesn't want to be in the child's life therefore the child is fatherless

The Father is deceased.

The child is in harm or danger, therefore it's an unfit home.

The child doesn't have parents

In the event the child's mother dies, custody can be established through court order......Find out the process. I really don't know.

If I would have adopted Josiah.

JoJo will get to a point where he seeks information and understanding for himself and he would approach his father asking, why didn't he make an effort to be in his life. His Father would more than likely respond, your parents didn't allow me to be a part of your life and pushed me out. JoJo can possibly develop resentment due to our actions, even if we felt it was in his best interest.

This is a great segway into the definition of "Dad." Dads come in all different forms, types, relationships and can be interchangeable for almost anyone providing support that uplifts positive change and growth. When my father wasn't around, coaches became father figures to me including men in the community that taught me fundamentals of manhood. When my father wasn't around, men in the community would hire me and my brother to pickup leaves. It probably was one of the worst jobs I've ever experienced but it built character and work ethic that I wouldn't trade for the world. There is a village that becomes available to instill the lessons children need to learn and the role of "dad" can often be spread throughout the village to ensure children learn fundamentals of life. This concept also applies when the dad is around. Everyone is limited on the amount of information we know. If someone excels in a certain area, send the child to exceed your own understanding as the future depends on our children being smarter and more skilled than us.

Confidence I'm a firm believer that what's for me is for me and no one can take it away. If something isn't for me, then it was only supposed to be in my life for a season and I'm fine.

Being okay with JoJo's biological dad coming into the picture Studies show, 85% of blended familes are dysfunctional. While Drew and I were dating, she was very intentional not to allow me to play the dad role. She didn't want to scare me off or put responsibility on me before we had a chance to know if our relationship would last. Her family also assisted in our dating process. Their goal was to help Drew find the man of her dreams and would take JoJo so she could go out on dates. Well, that strategy worked! Drew and I went on a date that lasted 12hrs. Her family wasn't very happy when I brought her home at 4am. To no despair, we stayed in contact and she became my wife. I would ask Drew if I could take JoJo for ice cream or take him to the park while she was working if I felt she needed a helping hand so I could build a stronger bond with him. I knew if I married Drew, he would become my son. JoJo's biological father currently wasn't around and I knew JoJo needed a male influence to help him navigate the world, instill moral and values and grow into the man he would become. I had great expectations however I didn't know what a son or father figure meant from my wifes's eyes. My thought was once we were married, I would automatically take on the father role.

In our scenario, we got married extremely fast and Drew was pregnant 2mo after. We had a huge decision to make, where do we stay to raise the kids. At the time we were in LA and didn't feel like we had much support. We could either go to NJ to my family or Chicago with her family. I spoke with Drew's mom and she said I really can't help you if you stay in LA. Drew has a big family, her mom and dad and 4 sisters. It was a no brainer and we relocated to Chicago before Machai was born. I didn't have a chance to fully assume the "Dad" role as everything was moving fast. We were living under the same roof however Drew was making moves the way she programmed and without much

involvement or opinion from my side. There were a few things that I didn't like entirely too much such as JoJo staying up until any time he wanted as if he was a little rockstar in a diaper and him sleeping in the same bed. Drew wasn't receptive to him staying up late and defended by saying she's an actress and her hours flucturate. To combat, I provided studies and reports on best practices for sleeping. I also provided a guidance for the tv staying on all night and she said her parents did it with them and everyone is okay so it's not that bad. I tried developing the "My House, My Rules" concept but it quickly fell on death ears as my concerns weren't enforced. Opposed to supporting, JoJo would cry and mom would come to the rescue. I began to see a common thread, where JoJo was also learning how to get his way and It then became an issue where it was Me vs. Them.

Boiling Point where I felt I couldn't parent

Due to JoJo not receiving adequate sleep, he struggled to get up for school in the morning. Being a man, I had my way of getting you to follow directions which was to place the fear of God in you because at the end of the day, I'm the parent. JoJo stood by the sink and didn't want to brush his teeth so I "acted" as if I was going to give him a pinch and he started crying, not because of pain but because of the act. His mother ran upstairs and grabbed JoJo, asking what happened. JoJo responded, daddy pinched me. Drew grabbed JoJo and reprimanded me saying I told you not to do that to him. I asked JoJo to demonstrate on his mother exactly how hard I pinched him and he barely touched his mother. I walked out the room as I felt emasculated and minimized below a child. I thought to myself if I wanted to stay in a relationship where I didn't have a parenting voice. Besides all that I've done and contributed, I should feel more respected. We ended up seeking out a marriage counselor that told us we're doing things all wrong. We didn't have a plan and it shows.

but she did ask for my thoughts to correct him sleeping in the bed.

Introduce Drew's mom, millinial

Support we had and lacked

Realistic / Unrealistic Expectations

It's either him or me

Village mindset, when JoJo's dad came home, Respect. Territorial. No this is my house.

Drew received a call from JoJo's biological dad that he came home from jail and wanted to see his son if possible. At the time Drew was still hurt by the lack of support and effort. Her perspective was, if you haven't been around or made an effort all this time, why now. JoJo doesn't need you. Besides she had me in her life which "filled" the void of JoJo's lack of a father figure. Once Drew brought the conversation and intention to my attention, I had a lot of thinking to do also. As a man or the other man in the situation, I had several thoughts run through my mind. As men, we can rightfully be territorial and protective of their castle. After I let my pride down, put myself in his shoes and think big picture, there were a few things I had to evaluate. Did JoJo's father approach the situation respectfully for my wife and also for me? Did he do anything to neglect the wellbeing and safety of JoJo? What is the intention? Is this relationship in the best interest for JoJo? I immediately thought of my father and our circumstances.

As a child, no one couldn't tell me that my father wasn't the best in the world and guess what, that's my perspective. If you measured or quantified the value of our relationship, there would be large gaps in his presence, missed games and events, missed birthdays, missed growth and bonding opportunities. Yet, my father was still the best thing that could have ever happened to me. How could this be, the heart doesn't measure value in the way our minds do. Love is blind and that's what makes love beautiful, innocent and cherished. Without love, we would be robots, incapable of forgiving or giving someone an opportunity to succeed. If we were robotic in our heart, we would leave a baby that didn't learn to walk fast enough or talk. Sometimes the greatest lessons on earth is experiencing life.

Interesting enough, Initially I didn't speak with JoJo's biological father as Drew had to feel comfortable with the interaction first however I was always by her side supporting the process. Change is very hard especially on a child therefore she wanted to make sure he wanted to really be part of his life before introducing his Father and he deciding he didn't want that role. Consistency is important to know if you're in this for the long run or if it's a nice experience because you think you should do it. Drew put JoJo's father on a call schedule to slowly introduce JoJo to his Father. JoJo visited with him as a baby but it's been years since they spoke and as a child, they don't know what a father means. The first few interactions was awkward just as any person that walks into a child's life that doesn't have kids, there is a learning process.

Adoption Because JoJo's father wasn't around, people would ask if I would adopt him, which is a great question. These are my rules on adopting in a blended family:

The Father doesn't want to be in the child's life therefore the child is fatherless

The Father is deceased.

The child is in harm or danger, therefore it's an unfit home.

The child doesn't have parents

In the event the child's mother dies, custody can be established through court order.....Find out the process. I really don't know.

If I would have adopted Josiah.

JoJo will get to a point where he seeks information and understanding for himself and he would approach his father asking, why didn't he make an effort to be in his life. His Father would more than likely respond, your parents didn't allow me to be a part of your life and pushed me out. JoJo can possibly develop resentment due to our actions, even if we felt it was in his best interest.

This is a great segway into the definition of "Dad." Dads come in all different forms, types, relationships and can be interchangeable for almost anyone providing support that uplifts positive

change and growth. When my father wasn't around, coaches became father figures to me including men in the community that taught me fundamentals of manhood. When my father wasn't around, men in the community would hire me and my brother to pickup leaves. It probably was one of the worst jobs I've ever experienced but it built character and work ethic that I wouldn't trade for the world. There is a village that becomes available to instill the lessons children need to learn and the role of "dad" can often be spread throughout the village to ensure children learn fundamentals of life. This concept also applies when the dad is around. Everyone is limited on the amount of information we know. If someone excels in a certain area, send the child to exceed your own understanding as the future depends on our children being smarter and more skilled than us.

Confidence I'm a firm believer that what's for me is for me and no one can take it away. If something isn't for me, then it was only supposed to be in my life for a season and I'm fine.

Being okay with JoJo's biological dad coming into the picture

Studies show, 85% of blended familes are dysfunctional. While Drew and I were dating, she was very intentional not to allow me to play the dad role. She didn't want to scare me off or put responsibility on me before we had a chance to know if our relationship would last. Her family also assisted in our dating process. Their goal was to help Drew find the man of her dreams and would take JoJo so she could go out on dates. Well, that strategy worked! Drew and I went on a date that lasted 12hrs. Her family wasn't very happy when I brought her home at 4am. To no despair, we stayed in contact and she became my wife. I would ask Drew if I could take JoJo for ice cream or take him to the park while she was working if I felt she needed a helping hand so I could build a stronger bond with him. I knew if I married Drew, he would become my son. JoJo's biological father currently wasn't around and I knew JoJo needed a male influence to help him navigate the world, instill moral and values and grow into the man he would become. I had great expectations however

I didn't know what a son or father figure meant from my wifes's eyes. My thought was once we were married, I would automatically take on the father role.

In our scenario, we got married extremely fast and Drew was pregnant 2mo after. We had a huge decision to make, where do we stay to raise the kids. At the time we were in LA and didn't feel like we had much support. We could either go to NJ to my family or Chicago with her family. I spoke with Drew's mom and she said I really can't help you if you stay in LA. Drew has a big family, her mom and dad and 4 sisters. It was a no brainer and we relocated to Chicago before Machai was born. I didn't have a chance to fully assume the "Dad" role as everything was moving fast. We were living under the same roof however Drew was making moves the way she programmed and without much involvement or opinion from my side. There were a few things that I didn't like entirely too much such as JoJo staying up until any time he wanted as if he was a little rockstar in a diaper and him sleeping in the same bed. Drew wasn't receptive to him staying up late and defended by saying she's an actress and her hours flucturate. To combat, I provided studies and reports on best practices for sleeping. I also provided a guidance for the tv staying on all night and she said her parents did it with them and everyone is okay so it's not that bad. I tried developing the "My House, My Rules" concept but it quickly fell on death ears as my concerns weren't enforced. Opposed to supporting, JoJo would cry and mom would come to the rescue. I began to see a common thread, where JoJo was also learning how to get his way and It then became an issue where it was Me vs. Them.

Boiling Point where I felt I couldn't parent

Due to JoJo not receiving adequate sleep, he struggled to get up for school in the morning. Being a man, I had my way of getting you to follow directions which was to place the fear of God in you because at the end of the day, I'm the parent. JoJo stood by the sink and didn't want to brush his teeth so I "acted" as if I was going to give him a pinch and he started crying, not because

of pain but because of the act. His mother ran upstairs and grabbed JoJo, asking what happened. JoJo responded, daddy pinched me. Drew grabbed JoJo and reprimanded me saying I told you not to do that to him. I asked JoJo to demonstrate on his mother exactly how hard I pinched him and he barely touched his mother. I walked out the room as I felt emasculated and minimized below a child. I thought to myself if I wanted to stay in a relationship where I didn't have a parenting voice. Besides all that I've done and contributed, I should feel more respected. We ended up seeking out a marriage counselor that told us we're doing things all wrong. We didn't have a plan and it shows.

but she did ask for my thoughts to correct him sleeping in the bed.

Introduce Drew's mom, millinial

Support we had and lacked

Realistic / Unrealistic Expectations

It's either him or me

Village mindset, when JoJo's dad came home, Respect. Territorial. No this is my house.

Drew received a call from JoJo's biological dad that he came home from jail and wanted to see his son if possible. At the time Drew was still hurt by the lack of support and effort. Her perspective was, if you haven't been around or made an effort all this time, why now. JoJo doesn't need you. Besides she had me in her life which "filled" the void of JoJo's lack of a father figure. Once Drew brought the conversation and intention to my attention, I had a lot of thinking to do also. As a man or the other man in the situation, I had several thoughts run through my mind. As men, we can rightfully be territorial and protective of their castle. After I let my pride down, put myself in his shoes and think big picture, there were a few things I had to evaluate. Did JoJo's father approach the situation respectfully for my wife and also for me? Did he do anything to neglect the wellbeing and safety of JoJo? What is the intention? Is this relationship in the

best interest for JoJo? I immediately thought of my father and our circumstances.

As a child, no one couldn't tell me that my father wasn't the best in the world and guess what, that's my perspective. If you measured or quantified the value of our relationship, there would be large gaps in his presence, missed games and events, missed birthdays, missed growth and bonding opportunities. Yet, my father was still the best thing that could have ever happened to me. How could this be, the heart doesn't measure value in the way our minds do. Love is blind and that's what makes love beautiful, innocent and cherished. Without love, we would be robots, incapable of forgiving or giving someone an opportunity to succeed. If we were robotic in our heart, we would leave a baby that didn't learn to walk fast enough or talk. Sometimes the greatest lessons on earth is experiencing life.

Interesting enough, Initially I didn't speak with JoJo's biological father as Drew had to feel comfortable with the interaction first however I was always by her side supporting the process. Change is very hard especially on a child therefore she wanted to make sure he wanted to really be part of his life before introducing his Father and he deciding he didn't want that role. Consistency is important to know if you're in this for the long run or if it's a nice experience because you think you should do it. Drew put JoJo's father on a call schedule to slowly introduce JoJo to his Father. JoJo visited with him as a baby but it's been years since they spoke and as a child, they don't know what a father means. The first few interactions was awkward just as any person that walks into a child's life that doesn't have kids, there is a learning process.

Adoption Because JoJo's father wasn't around, people would ask if I would adopt him, which is a great question. These are my rules on adopting in a blended family:

The Father doesn't want to be in the child's life therefore the child is fatherless

The Father is deceased.

The child is in harm or danger, therefore it's an unfit home.

The child doesn't have parents

In the event the child's mother dies, custody can be established through court order.....Find out the process. I really don't know.

If I would have adopted Josiah.

JoJo will get to a point where he seeks information and understanding for himself and he would approach his father asking, why didn't he make an effort to be in his life. His Father would more than likely respond, your parents didn't allow me to be a part of your life and pushed me out. JoJo can possibly develop resentment due to our actions, even if we felt it was in his best interest.

This is a great segway into the definition of "Dad." Dads come in all different forms, types, relationships and can be interchangeable for almost anyone providing support that uplifts positive change and growth. When my father wasn't around, coaches became father figures to me including men in the community that taught me fundamentals of manhood. When my father wasn't around, men in the community would hire me and my brother to pickup leaves. It probably was one of the worst jobs I've ever experienced but it built character and work ethic that I wouldn't trade for the world. There is a village that becomes available to instill the lessons children need to learn and the role of "dad" can often be spread throughout the village to ensure children learn fundamentals of life. This concept also applies when the dad is around. Everyone is limited on the amount of information we know. If someone excels in a certain area, send the child to exceed your own understanding as the future depends on our children being smarter and more skilled than us.

Confidence I'm a firm believer that what's for me is for me and no one can take it away. If something isn't for me, then it was only supposed to be in my life for a season and I'm fine.

Being okay with JoJo's biological dad coming into the picture

Studies show, 85% of blended familes are dysfunctional. While Drew and I were dating, she was very intentional not to

allow me to play the dad role. She didn't want to scare me off or put responsibility on me before we had a chance to know if our relationship would last. Her family also assisted in our dating process. Their goal was to help Drew find the man of her dreams and would take JoJo so she could go out on dates. Well, that strategy worked! Drew and I went on a date that lasted 12hrs. Her family wasn't very happy when I brought her home at 4am. To no despair, we stayed in contact and she became my wife. I would ask Drew if I could take JoJo for ice cream or take him to the park while she was working if I felt she needed a helping hand so I could build a stronger bond with him. I knew if I married Drew, he would become my son. JoJo's biological father currently wasn't around and I knew JoJo needed a male influence to help him navigate the world, instill moral and values and grow into the man he would become. I had great expectations however I didn't know what a son or father figure meant from my wifes's eyes. My thought was once we were married, I would automatically take on the father role.

In our scenario, we got married extremely fast and Drew was pregnant 2mo after. We had a huge decision to make, where do we stay to raise the kids. At the time we were in LA and didn't feel like we had much support. We could either go to NJ to my family or Chicago with her family. I spoke with Drew's mom and she said I really can't help you if you stay in LA. Drew has a big family, her mom and dad and 4 sisters. It was a no brainer and we relocated to Chicago before Machai was born. I didn't have a chance to fully assume the "Dad" role as everything was moving fast. We were living under the same roof however Drew was making moves the way she programmed and without much involvement or opinion from my side. There were a few things that I didn't like entirely too much such as JoJo staying up until any time he wanted as if he was a little rockstar in a diaper and him sleeping in the same bed. Drew wasn't receptive to him staying up late and defended by saying she's an actress and her hours flucturate. To combat, I provided studies and reports on

best practices for sleeping. I also provided a guidance for the tv staying on all night and she said her parents did it with them and everyone is okay so it's not that bad. I tried developing the "My House, My Rules" concept but it quickly fell on death ears as my concerns weren't enforced. Opposed to supporting, JoJo would cry and mom would come to the rescue. I began to see a common thread, where JoJo was also learning how to get his way and It then became an issue where it was Me vs. Them.

Boiling Point where I felt I couldn't parent

Due to JoJo not receiving adequate sleep, he struggled to get up for school in the morning. Being a man, I had my way of getting you to follow directions which was to place the fear of God in you because at the end of the day, I'm the parent. JoJo stood by the sink and didn't want to brush his teeth so I "acted" as if I was going to give him a pinch and he started crying, not because of pain but because of the act. His mother ran upstairs and grabbed JoJo, asking what happened. JoJo responded, daddy pinched me. Drew grabbed JoJo and repremanded me saying I told you not to do that to him. I asked JoJo to demonstrate on his mother exactly how hard I pinched him and he barely touched his mother. I walked out the room as I felt emasculated and minimized below a child. I thought to myself if I wanted to stay in a relationship where I didn't have a parenting voice. Besides all that I've done and contributed, I should feel more respected. We ended up seeking out a marriage counselor that told us we're doing things all wrong. We didn't have a plan and it shows.

but she did ask for my thoughts to correct him sleeping in the bed.

Introduce Drew's mom, millinial

Support we had and lacked

Realistic / Unrealistic Expectations

It's either him or me

Village mindset, when JoJo's dad came home, Respect. Territorial. No this is my house.

Drew received a call from JoJo's biological dad that he came home from jail and wanted to see his son if possible. At the time Drew was still hurt by the lack of support and effort. Her perspective was, if you haven't been around or made an effort all this time, why now. JoJo doesn't need you. Besides she had me in her life which "filled" the void of JoJo's lack of a father figure. Once Drew brought the conversation and intention to my attention, I had a lot of thinking to do also. As a man or the other man in the situation, I had several thoughts run through my mind. As men, we can rightfully be territorial and protective of their castle. After I let my pride down, put myself in his shoes and think big picture, there were a few things I had to evaluate. Did JoJo's father approach the situation respectfully for my wife and also for me? Did he do anything to neglect the wellbeing and safety of JoJo? What is the intention? Is this relationship in the best interest for JoJo? I immediately thought of my father and our circumstances.

As a child, no one couldn't tell me that my father wasn't the best in the world and guess what, that's my perspective. If you measured or quantified the value of our relationship, there would be large gaps in his presence, missed games and events, missed birthdays, missed growth and bonding opportunities. Yet, my father was still the best thing that could have ever happened to me. How could this be, the heart doesn't measure value in the way our minds do. Love is blind and that's what makes love beautiful, innocent and cherished. Without love, we would be robots, incapable of forgiving or giving someone an opportunity to succeed. If we were robotic in our heart, we would leave a baby that didn't learn to walk fast enough or talk. Sometimes the greatest lessons on earth is experiencing life.

Interesting enough, Initially I didn't speak with JoJo's biological father as Drew had to feel comfortable with the interaction first however I was always by her side supporting the process. Change is very hard especially on a child therefore she wanted to make sure he wanted to really be part of his life before

introducing his Father and he deciding he didn't want that role. Consistency is important to know if you're in this for the long run or if it's a nice experience because you think you should do it. Drew put JoJo's father on a call schedule to slowly introduce JoJo to his Father. JoJo visited with him as a baby but it's been years since they spoke and as a child, they don't know what a father means. The first few interactions was awkward just as any person that walks into a child's life that doesn't have kids, there is a learning process.

Adoption Because JoJo's father wasn't around, people would ask if I would adopt him, which is a great question. These are my rules on adopting in a blended family:

The Father doesn't want to be in the child's life therefore the child is fatherless

The Father is deceased.

The child is in harm or danger, therefore it's an unfit home.

The child doesn't have parents

In the event the child's mother dies, custody can be established through court order.....Find out the process. I really don't know.

If I would have adopted Josiah.

JoJo will get to a point where he seeks information and understanding for himself and he would approach his father asking, why didn't he make an effort to be in his life. His Father would more than likely respond, your parents didn't allow me to be a part of your life and pushed me out. JoJo can possibly develop resentment due to our actions, even if we felt it was in his best interest.

This is a great segway into the definition of "Dad." Dads come in all different forms, types, relationships and can be interchangeable for almost anyone providing support that uplifts positive change and growth. When my father wasn't around, coaches became father figures to me including men in the community that taught me fundamentals of manhood. When my father wasn't around, men in the community would hire me and my brother to pickup leaves. It probably was one of the worst jobs I've ever

experienced but it built character and work ethic that I wouldn't trade for the world. There is a village that becomes available to instill the lessons children need to learn and the role of "dad" can often be spread throughout the village to ensure children learn fundamentals of life. This concept also applies when the dad is around. Everyone is limited on the amount of information we know. If someone excels in a certain area, send the child to exceed your own understanding as the future depends on our children being smarter and more skilled than us.

Confidence I'm a firm believer that what's for me is for me and no one can take it away. If something isn't for me, then it was only supposed to be in my life for a season and I'm fine.

Being okay with JoJo's biological dad coming into the picture Studies show, 85% of blended familes are dysfunctional. While Drew and I were dating, she was very intentional not to allow me to play the dad role. She didn't want to scare me off or put responsibility on me before we had a chance to know if our relationship would last. Her family also assisted in our dating process. Their goal was to help Drew find the man of her dreams and would take JoJo so she could go out on dates. Well, that strategy worked! Drew and I went on a date that lasted 12hrs. Her family wasn't very happy when I brought her home at 4am. To no despair, we stayed in contact and she became my wife. I would ask Drew if I could take JoJo for ice cream or take him to the park while she was working if I felt she needed a helping hand so I could build a stronger bond with him. I knew if I married Drew, he would become my son. JoJo's biological father currently wasn't around and I knew JoJo needed a male influence to help him navigate the world, instill moral and values and grow into the man he would become. I had great expectations however I didn't know what a son or father figure meant from my wifes's eyes. My thought was once we were married, I would automatically take on the father role.

In our scenario, we got married extremely fast and Drew was pregnant 2mo after. We had a huge decision to make, where do

we stay to raise the kids. At the time we were in LA and didn't feel like we had much support. We could either go to NJ to my family or Chicago with her family. I spoke with Drew's mom and she said I really can't help you if you stay in LA. Drew has a big family, her mom and dad and 4 sisters. It was a no brainer and we relocated to Chicago before Machai was born. I didn't have a chance to fully assume the "Dad" role as everything was moving fast. We were living under the same roof however Drew was making moves the way she programmed and without much involvement or opinion from my side. There were a few things that I didn't like entirely too much such as JoJo staying up until any time he wanted as if he was a little rockstar in a diaper and him sleeping in the same bed. Drew wasn't receptive to him staying up late and defended by saying she's an actress and her hours flucturate. To combat, I provided studies and reports on best practices for sleeping. I also provided a guidance for the tv staying on all night and she said her parents did it with them and everyone is okay so it's not that bad. I tried developing the "My House, My Rules" concept but it quickly fell on death ears as my concerns weren't enforced. Opposed to supporting, JoJo would cry and mom would come to the rescue. I began to see a common thread, where JoJo was also learning how to get his way and It then became an issue where it was Me vs. Them.

Boiling Point where I felt I couldn't parent

Due to JoJo not receiving adequate sleep, he struggled to get up for school in the morning. Being a man, I had my way of getting you to follow directions which was to place the fear of God in you because at the end of the day, I'm the parent. JoJo stood by the sink and didn't want to brush his teeth so I "acted" as if I was going to give him a pinch and he started crying, not because of pain but because of the act. His mother ran upstairs and grabbed JoJo, asking what happened. JoJo responded, daddy pinched me. Drew grabbed JoJo and repremanded me saying I told you not to do that to him. I asked JoJo to demonstrate on his mother exactly how hard I pinched him and he barely touched

his mother. I walked out the room as I felt emasculated and minimized below a child. I thought to myself if I wanted to stay in a relationship where I didn't have a parenting voice. Besides all that I've done and contributed, I should feel more respected. We ended up seeking out a marriage counselor that told us we're doing things all wrong. We didn't have a plan and it shows.

but she did ask for my thoughts to correct him sleeping in the bed.

Introduce Drew's mom, millinial

Support we had and lacked

Realistic / Unrealistic Expectations

It's either him or me

Village mindset, when JoJo's dad came home, Respect. Territorial. No this is my house.

Drew received a call from JoJo's biological dad that he came home from jail and wanted to see his son if possible. At the time Drew was still hurt by the lack of support and effort. Her perspective was, if you haven't been around or made an effort all this time, why now. JoJo doesn't need you. Besides she had me in her life which "filled" the void of JoJo's lack of a father figure. Once Drew brought the conversation and intention to my attention, I had a lot of thinking to do also. As a man or the other man in the situation, I had several thoughts run through my mind. As men, we can rightfully be territorial and protective of their castle. After I let my pride down, put myself in his shoes and think big picture, there were a few things I had to evaluate. Did JoJo's father approach the situation respectfully for my wife and also for me? Did he do anything to neglect the wellbeing and safety of JoJo? What is the intention? Is this relationship in the best interest for JoJo? I immediately thought of my father and our circumstances.

As a child, no one couldn't tell me that my father wasn't the best in the world and guess what, that's my perspective. If you measured or quantified the value of our relationship, there would be large gaps in his presence, missed games and events,

missed birthdays, missed growth and bonding opportunities. Yet, my father was still the best thing that could have ever happened to me. How could this be, the heart doesn't measure value in the way our minds do. Love is blind and that's what makes love beautiful, innocent and cherished. Without love, we would be robots, incapable of forgiving or giving someone an opportunity to succeed. If we were robotic in our heart, we would leave a baby that didn't learn to walk fast enough or talk. Sometimes the greatest lessons on earth is experiencing life.

Interesting enough, Initially I didn't speak with JoJo's biological father as Drew had to feel comfortable with the interaction first however I was always by her side supporting the process. Change is very hard especially on a child therefore she wanted to make sure he wanted to really be part of his life before introducing his Father and he deciding he didn't want that role. Consistency is important to know if you're in this for the long run or if it's a nice experience because you think you should do it. Drew put JoJo's father on a call schedule to slowly introduce JoJo to his Father. JoJo visited with him as a baby but it's been years since they spoke and as a child, they don't know what a father means. The first few interactions was awkward just as any person that walks into a child's life that doesn't have kids, there is a learning process.

Adoption Because JoJo's father wasn't around, people would ask if I would adopt him, which is a great question. These are my rules on adopting in a blended family:

The Father doesn't want to be in the child's life therefore the child is fatherless

The Father is deceased.

The child is in harm or danger, therefore it's an unfit home.

The child doesn't have parents

In the event the child's mother dies, custody can be established through court order.....Find out the process. I really don't know.

If I would have adopted Josiah.

JoJo will get to a point where he seeks information and under-standing for himself and he would approach his father asking, why didn't he make an effort to be in his life. His Father would more than likely respond, your parents didn't allow me to be a part of your life and pushed me out. JoJo can possibly develop resentment due to our actions, even if we felt it was in his best interest.

This is a great segway into the definition of "Dad." Dads come in all different forms, types, relationships and can be interchange-able for almost anyone providing support that uplifts positive change and growth. When my father wasn't around, coaches became father figures to me including men in the community that taught me fundamentals of manhood. When my father wasn't around, men in the community would hire me and my brother to pickup leaves. It probably was one of the worst jobs I've ever experienced but it built character and work ethic that I wouldn't trade for the world. There is a village that becomes available to instill the lessons children need to learn and the role of "dad" can often be spread throughout the village to ensure children learn fundamentals of life. This concept also applies when the dad is around. Everyone is limited on the amount of information we know. If someone excels in a certain area, send the child to exceed your own understanding as the future depends on our children being smarter and more skilled than us.

Confidence I'm a firm believer that what's for me is for me and no one can take it away. If something isn't for me, then it was only supposed to be in my life for a season and I'm fine.

Being okay with JoJo's biological dad coming into the picture Studies show, 85% of blended familes are dysfunctional. While Drew and I were dating, she was very intentional not to allow me to play the dad role. She didn't want to scare me off or put responsibility on me before we had a chance to know if our relationship would last. Her family also assisted in our dating process. Their goal was to help Drew find the man of her dreams and would take JoJo so she could go out on dates. Well, that

strategy worked! Drew and I went on a date that lasted 12hrs. Her family wasn't very happy when I brought her home at 4am. To no despair, we stayed in contact and she became my wife. I would ask Drew if I could take JoJo for ice cream or take him to the park while she was working if I felt she needed a helping hand so I could build a stronger bond with him. I knew if I married Drew, he would become my son. JoJo's biological father currently wasn't around and I knew JoJo needed a male influence to help him navigate the world, instill moral and values and grow into the man he would become. I had great expectations however I didn't know what a son or father figure meant from my wifes's eyes. My thought was once we were married, I would automatically take on the father role.

In our scenario, we got married extremely fast and Drew was pregnant 2mo after. We had a huge decision to make, where do we stay to raise the kids. At the time we were in LA and didn't feel like we had much support. We could either go to NJ to my family or Chicago with her family. I spoke with Drew's mom and she said I really can't help you if you stay in LA. Drew has a big family, her mom and dad and 4 sisters. It was a no brainer and we relocated to Chicago before Machai was born. I didn't have a chance to fully assume the "Dad" role as everything was moving fast. We were living under the same roof however Drew was making moves the way she programmed and without much involvement or opinion from my side. There were a few things that I didn't like entirely too much such as JoJo staying up until any time he wanted as if he was a little rockstar in a diaper and him sleeping in the same bed. Drew wasn't receptive to him staying up late and defended by saying she's an actress and her hours flucturate. To combat, I provided studies and reports on best practices for sleeping. I also provided a guidance for the tv staying on all night and she said her parents did it with them and everyone is okay so it's not that bad. I tried developing the "My House, My Rules" concept but it quickly fell on death ears as my concerns weren't enforced. Opposed to supporting, JoJo would

cry and mom would come to the rescue. I began to see a common thread, where JoJo was also learning how to get his way and It then became an issue where it was Me vs. Them.

Boiling Point where I felt I couldn't parent

Due to JoJo not receiving adequate sleep, he struggled to get up for school in the morning. Being a man, I had my way of getting you to follow directions which was to place the fear of God in you because at the end of the day, I'm the parent. JoJo stood by the sink and didn't want to brush his teeth so I "acted" as if I was going to give him a pinch and he started crying, not because of pain but because of the act. His mother ran upstairs and grabbed JoJo, asking what happened. JoJo responded, daddy pinched me. Drew grabbed JoJo and repremanded me saying I told you not to do that to him. I asked JoJo to demonstrate on his mother exactly how hard I pinched him and he barely touched his mother. I walked out the room as I felt emasculated and minimized below a child. I thought to myself if I wanted to stay in a relationship where I didn't have a parenting voice. Besides all that I've done and contributed, I should feel more respected. We ended up seeking out a marriage counselor that told us we're doing things all wrong. We didn't have a plan and it shows.

but she did ask for my thoughts to correct him sleeping in the bed.

Introduce Drew's mom, millinial

Support we had and lacked

Realistic / Unrealistic Expectations

It's either him or me

Village mindset, when JoJo's dad came home, Respect. Territorial. No this is my house.

Drew received a call from JoJo's biological dad that he came home from jail and wanted to see his son if possible. At the time Drew was still hurt by the lack of support and effort. Her perspective was, if you haven't been around or made an effort all this time, why now. JoJo doesn't need you. Besides she had me in her life which "filled" the void of JoJo's lack of a father figure.

Once Drew brought the conversation and intention to my attention, I had a lot of thinking to do also. As a man or the other man in the situation, I had several thoughts run through my mind. As men, we can rightfully be territorial and protective of their castle. After I let my pride down, put myself in his shoes and think big picture, there were a few things I had to evaluate. Did JoJo's father approach the situation respectfully for my wife and also for me? Did he do anything to neglect the wellbeing and safety of JoJo? What is the intention? Is this relationship in the best interest for JoJo? I immediately thought of my father and our circumstances.

As a child, no one couldn't tell me that my father wasn't the best in the world and guess what, that's my perspective. If you measured or quantified the value of our relationship, there would be large gaps in his presence, missed games and events, missed birthdays, missed growth and bonding opportunities. Yet, my father was still the best thing that could have ever happened to me. How could this be, the heart doesn't measure value in the way our minds do. Love is blind and that's what makes love beautiful, innocent and cherished. Without love, we would be robots, incapable of forgiving or giving someone an opportunity to succeed. If we were robotic in our heart, we would leave a baby that didn't learn to walk fast enough or talk. Sometimes the greatest lessons on earth is experiencing life.

Interesting enough, Initially I didn't speak with JoJo's biological father as Drew had to feel comfortable with the interaction first however I was always by her side supporting the process. Change is very hard especially on a child therefore she wanted to make sure he wanted to really be part of his life before introducing his Father and he deciding he didn't want that role. Consistency is important to know if you're in this for the long run or if it's a nice experience because you think you should do it. Drew put JoJo's father on a call schedule to slowly introduce JoJo to his Father. JoJo visited with him as a baby but it's been years since they spoke and as a child, they don't know what a

father means. The first few interactions was awkward just as any person that walks into a child's life that doesn't have kids, there is a learning process.

Adoption Because JoJo's father wasn't around, people would ask if I would adopt him, which is a great question. These are my rules on adopting in a blended family:

The Father doesn't want to be in the child's life therefore the child is fatherless

The Father is deceased.

The child is in harm or danger, therefore it's an unfit home.

The child doesn't have parents

In the event the child's mother dies, custody can be established through court order.....Find out the process. I really don't know.

If I would have adopted Josiah.

JoJo will get to a point where he seeks information and understanding for himself and he would approach his father asking, why didn't he make an effort to be in his life. His Father would more than likely respond, your parents didn't allow me to be a part of your life and pushed me out. JoJo can possibly develop resentment due to our actions, even if we felt it was in his best interest.

This is a great segway into the definition of "Dad." Dads come in all different forms, types, relationships and can be interchangeable for almost anyone providing support that uplifts positive change and growth. When my father wasn't around, coaches became father figures to me including men in the community that taught me fundamentals of manhood. When my father wasn't around, men in the community would hire me and my brother to pickup leaves. It probably was one of the worst jobs I've ever experienced but it built character and work ethic that I wouldn't trade for the world. There is a village that becomes available to instill the lessons children need to learn and the role of "dad" can often be spread throughout the village to ensure children learn fundamentals of life. This concept also applies when the dad is around. Everyone is limited on the amount of information

we know. If someone excels in a certain area, send the child to exceed your own understanding as the future depends on our children being smarter and more skilled than us.

Confidence I'm a firm believer that what's for me is for me and no one can take it away. If something isn't for me, then it was only supposed to be in my life for a season and I'm fine.

Being okay with JoJo's biological dad coming into the picture Studies show, 85% of blended familes are dysfunctional. While Drew and I were dating, she was very intentional not to allow me to play the dad role. She didn't want to scare me off or put responsibility on me before we had a chance to know if our relationship would last. Her family also assisted in our dating process. Their goal was to help Drew find the man of her dreams and would take JoJo so she could go out on dates. Well, that strategy worked! Drew and I went on a date that lasted 12hrs. Her family wasn't very happy when I brought her home at 4am. To no despair, we stayed in contact and she became my wife. I would ask Drew if I could take JoJo for ice cream or take him to the park while she was working if I felt she needed a helping hand so I could build a stronger bond with him. I knew if I married Drew, he would become my son. JoJo's biological father currently wasn't around and I knew JoJo needed a male influence to help him navigate the world, instill moral and values and grow into the man he would become. I had great expectations however I didn't know what a son or father figure meant from my wifes's eyes. My thought was once we were married, I would automatically take on the father role.

In our scenario, we got married extremely fast and Drew was pregnant 2mo after. We had a huge decision to make, where do we stay to raise the kids. At the time we were in LA and didn't feel like we had much support. We could either go to NJ to my family or Chicago with her family. I spoke with Drew's mom and she said I really can't help you if you stay in LA. Drew has a big family, her mom and dad and 4 sisters. It was a no brainer and we relocated to Chicago before Machai was born. I didn't

have a chance to fully assume the "Dad" role as everything was moving fast. We were living under the same roof however Drew was making moves the way she programmed and without much involvement or opinion from my side. There were a few things that I didn't like entirely too much such as JoJo staying up until any time he wanted as if he was a little rockstar in a diaper and him sleeping in the same bed. Drew wasn't receptive to him staying up late and defended by saying she's an actress and her hours flucturate. To combat, I provided studies and reports on best practices for sleeping. I also provided a guidance for the tv staying on all night and she said her parents did it with them and everyone is okay so it's not that bad. I tried developing the "My House, My Rules" concept but it quickly fell on death ears as my concerns weren't enforced. Opposed to supporting, JoJo would cry and mom would come to the rescue. I began to see a common thread, where JoJo was also learning how to get his way and It then became an issue where it was Me vs. Them.

Boiling Point where I felt I couldn't parent

Due to JoJo not receiving adequate sleep, he struggled to get up for school in the morning. Being a man, I had my way of getting you to follow directions which was to place the fear of God in you because at the end of the day, I'm the parent. JoJo stood by the sink and didn't want to brush his teeth so I "acted" as if I was going to give him a pinch and he started crying, not because of pain but because of the act. His mother ran upstairs and grabbed JoJo, asking what happened. JoJo responded, daddy pinched me. Drew grabbed JoJo and repremanded me saying I told you not to do that to him. I asked JoJo to demonstrate on his mother exactly how hard I pinched him and he barely touched his mother. I walked out the room as I felt emasculated and minimized below a child. I thought to myself if I wanted to stay in a relationship where I didn't have a parenting voice. Besides all that I've done and contributed, I should feel more respected. We ended up seeking out a marriage counselor that told us we're doing things all wrong. We didn't have a plan and it shows.

but she did ask for my thoughts to correct him sleeping in the bed.

Introduce Drew's mom, millinial

Support we had and lacked

Realistic / Unrealistic Expectations

It's either him or me

Village mindset, when JoJo's dad came home, Respect. Territorial. No this is my house.

Drew received a call from JoJo's biological dad that he came home from jail and wanted to see his son if possible. At the time Drew was still hurt by the lack of support and effort. Her perspective was, if you haven't been around or made an effort all this time, why now. JoJo doesn't need you. Besides she had me in her life which "filled" the void of JoJo's lack of a father figure. Once Drew brought the conversation and intention to my attention, I had a lot of thinking to do also. As a man or the other man in the situation, I had several thoughts run through my mind. As men, we can rightfully be territorial and protective of their castle. After I let my pride down, put myself in his shoes and think big picture, there were a few things I had to evaluate. Did JoJo's father approach the situation respectfully for my wife and also for me? Did he do anything to neglect the wellbeing and safety of JoJo? What is the intention? Is this relationship in the best interest for JoJo? I immediately thought of my father and our circumstances.

As a child, no one couldn't tell me that my father wasn't the best in the world and guess what, that's my perspective. If you measured or quantified the value of our relationship, there would be large gaps in his presence, missed games and events, missed birthdays, missed growth and bonding opportunities. Yet, my father was still the best thing that could have ever happened to me. How could this be, the heart doesn't measure value in the way our minds do. Love is blind and that's what makes love beautiful, innocent and cherished. Without love, we would be robots, incapable of forgiving or giving someone an opportunity to succeed.

If we were robotic in our heart, we would leave a baby that didn't learn to walk fast enough or talk. Sometimes the greatest lessons on earth is experiencing life.

Interesting enough, Initially I didn't speak with JoJo's biological father as Drew had to feel comfortable with the interaction first however I was always by her side supporting the process. Change is very hard especially on a child therefore she wanted to make sure he wanted to really be part of his life before introducing his Father and he deciding he didn't want that role. Consistency is important to know if you're in this for the long run or if it's a nice experience because you think you should do it. Drew put JoJo's father on a call schedule to slowly introduce JoJo to his Father. JoJo visited with him as a baby but it's been years since they spoke and as a child, they don't know what a father means. The first few interactions was awkward just as any person that walks into a child's life that doesn't have kids, there is a learning process.

Adoption Because JoJo's father wasn't around, people would ask if I would adopt him, which is a great question. These are my rules on adopting in a blended family:

The Father doesn't want to be in the child's life therefore the child is fatherless

The Father is deceased.

The child is in harm or danger, therefore it's an unfit home.

The child doesn't have parents

In the event the child's mother dies, custody can be established through court order.....Find out the process. I really don't know.

If I would have adopted Josiah.

JoJo will get to a point where he seeks information and understanding for himself and he would approach his father asking, why didn't he make an effort to be in his life. His Father would more than likely respond, your parents didn't allow me to be a part of your life and pushed me out. JoJo can possibly develop resentment due to our actions, even if we felt it was in his best interest.

This is a great segway into the definition of "Dad." Dads come in all different forms, types, relationships and can be interchangeable for almost anyone providing support that uplifts positive change and growth. When my father wasn't around, coaches became father figures to me including men in the community that taught me fundamentals of manhood. When my father wasn't around, men in the community would hire me and my brother to pickup leaves. It probably was one of the worst jobs I've ever experienced but it built character and work ethic that I wouldn't trade for the world. There is a village that becomes available to instill the lessons children need to learn and the role of "dad" can often be spread throughout the village to ensure children learn fundamentals of life. This concept also applies when the dad is around. Everyone is limited on the amount of information we know. If someone excels in a certain area, send the child to exceed your own understanding as the future depends on our children being smarter and more skilled than us.

Confidence I'm a firm believer that what's for me is for me and no one can take it away. If something isn't for me, then it was only supposed to be in my life for a season and I'm fine.

Being okay with JoJo's biological dad coming into the picture Studies show, 85% of blended familes are dysfunctional. While Drew and I were dating, she was very intentional not to allow me to play the dad role. She didn't want to scare me off or put responsibility on me before we had a chance to know if our relationship would last. Her family also assisted in our dating process. Their goal was to help Drew find the man of her dreams and would take JoJo so she could go out on dates. Well, that strategy worked! Drew and I went on a date that lasted 12hrs. Her family wasn't very happy when I brought her home at 4am. To no despair, we stayed in contact and she became my wife. I would ask Drew if I could take JoJo for ice cream or take him to the park while she was working if I felt she needed a helping hand so I could build a stronger bond with him. I knew if I married Drew, he would become my son. JoJo's biological father currently

wasn't around and I knew JoJo needed a male influence to help him navigate the world, instill moral and values and grow into the man he would become. I had great expectations however I didn't know what a son or father figure meant from my wifes's eyes. My thought was once we were married, I would automatically take on the father role.

In our scenario, we got married extremely fast and Drew was pregnant 2mo after. We had a huge decision to make, where do we stay to raise the kids. At the time we were in LA and didn't feel like we had much support. We could either go to NJ to my family or Chicago with her family. I spoke with Drew's mom and she said I really can't help you if you stay in LA. Drew has a big family, her mom and dad and 4 sisters. It was a no brainer and we relocated to Chicago before Machai was born. I didn't have a chance to fully assume the "Dad" role as everything was moving fast. We were living under the same roof however Drew was making moves the way she programmed and without much involvement or opinion from my side. There were a few things that I didn't like entirely too much such as JoJo staying up until any time he wanted as if he was a little rockstar in a diaper and him sleeping in the same bed. Drew wasn't receptive to him staying up late and defended by saying she's an actress and her hours flucturate. To combat, I provided studies and reports on best practices for sleeping. I also provided a guidance for the tv staying on all night and she said her parents did it with them and everyone is okay so it's not that bad. I tried developing the "My House, My Rules" concept but it quickly fell on death ears as my concerns weren't enforced. Opposed to supporting, JoJo would cry and mom would come to the rescue. I began to see a common thread, where JoJo was also learning how to get his way and It then became an issue where it was Me vs. Them.

Boiling Point where I felt I couldn't parent

Due to JoJo not receiving adequate sleep, he struggled to get up for school in the morning. Being a man, I had my way of getting you to follow directions which was to place the fear of God

in you because at the end of the day, I'm the parent. JoJo stood by the sink and didn't want to brush his teeth so I "acted" as if I was going to give him a pinch and he started crying, not because of pain but because of the act. His mother ran upstairs and grabbed JoJo, asking what happened. JoJo responded, daddy pinched me. Drew grabbed JoJo and repremanded me saying I told you not to do that to him. I asked JoJo to demonstrate on his mother exactly how hard I pinched him and he barely touched his mother. I walked out the room as I felt emasculated and minimized below a child. I thought to myself if I wanted to stay in a relationship where I didn't have a parenting voice. Besides all that I've done and contributed, I should feel more respected. We ended up seeking out a marriage counselor that told us we're doing things all wrong. We didn't have a plan and it shows.

but she did ask for my thoughts to correct him sleeping in the bed.

Introduce Drew's mom, millinial

Support we had and lacked

Realistic / Unrealistic Expectations

It's either him or me

Village mindset, when JoJo's dad came home, Respect. Territorial. No this is my house.

Drew received a call from JoJo's biological dad that he came home from jail and wanted to see his son if possible. At the time Drew was still hurt by the lack of support and effort. Her perspective was, if you haven't been around or made an effort all this time, why now. JoJo doesn't need you. Besides she had me in her life which "filled" the void of JoJo's lack of a father figure. Once Drew brought the conversation and intention to my attention, I had a lot of thinking to do also. As a man or the other man in the situation, I had several thoughts run through my mind. As men, we can rightfully be territorial and protective of their castle. After I let my pride down, put myself in his shoes and think big picture, there were a few things I had to evaluate. Did JoJo's father approach the situation respectfully for my wife and

also for me? Did he do anything to neglect the wellbeing and safety of JoJo? What is the intention? Is this relationship in the best interest for JoJo? I immediately thought of my father and our circumstances.

Village Mindset

A **S A CHILD,** no one couldn't tell me that my father wasn't the best in the world and guess what, that's my perspective. If you measured or quantified the value of our relationship, there would be large gaps in his presence, missed games and events, missed birthdays, missed growth and bonding opportunities. Yet, my father was still the best thing that could have ever happened to me. How could this be, the heart doesn't measure value in the way our minds do. Love is blind and that's what makes love beautiful, innocent and cherished. Without love, we would be robots, incapable of forgiving or giving someone an opportunity to succeed. If we were robotic in our heart, we would leave a baby that didn't learn to walk fast enough or talk. Sometimes the greatest lessons on earth is experiencing life.

Interesting enough, Initially I didn't speak with JoJo's biological father as Drew had to feel comfortable with the interaction first however I was always by her side supporting the process. Change is very hard especially on a child therefore she wanted to make sure he wanted to really be part of his life before introducing his Father and he deciding he didn't want that role. Consistency is important to know if you're in this for the long run or if it's a nice experience because you think you should do

it. Drew put JoJo's father on a call schedule to slowly introduce JoJo to his Father. JoJo visited with him as a baby but it's been years since they spoke and as a child, they don't know what a father means. The first few interactions was awkward just as any person that walks into a child's life that doesn't have kids, there is a learning process.

Adoption Because JoJo's father wasn't around, people would ask if I would adopt him, which is a great question. These are my rules on adopting in a blended family:

The Father doesn't want to be in the child's life therefore the child is fatherless

The Father is deceased.

The child is in harm or danger, therefore it's an unfit home.

The child doesn't have parents

In the event the child's mother dies, custody can be established through court order.....Find out the process. I really don't know.

If I would have adopted Josiah.

JoJo will get to a point where he seeks information and understanding for himself and he would approach his father asking, why didn't he make an effort to be in his life. His Father would more than likely respond, your parents didn't allow me to be a part of your life and pushed me out. JoJo can possibly develop resentment due to our actions, even if we felt it was in his best interest.

This is a great segway into the definition of "Dad." Dads come in all different forms, types, relationships and can be interchangeable for almost anyone providing support that uplifts positive change and growth. When my father wasn't around, coaches became father figures to me including men in the community that taught me fundamentals of manhood. When my father wasn't around, men in the community would hire me and my brother to pickup leaves. It probably was one of the worst jobs I've ever experienced but it built character and work ethic that I wouldn't trade for the world. There is a village that becomes available to instill the lessons children need to learn and the role of "dad"

can often be spread throughout the village to ensure children learn fundamentals of life. This concept also applies when the dad is around. Everyone is limited on the amount of information we know. If someone excels in a certain area, send the child to exceed your own understanding as the future depends on our children being smarter and more skilled than us.

Confidence I'm a firm believer that what's for me is for me and no one can take it away. If something isn't for me, then it was only supposed to be in my life for a season and I'm fine.

Being okay with JoJo's biological dad coming into the picture Studies show, 85% of blended familes are dysfunctional. While Drew and I were dating, she was very intentional not to allow me to play the dad role. She didn't want to scare me off or put responsibility on me before we had a chance to know if our relationship would last. Her family also assisted in our dating process. Their goal was to help Drew find the man of her dreams and would take JoJo so she could go out on dates. Well, that strategy worked! Drew and I went on a date that lasted 12hrs. Her family wasn't very happy when I brought her home at 4am. To no despair, we stayed in contact and she became my wife. I would ask Drew if I could take JoJo for ice cream or take him to the park while she was working if I felt she needed a helping hand so I could build a stronger bond with him. I knew if I married Drew, he would become my son. JoJo's biological father currently wasn't around and I knew JoJo needed a male influence to help him navigate the world, instill moral and values and grow into the man he would become. I had great expectations however I didn't know what a son or father figure meant from my wifes's eyes. My thought was once we were married, I would automatically take on the father role.

In our scenario, we got married extremely fast and Drew was pregnant 2mo after. We had a huge decision to make, where do we stay to raise the kids. At the time we were in LA and didn't feel like we had much support. We could either go to NJ to my family or Chicago with her family. I spoke with Drew's mom

and she said I really can't help you if you stay in LA. Drew has a big family, her mom and dad and 4 sisters. It was a no brainer and we relocated to Chicago before Machai was born. I didn't have a chance to fully assume the "Dad" role as everything was moving fast. We were living under the same roof however Drew was making moves the way she programmed and without much involvement or opinion from my side. There were a few things that I didn't like entirely too much such as JoJo staying up until any time he wanted as if he was a little rockstar in a diaper and him sleeping in the same bed. Drew wasn't receptive to him staying up late and defended by saying she's an actress and her hours flucturate. To combat, I provided studies and reports on best practices for sleeping. I also provided a guidance for the tv staying on all night and she said her parents did it with them and everyone is okay so it's not that bad. I tried developing the "My House, My Rules" concept but it quickly fell on death ears as my concerns weren't enforced. Opposed to supporting, JoJo would cry and mom would come to the rescue. I began to see a common thread, where JoJo was also learning how to get his way and It then became an issue where it was Me vs. Them.

Boiling Point where I felt I couldn't parent

Due to JoJo not receiving adequate sleep, he struggled to get up for school in the morning. Being a man, I had my way of getting you to follow directions which was to place the fear of God in you because at the end of the day, I'm the parent. JoJo stood by the sink and didn't want to brush his teeth so I "acted" as if I was going to give him a pinch and he started crying, not because of pain but because of the act. His mother ran upstairs and grabbed JoJo, asking what happened. JoJo responded, daddy pinched me. Drew grabbed JoJo and reprimanded me saying I told you not to do that to him. I asked JoJo to demonstrate on his mother exactly how hard I pinched him and he barely touched his mother. I walked out the room as I felt emasculated and minimized below a child. I thought to myself if I wanted to stay in a relationship where I didn't have a parenting voice. Besides all

that I've done and contributed, I should feel more respected. We ended up seeking out a marriage counselor that told us we're doing things all wrong. We didn't have a plan and it shows.

but she did ask for my thoughts to correct him sleeping in the bed.

Introduce Drew's mom, millinial

Support we had and lacked

Realistic / Unrealistic Expectations

It's either him or me

Village mindset, when JoJo's dad came home, Respect. Territorial. No this is my house.

Drew received a call from JoJo's biological dad that he came home from jail and wanted to see his son if possible. At the time Drew was still hurt by the lack of support and effort. Her perspective was, if you haven't been around or made an effort all this time, why now. JoJo doesn't need you. Besides she had me in her life which "filled" the void of JoJo's lack of a father figure. Once Drew brought the conversation and intention to my attention, I had a lot of thinking to do also. As a man or the other man in the situation, I had several thoughts run through my mind. As men, we can rightfully be territorial and protective of their castle. After I let my pride down, put myself in his shoes and think big picture, there were a few things I had to evaluate. Did JoJo's father approach the situation respectfully for my wife and also for me? Did he do anything to neglect the wellbeing and safety of JoJo? What is the intention? Is this relationship in the best interest for JoJo? I immediately thought of my father and our circumstances.

As a child, no one couldn't tell me that my father wasn't the best in the world and guess what, that's my perspective. If you measured or quantified the value of our relationship, there would be large gaps in his presence, missed games and events, missed birthdays, missed growth and bonding opportunities. Yet, my father was still the best thing that could have ever happened to me. How could this be, the heart doesn't measure value

in the way our minds do. Love is blind and that's what makes love beautiful, innocent and cherished. Without love, we would be robots, incapable of forgiving or giving someone an opportunity to succeed. If we were robotic in our heart, we would leave a baby that didn't learn to walk fast enough or talk. Sometimes the greatest lessons on earth is experiencing life.

Interesting enough, Initially I didn't speak with JoJo's biological father as Drew had to feel comfortable with the interaction first however I was always by her side supporting the process. Change is very hard especially on a child therefore she wanted to make sure he wanted to really be part of his life before introducing his Father and he deciding he didn't want that role. Consistency is important to know if you're in this for the long run or if it's a nice experience because you think you should do it. Drew put JoJo's father on a call schedule to slowly introduce JoJo to his Father. JoJo visited with him as a baby but it's been years since they spoke and as a child, they don't know what a father means. The first few interactions was awkward just as any person that walks into a child's life that doesn't have kids, there is a learning process.

Adoption Because JoJo's father wasn't around, people would ask if I would adopt him, which is a great question. These are my rules on adopting in a blended family:

The Father doesn't want to be in the child's life therefore the child is fatherless

The Father is deceased.

The child is in harm or danger, therefore it's an unfit home.

The child doesn't have parents

In the event the child's mother dies, custody can be established through court order.....Find out the process. I really don't know.

If I would have adopted Josiah.

JoJo will get to a point where he seeks information and understanding for himself and he would approach his father asking, why didn't he make an effort to be in his life. His Father would more than likely respond, your parents didn't allow me to be a

part of your life and pushed me out. JoJo can possibly develop resentment due to our actions, even if we felt it was in his best interest.

This is a great segway into the definition of "Dad." Dads come in all different forms, types, relationships and can be interchangeable for almost anyone providing support that uplifts positive change and growth. When my father wasn't around, coaches became father figures to me including men in the community that taught me fundamentals of manhood. When my father wasn't around, men in the community would hire me and my brother to pickup leaves. It probably was one of the worst jobs I've ever experienced but it built character and work ethic that I wouldn't trade for the world. There is a village that becomes available to instill the lessons children need to learn and the role of "dad" can often be spread throughout the village to ensure children learn fundamentals of life. This concept also applies when the dad is around. Everyone is limited on the amount of information we know. If someone excels in a certain area, send the child to exceed your own understanding as the future depends on our children being smarter and more skilled than us.

Confidence I'm a firm believer that what's for me is for me and no one can take it away. If something isn't for me, then it was only supposed to be in my life for a season and I'm fine.

Being okay with JoJo's biological dad coming into the picture Studies show, 85% of blended familes are dysfunctional.

While Drew and I were dating, she was very intentional not to allow me to play the dad role. She didn't want to scare me off or put responsibility on me before we had a chance to know if our relationship would last. Her family also assisted in our dating process. Their goal was to help Drew find the man of her dreams and would take JoJo so she could go out on dates. Well, that strategy worked! Drew and I went on a date that lasted 12hrs. Her family wasn't very happy when I brought her home at 4am. To no despair, we stayed in contact and she became my wife. I would ask Drew if I could take JoJo for ice cream or take him to the

park while she was working if I felt she needed a helping hand so I could build a stronger bond with him. I knew if I married Drew, he would become my son. JoJo's biological father currently wasn't around and I knew JoJo needed a male influence to help him navigate the world, instill moral and values and grow into the man he would become. I had great expectations however I didn't know what a son or father figure meant from my wifes's eyes. My thought was once we were married, I would automatically take on the father role.

In our scenario, we got married extremely fast and Drew was pregnant 2mo after. We had a huge decision to make, where do we stay to raise the kids. At the time we were in LA and didn't feel like we had much support. We could either go to NJ to my family or Chicago with her family. I spoke with Drew's mom and she said I really can't help you if you stay in LA. Drew has a big family, her mom and dad and 4 sisters. It was a no brainer and we relocated to Chicago before Machai was born. I didn't have a chance to fully assume the "Dad" role as everything was moving fast. We were living under the same roof however Drew was making moves the way she programmed and without much involvement or opinion from my side. There were a few things that I didn't like entirely too much such as JoJo staying up until any time he wanted as if he was a little rockstar in a diaper and him sleeping in the same bed. Drew wasn't receptive to him staying up late and defended by saying she's an actress and her hours flucturate. To combat, I provided studies and reports on best practices for sleeping. I also provided a guidance for the tv staying on all night and she said her parents did it with them and everyone is okay so it's not that bad. I tried developing the "My House, My Rules" concept but it quickly fell on death ears as my concerns weren't enforced. Opposed to supporting, JoJo would cry and mom would come to the rescue. I began to see a common thread, where JoJo was also learning how to get his way and It then became an issue where it was Me vs. Them.

Boiling Point where I felt I couldn't parent

Due to JoJo not receiving adequate sleep, he struggled to get up for school in the morning. Being a man, I had my way of getting you to follow directions which was to place the fear of God in you because at the end of the day, I'm the parent. JoJo stood by the sink and didn't want to brush his teeth so I "acted" as if I was going to give him a pinch and he started crying, not because of pain but because of the act. His mother ran upstairs and grabbed JoJo, asking what happened. JoJo responded, daddy pinched me. Drew grabbed JoJo and repremanded me saying I told you not to do that to him. I asked JoJo to demonstrate on his mother exactly how hard I pinched him and he barely touched his mother. I walked out the room as I felt emasculated and minimized below a child. I thought to myself if I wanted to stay in a relationship where I didn't have a parenting voice. Besides all that I've done and contributed, I should feel more respected. We ended up seeking out a marriage counselor that told us we're doing things all wrong. We didn't have a plan and it shows.

but she did ask for my thoughts to correct him sleeping in the bed.

Introduce Drew's mom, millinial

Support we had and lacked

Realistic / Unrealistic Expectations

It's either him or me

Village mindset, when JoJo's dad came home, Respect. Territorial. No this is my house.

Drew received a call from JoJo's biological dad that he came home from jail and wanted to see his son if possible. At the time Drew was still hurt by the lack of support and effort. Her perspective was, if you haven't been around or made an effort all this time, why now. JoJo doesn't need you. Besides she had me in her life which "filled" the void of JoJo's lack of a father figure. Once Drew brought the conversation and intention to my attention, I had a lot of thinking to do also. As a man or the other man in the situation, I had several thoughts run through my mind. As men, we can rightfully be territorial and protective of their

castle. After I let my pride down, put myself in his shoes and think big picture, there were a few things I had to evaluate. Did JoJo's father approach the situation respectfully for my wife and also for me? Did he do anything to neglect the wellbeing and safety of JoJo? What is the intention? Is this relationship in the best interest for JoJo? I immediately thought of my father and our circumstances.

As a child, no one couldn't tell me that my father wasn't the best in the world and guess what, that's my perspective. If you measured or quantified the value of our relationship, there would be large gaps in his presence, missed games and events, missed birthdays, missed growth and bonding opportunities. Yet, my father was still the best thing that could have ever happened to me. How could this be, the heart doesn't measure value in the way our minds do. Love is blind and that's what makes love beautiful, innocent and cherished. Without love, we would be robots, incapable of forgiving or giving someone an opportunity to succeed. If we were robotic in our heart, we would leave a baby that didn't learn to walk fast enough or talk. Sometimes the greatest lessons on earth is experiencing life.

Interesting enough, Initially I didn't speak with JoJo's biological father as Drew had to feel comfortable with the interaction first however I was always by her side supporting the process. Change is very hard especially on a child therefore she wanted to make sure he wanted to really be part of his life before introducing his Father and he deciding he didn't want that role. Consistency is important to know if you're in this for the long run or if it's a nice experience because you think you should do it. Drew put JoJo's father on a call schedule to slowly introduce JoJo to his Father. JoJo visited with him as a baby but it's been years since they spoke and as a child, they don't know what a father means. The first few interactions was awkward just as any person that walks into a child's life that doesn't have kids, there is a learning process.

Adoption Because JoJo's father wasn't around, people would ask if I would adopt him, which is a great question. These are my rules on adopting in a blended family:

The Father doesn't want to be in the child's life therefore the child is fatherless

The Father is deceased.

The child is in harm or danger, therefore it's an unfit home.

The child doesn't have parents

In the event the child's mother dies, custody can be established through court order.....Find out the process. I really don't know.

If I would have adopted Josiah.

JoJo will get to a point where he seeks information and understanding for himself and he would approach his father asking, why didn't he make an effort to be in his life. His Father would more than likely respond, your parents didn't allow me to be a part of your life and pushed me out. JoJo can possibly develop resentment due to our actions, even if we felt it was in his best interest.

This is a great segway into the definition of "Dad." Dads come in all different forms, types, relationships and can be interchangeable for almost anyone providing support that uplifts positive change and growth. When my father wasn't around, coaches became father figures to me including men in the community that taught me fundamentals of manhood. When my father wasn't around, men in the community would hire me and my brother to pickup leaves. It probably was one of the worst jobs I've ever experienced but it built character and work ethic that I wouldn't trade for the world. There is a village that becomes available to instill the lessons children need to learn and the role of "dad" can often be spread throughout the village to ensure children learn fundamentals of life. This concept also applies when the dad is around. Everyone is limited on the amount of information we know. If someone excels in a certain area, send the child to exceed your own understanding as the future depends on our children being smarter and more skilled than us.

Confidence I'm a firm believer that what's for me is for me and no one can take it away. If something isn't for me, then it was only supposed to be in my life for a season and I'm fine.

Being okay with JoJo's biological dad coming into the picture Studies show, 85% of blended familes are dysfunctional. While Drew and I were dating, she was very intentional not to allow me to play the dad role. She didn't want to scare me off or put responsibility on me before we had a chance to know if our relationship would last. Her family also assisted in our dating process. Their goal was to help Drew find the man of her dreams and would take JoJo so she could go out on dates. Well, that strategy worked! Drew and I went on a date that lasted 12hrs. Her family wasn't very happy when I brought her home at 4am. To no despair, we stayed in contact and she became my wife. I would ask Drew if I could take JoJo for ice cream or take him to the park while she was working if I felt she needed a helping hand so I could build a stronger bond with him. I knew if I married Drew, he would become my son. JoJo's biological father currently wasn't around and I knew JoJo needed a male influence to help him navigate the world, instill moral and values and grow into the man he would become. I had great expectations however I didn't know what a son or father figure meant from my wifes's eyes. My thought was once we were married, I would automatically take on the father role.

In our scenario, we got married extremely fast and Drew was pregnant 2mo after. We had a huge decision to make, where do we stay to raise the kids. At the time we were in LA and didn't feel like we had much support. We could either go to NJ to my family or Chicago with her family. I spoke with Drew's mom and she said I really can't help you if you stay in LA. Drew has a big family, her mom and dad and 4 sisters. It was a no brainer and we relocated to Chicago before Machai was born. I didn't have a chance to fully assume the "Dad" role as everything was moving fast. We were living under the same roof however Drew was making moves the way she programmed and without much

involvement or opinion from my side. There were a few things that I didn't like entirely too much such as JoJo staying up until any time he wanted as if he was a little rockstar in a diaper and him sleeping in the same bed. Drew wasn't receptive to him staying up late and defended by saying she's an actress and her hours flucturate. To combat, I provided studies and reports on best practices for sleeping. I also provided a guidance for the tv staying on all night and she said her parents did it with them and everyone is okay so it's not that bad. I tried developing the "My House, My Rules" concept but it quickly fell on death ears as my concerns weren't enforced. Opposed to supporting, JoJo would cry and mom would come to the rescue. I began to see a common thread, where JoJo was also learning how to get his way and It then became an issue where it was Me vs. Them.

Boiling Point where I felt I couldn't parent

Due to JoJo not receiving adequate sleep, he struggled to get up for school in the morning. Being a man, I had my way of getting you to follow directions which was to place the fear of God in you because at the end of the day, I'm the parent. JoJo stood by the sink and didn't want to brush his teeth so I "acted" as if I was going to give him a pinch and he started crying, not because of pain but because of the act. His mother ran upstairs and grabbed JoJo, asking what happened. JoJo responded, daddy pinched me. Drew grabbed JoJo and repremanded me saying I told you not to do that to him. I asked JoJo to demonstrate on his mother exactly how hard I pinched him and he barely touched his mother. I walked out the room as I felt emasculated and minimized below a child. I thought to myself if I wanted to stay in a relationship where I didn't have a parenting voice. Besides all that I've done and contributed, I should feel more respected. We ended up seeking out a marriage counselor that told us we're doing things all wrong. We didn't have a plan and it shows.

but she did ask for my thoughts to correct him sleeping in the bed.

Introduce Drew's mom, millinial

Support we had and lacked
Realistic / Unrealistic Expectations
It's either him or me
Village mindset, when JoJo's dad came home, Respect. Territorial. No this is my house.

Drew received a call from JoJo's biological dad that he came home from jail and wanted to see his son if possible. At the time Drew was still hurt by the lack of support and effort. Her perspective was, if you haven't been around or made an effort all this time, why now. JoJo doesn't need you. Besides she had me in her life which "filled" the void of JoJo's lack of a father figure. Once Drew brought the conversation and intention to my attention, I had a lot of thinking to do also. As a man or the other man in the situation, I had several thoughts run through my mind. As men, we can rightfully be territorial and protective of their castle. After I let my pride down, put myself in his shoes and think big picture, there were a few things I had to evaluate. Did JoJo's father approach the situation respectfully for my wife and also for me? Did he do anything to neglect the wellbeing and safety of JoJo? What is the intention? Is this relationship in the best interest for JoJo? I immediately thought of my father and our circumstances.

As a child, no one couldn't tell me that my father wasn't the best in the world and guess what, that's my perspective. If you measured or quantified the value of our relationship, there would be large gaps in his presence, missed games and events, missed birthdays, missed growth and bonding opportunities. Yet, my father was still the best thing that could have ever happened to me. How could this be, the heart doesn't measure value in the way our minds do. Love is blind and that's what makes love beautiful, innocent and cherished. Without love, we would be robots, incapable of forgiving or giving someone an opportunity to succeed. If we were robotic in our heart, we would leave a baby that didn't learn to walk fast enough or talk. Sometimes the greatest lessons on earth is experiencing life.

Interesting enough, Initially I didn't speak with JoJo's biological father as Drew had to feel comfortable with the interaction first however I was always by her side supporting the process. Change is very hard especially on a child therefore she wanted to make sure he wanted to really be part of his life before introducing his Father and he deciding he didn't want that role. Consistency is important to know if you're in this for the long run or if it's a nice experience because you think you should do it. Drew put JoJo's father on a call schedule to slowly introduce JoJo to his Father. JoJo visited with him as a baby but it's been years since they spoke and as a child, they don't know what a father means. The first few interactions was awkward just as any person that walks into a child's life that doesn't have kids, there is a learning process.

Adoption Because JoJo's father wasn't around, people would ask if I would adopt him, which is a great question. These are my rules on adopting in a blended family:

The Father doesn't want to be in the child's life therefore the child is fatherless

The Father is deceased.

The child is in harm or danger, therefore it's an unfit home.

The child doesn't have parents

In the event the child's mother dies, custody can be established through court order.....Find out the process. I really don't know.

If I would have adopted Josiah.

JoJo will get to a point where he seeks information and understanding for himself and he would approach his father asking, why didn't he make an effort to be in his life. His Father would more than likely respond, your parents didn't allow me to be a part of your life and pushed me out. JoJo can possibly develop resentment due to our actions, even if we felt it was in his best interest.

This is a great segway into the definition of "Dad." Dads come in all different forms, types, relationships and can be interchangeable for almost anyone providing support that uplifts positive

change and growth. When my father wasn't around, coaches became father figures to me including men in the community that taught me fundamentals of manhood. When my father wasn't around, men in the community would hire me and my brother to pickup leaves. It probably was one of the worst jobs I've ever experienced but it built character and work ethic that I wouldn't trade for the world. There is a village that becomes available to instill the lessons children need to learn and the role of "dad" can often be spread throughout the village to ensure children learn fundamentals of life. This concept also applies when the dad is around. Everyone is limited on the amount of information we know. If someone excels in a certain area, send the child to exceed your own understanding as the future depends on our children being smarter and more skilled than us.

Confidence I'm a firm believer that what's for me is for me and no one can take it away. If something isn't for me, then it was only supposed to be in my life for a season and I'm fine.

Being okay with JoJo's biological dad coming into the picture Studies show, 85% of blended familes are dysfunctional. While Drew and I were dating, she was very intentional not to allow me to play the dad role. She didn't want to scare me off or put responsibility on me before we had a chance to know if our relationship would last. Her family also assisted in our dating process. Their goal was to help Drew find the man of her dreams and would take JoJo so she could go out on dates. Well, that strategy worked! Drew and I went on a date that lasted 12hrs. Her family wasn't very happy when I brought her home at 4am. To no despair, we stayed in contact and she became my wife. I would ask Drew if I could take JoJo for ice cream or take him to the park while she was working if I felt she needed a helping hand so I could build a stronger bond with him. I knew if I married Drew, he would become my son. JoJo's biological father currently wasn't around and I knew JoJo needed a male influence to help him navigate the world, instill moral and values and grow into the man he would become. I had great expectations however

I didn't know what a son or father figure meant from my wifes's eyes. My thought was once we were married, I would automatically take on the father role.

In our scenario, we got married extremely fast and Drew was pregnant 2mo after. We had a huge decision to make, where do we stay to raise the kids. At the time we were in LA and didn't feel like we had much support. We could either go to NJ to my family or Chicago with her family. I spoke with Drew's mom and she said I really can't help you if you stay in LA. Drew has a big family, her mom and dad and 4 sisters. It was a no brainer and we relocated to Chicago before Machai was born. I didn't have a chance to fully assume the "Dad" role as everything was moving fast. We were living under the same roof however Drew was making moves the way she programmed and without much involvement or opinion from my side. There were a few things that I didn't like entirely too much such as JoJo staying up until any time he wanted as if he was a little rockstar in a diaper and him sleeping in the same bed. Drew wasn't receptive to him staying up late and defended by saying she's an actress and her hours flucturate. To combat, I provided studies and reports on best practices for sleeping. I also provided a guidance for the tv staying on all night and she said her parents did it with them and everyone is okay so it's not that bad. I tried developing the "My House, My Rules" concept but it quickly fell on death ears as my concerns weren't enforced. Opposed to supporting, JoJo would cry and mom would come to the rescue. I began to see a common thread, where JoJo was also learning how to get his way and It then became an issue where it was Me vs. Them.

Boiling Point where I felt I couldn't parent

Due to JoJo not receiving adequate sleep, he struggled to get up for school in the morning. Being a man, I had my way of getting you to follow directions which was to place the fear of God in you because at the end of the day, I'm the parent. JoJo stood by the sink and didn't want to brush his teeth so I "acted" as if I was going to give him a pinch and he started crying, not because

of pain but because of the act. His mother ran upstairs and grabbed JoJo, asking what happened. JoJo responded, daddy pinched me. Drew grabbed JoJo and repremanded me saying I told you not to do that to him. I asked JoJo to demonstrate on his mother exactly how hard I pinched him and he barely touched his mother. I walked out the room as I felt emasculated and minimized below a child. I thought to myself if I wanted to stay in a relationship where I didn't have a parenting voice. Besides all that I've done and contributed, I should feel more respected. We ended up seeking out a marriage counselor that told us we're doing things all wrong. We didn't have a plan and it shows.

but she did ask for my thoughts to correct him sleeping in the bed.

Introduce Drew's mom, millinial

Support we had and lacked

Realistic / Unrealistic Expectations

It's either him or me

Village mindset, when JoJo's dad came home, Respect. Territorial. No this is my house.

Drew received a call from JoJo's biological dad that he came home from jail and wanted to see his son if possible. At the time Drew was still hurt by the lack of support and effort. Her perspective was, if you haven't been around or made an effort all this time, why now. JoJo doesn't need you. Besides she had me in her life which "filled" the void of JoJo's lack of a father figure. Once Drew brought the conversation and intention to my attention, I had a lot of thinking to do also. As a man or the other man in the situation, I had several thoughts run through my mind. As men, we can rightfully be territorial and protective of their castle. After I let my pride down, put myself in his shoes and think big picture, there were a few things I had to evaluate. Did JoJo's father approach the situation respectfully for my wife and also for me? Did he do anything to neglect the wellbeing and safety of JoJo? What is the intention? Is this relationship in the

best interest for JoJo? I immediately thought of my father and our circumstances.

As a child, no one couldn't tell me that my father wasn't the best in the world and guess what, that's my perspective. If you measured or quantified the value of our relationship, there would be large gaps in his presence, missed games and events, missed birthdays, missed growth and bonding opportunities. Yet, my father was still the best thing that could have ever happened to me. How could this be, the heart doesn't measure value in the way our minds do. Love is blind and that's what makes love beautiful, innocent and cherished. Without love, we would be robots, incapable of forgiving or giving someone an opportunity to succeed. If we were robotic in our heart, we would leave a baby that didn't learn to walk fast enough or talk. Sometimes the greatest lessons on earth is experiencing life.

Interesting enough, Initially I didn't speak with JoJo's biological father as Drew had to feel comfortable with the interaction first however I was always by her side supporting the process. Change is very hard especially on a child therefore she wanted to make sure he wanted to really be part of his life before introducing his Father and he deciding he didn't want that role. Consistency is important to know if you're in this for the long run or if it's a nice experience because you think you should do it. Drew put JoJo's father on a call schedule to slowly introduce JoJo to his Father. JoJo visited with him as a baby but it's been years since they spoke and as a child, they don't know what a father means. The first few interactions was awkward just as any person that walks into a child's life that doesn't have kids, there is a learning process.

Adoption Because JoJo's father wasn't around, people would ask if I would adopt him, which is a great question. These are my rules on adopting in a blended family:

The Father doesn't want to be in the child's life therefore the child is fatherless

The Father is deceased.

The child is in harm or danger, therefore it's an unfit home.

The child doesn't have parents

In the event the child's mother dies, custody can be established through court order.....Find out the process. I really don't know.

If I would have adopted Josiah.

JoJo will get to a point where he seeks information and understanding for himself and he would approach his father asking, why didn't he make an effort to be in his life. His Father would more than likely respond, your parents didn't allow me to be a part of your life and pushed me out. JoJo can possibly develop resentment due to our actions, even if we felt it was in his best interest.

This is a great segway into the definition of "Dad." Dads come in all different forms, types, relationships and can be interchangeable for almost anyone providing support that uplifts positive change and growth. When my father wasn't around, coaches became father figures to me including men in the community that taught me fundamentals of manhood. When my father wasn't around, men in the community would hire me and my brother to pickup leaves. It probably was one of the worst jobs I've ever experienced but it built character and work ethic that I wouldn't trade for the world. There is a village that becomes available to instill the lessons children need to learn and the role of "dad" can often be spread throughout the village to ensure children learn fundamentals of life. This concept also applies when the dad is around. Everyone is limited on the amount of information we know. If someone excels in a certain area, send the child to exceed your own understanding as the future depends on our children being smarter and more skilled than us.

Confidence I'm a firm believer that what's for me is for me and no one can take it away. If something isn't for me, then it was only supposed to be in my life for a season and I'm fine.

Being okay with JoJo's biological dad coming into the picture

Studies show, 85% of blended familes are dysfunctional. While Drew and I were dating, she was very intentional not to

allow me to play the dad role. She didn't want to scare me off or put responsibility on me before we had a chance to know if our relationship would last. Her family also assisted in our dating process. Their goal was to help Drew find the man of her dreams and would take JoJo so she could go out on dates. Well, that strategy worked! Drew and I went on a date that lasted 12hrs. Her family wasn't very happy when I brought her home at 4am. To no despair, we stayed in contact and she became my wife. I would ask Drew if I could take JoJo for ice cream or take him to the park while she was working if I felt she needed a helping hand so I could build a stronger bond with him. I knew if I married Drew, he would become my son. JoJo's biological father currently wasn't around and I knew JoJo needed a male influence to help him navigate the world, instill moral and values and grow into the man he would become. I had great expectations however I didn't know what a son or father figure meant from my wifes's eyes. My thought was once we were married, I would automatically take on the father role.

In our scenario, we got married extremely fast and Drew was pregnant 2mo after. We had a huge decision to make, where do we stay to raise the kids. At the time we were in LA and didn't feel like we had much support. We could either go to NJ to my family or Chicago with her family. I spoke with Drew's mom and she said I really can't help you if you stay in LA. Drew has a big family, her mom and dad and 4 sisters. It was a no brainer and we relocated to Chicago before Machai was born. I didn't have a chance to fully assume the "Dad" role as everything was moving fast. We were living under the same roof however Drew was making moves the way she programmed and without much involvement or opinion from my side. There were a few things that I didn't like entirely too much such as JoJo staying up until any time he wanted as if he was a little rockstar in a diaper and him sleeping in the same bed. Drew wasn't receptive to him staying up late and defended by saying she's an actress and her hours flucturate. To combat, I provided studies and reports on

best practices for sleeping. I also provided a guidance for the tv staying on all night and she said her parents did it with them and everyone is okay so it's not that bad. I tried developing the "My House, My Rules" concept but it quickly fell on death ears as my concerns weren't enforced. Opposed to supporting, JoJo would cry and mom would come to the rescue. I began to see a common thread, where JoJo was also learning how to get his way and It then became an issue where it was Me vs. Them.

Boiling Point where I felt I couldn't parent

Due to JoJo not receiving adequate sleep, he struggled to get up for school in the morning. Being a man, I had my way of getting you to follow directions which was to place the fear of God in you because at the end of the day, I'm the parent. JoJo stood by the sink and didn't want to brush his teeth so I "acted" as if I was going to give him a pinch and he started crying, not because of pain but because of the act. His mother ran upstairs and grabbed JoJo, asking what happened. JoJo responded, daddy pinched me. Drew grabbed JoJo and repremanded me saying I told you not to do that to him. I asked JoJo to demonstrate on his mother exactly how hard I pinched him and he barely touched his mother. I walked out the room as I felt emasculated and minimized below a child. I thought to myself if I wanted to stay in a relationship where I didn't have a parenting voice. Besides all that I've done and contributed, I should feel more respected. We ended up seeking out a marriage counselor that told us we're doing things all wrong. We didn't have a plan and it shows.

but she did ask for my thoughts to correct him sleeping in the bed.

Introduce Drew's mom, millinial

Support we had and lacked

Realistic / Unrealistic Expectations

It's either him or me

Village mindset, when JoJo's dad came home, Respect. Territorial. No this is my house.

Drew received a call from JoJo's biological dad that he came home from jail and wanted to see his son if possible. At the time Drew was still hurt by the lack of support and effort. Her perspective was, if you haven't been around or made an effort all this time, why now. JoJo doesn't need you. Besides she had me in her life which "filled" the void of JoJo's lack of a father figure. Once Drew brought the conversation and intention to my attention, I had a lot of thinking to do also. As a man or the other man in the situation, I had several thoughts run through my mind. As men, we can rightfully be territorial and protective of their castle. After I let my pride down, put myself in his shoes and think big picture, there were a few things I had to evaluate. Did JoJo's father approach the situation respectfully for my wife and also for me? Did he do anything to neglect the wellbeing and safety of JoJo? What is the intention? Is this relationship in the best interest for JoJo? I immediately thought of my father and our circumstances.

As a child, no one couldn't tell me that my father wasn't the best in the world and guess what, that's my perspective. If you measured or quantified the value of our relationship, there would be large gaps in his presence, missed games and events, missed birthdays, missed growth and bonding opportunities. Yet, my father was still the best thing that could have ever happened to me. How could this be, the heart doesn't measure value in the way our minds do. Love is blind and that's what makes love beautiful, innocent and cherished. Without love, we would be robots, incapable of forgiving or giving someone an opportunity to succeed. If we were robotic in our heart, we would leave a baby that didn't learn to walk fast enough or talk. Sometimes the greatest lessons on earth is experiencing life.

Interesting enough, Initially I didn't speak with JoJo's biological father as Drew had to feel comfortable with the interaction first however I was always by her side supporting the process. Change is very hard especially on a child therefore she wanted to make sure he wanted to really be part of his life before

introducing his Father and he deciding he didn't want that role. Consistency is important to know if you're in this for the long run or if it's a nice experience because you think you should do it. Drew put JoJo's father on a call schedule to slowly introduce JoJo to his Father. JoJo visited with him as a baby but it's been years since they spoke and as a child, they don't know what a father means. The first few interactions was awkward just as any person that walks into a child's life that doesn't have kids, there is a learning process.

Adoption Because JoJo's father wasn't around, people would ask if I would adopt him, which is a great question. These are my rules on adopting in a blended family:

The Father doesn't want to be in the child's life therefore the child is fatherless

The Father is deceased.

The child is in harm or danger, therefore it's an unfit home.

The child doesn't have parents

In the event the child's mother dies, custody can be established through court order.....Find out the process. I really don't know.

If I would have adopted Josiah.

JoJo will get to a point where he seeks information and understanding for himself and he would approach his father asking, why didn't he make an effort to be in his life. His Father would more than likely respond, your parents didn't allow me to be a part of your life and pushed me out. JoJo can possibly develop resentment due to our actions, even if we felt it was in his best interest.

This is a great segway into the definition of "Dad." Dads come in all different forms, types, relationships and can be interchangeable for almost anyone providing support that uplifts positive change and growth. When my father wasn't around, coaches became father figures to me including men in the community that taught me fundamentals of manhood. When my father wasn't around, men in the community would hire me and my brother to pickup leaves. It probably was one of the worst jobs I've ever

experienced but it built character and work ethic that I wouldn't trade for the world. There is a village that becomes available to instill the lessons children need to learn and the role of "dad" can often be spread throughout the village to ensure children learn fundamentals of life. This concept also applies when the dad is around. Everyone is limited on the amount of information we know. If someone excels in a certain area, send the child to exceed your own understanding as the future depends on our children being smarter and more skilled than us.

Confidence I'm a firm believer that what's for me is for me and no one can take it away. If something isn't for me, then it was only supposed to be in my life for a season and I'm fine.

Being okay with JoJo's biological dad coming into the picture Studies show, 85% of blended familes are dysfunctional. While Drew and I were dating, she was very intentional not to allow me to play the dad role. She didn't want to scare me off or put responsibility on me before we had a chance to know if our relationship would last. Her family also assisted in our dating process. Their goal was to help Drew find the man of her dreams and would take JoJo so she could go out on dates. Well, that strategy worked! Drew and I went on a date that lasted 12hrs. Her family wasn't very happy when I brought her home at 4am. To no despair, we stayed in contact and she became my wife. I would ask Drew if I could take JoJo for ice cream or take him to the park while she was working if I felt she needed a helping hand so I could build a stronger bond with him. I knew if I married Drew, he would become my son. JoJo's biological father currently wasn't around and I knew JoJo needed a male influence to help him navigate the world, instill moral and values and grow into the man he would become. I had great expectations however I didn't know what a son or father figure meant from my wifes's eyes. My thought was once we were married, I would automatically take on the father role.

In our scenario, we got married extremely fast and Drew was pregnant 2mo after. We had a huge decision to make, where do

we stay to raise the kids. At the time we were in LA and didn't feel like we had much support. We could either go to NJ to my family or Chicago with her family. I spoke with Drew's mom and she said I really can't help you if you stay in LA. Drew has a big family, her mom and dad and 4 sisters. It was a no brainer and we relocated to Chicago before Machai was born. I didn't have a chance to fully assume the "Dad" role as everything was moving fast. We were living under the same roof however Drew was making moves the way she programmed and without much involvement or opinion from my side. There were a few things that I didn't like entirely too much such as JoJo staying up until any time he wanted as if he was a little rockstar in a diaper and him sleeping in the same bed. Drew wasn't receptive to him staying up late and defended by saying she's an actress and her hours flucturate. To combat, I provided studies and reports on best practices for sleeping. I also provided a guidance for the tv staying on all night and she said her parents did it with them and everyone is okay so it's not that bad. I tried developing the "My House, My Rules" concept but it quickly fell on death ears as my concerns weren't enforced. Opposed to supporting, JoJo would cry and mom would come to the rescue. I began to see a common thread, where JoJo was also learning how to get his way and It then became an issue where it was Me vs. Them.

Boiling Point where I felt I couldn't parent

Due to JoJo not receiving adequate sleep, he struggled to get up for school in the morning. Being a man, I had my way of getting you to follow directions which was to place the fear of God in you because at the end of the day, I'm the parent. JoJo stood by the sink and didn't want to brush his teeth so I "acted" as if I was going to give him a pinch and he started crying, not because of pain but because of the act. His mother ran upstairs and grabbed JoJo, asking what happened. JoJo responded, daddy pinched me. Drew grabbed JoJo and reprimanded me saying I told you not to do that to him. I asked JoJo to demonstrate on his mother exactly how hard I pinched him and he barely touched

his mother. I walked out the room as I felt emasculated and minimized below a child. I thought to myself if I wanted to stay in a relationship where I didn't have a parenting voice. Besides all that I've done and contributed, I should feel more respected. We ended up seeking out a marriage counselor that told us we're doing things all wrong. We didn't have a plan and it shows.

but she did ask for my thoughts to correct him sleeping in the bed.

Introduce Drew's mom, millinial

Support we had and lacked

Realistic / Unrealistic Expectations

It's either him or me

Village mindset, when JoJo's dad came home, Respect. Territorial. No this is my house.

Drew received a call from JoJo's biological dad that he came home from jail and wanted to see his son if possible. At the time Drew was still hurt by the lack of support and effort. Her perspective was, if you haven't been around or made an effort all this time, why now. JoJo doesn't need you. Besides she had me in her life which "filled" the void of JoJo's lack of a father figure. Once Drew brought the conversation and intention to my attention, I had a lot of thinking to do also. As a man or the other man in the situation, I had several thoughts run through my mind. As men, we can rightfully be territorial and protective of their castle. After I let my pride down, put myself in his shoes and think big picture, there were a few things I had to evaluate. Did JoJo's father approach the situation respectfully for my wife and also for me? Did he do anything to neglect the wellbeing and safety of JoJo? What is the intention? Is this relationship in the best interest for JoJo? I immediately thought of my father and our circumstances.

As a child, no one couldn't tell me that my father wasn't the best in the world and guess what, that's my perspective. If you measured or quantified the value of our relationship, there would be large gaps in his presence, missed games and events,

missed birthdays, missed growth and bonding opportunities. Yet, my father was still the best thing that could have ever happened to me. How could this be, the heart doesn't measure value in the way our minds do. Love is blind and that's what makes love beautiful, innocent and cherished. Without love, we would be robots, incapable of forgiving or giving someone an opportunity to succeed. If we were robotic in our heart, we would leave a baby that didn't learn to walk fast enough or talk. Sometimes the greatest lessons on earth is experiencing life.

Interesting enough, Initially I didn't speak with JoJo's biological father as Drew had to feel comfortable with the interaction first however I was always by her side supporting the process. Change is very hard especially on a child therefore she wanted to make sure he wanted to really be part of his life before introducing his Father and he deciding he didn't want that role. Consistency is important to know if you're in this for the long run or if it's a nice experience because you think you should do it. Drew put JoJo's father on a call schedule to slowly introduce JoJo to his Father. JoJo visited with him as a baby but it's been years since they spoke and as a child, they don't know what a father means. The first few interactions was awkward just as any person that walks into a child's life that doesn't have kids, there is a learning process.

Adoption Because JoJo's father wasn't around, people would ask if I would adopt him, which is a great question. These are my rules on adopting in a blended family:

The Father doesn't want to be in the child's life therefore the child is fatherless

The Father is deceased.

The child is in harm or danger, therefore it's an unfit home.

The child doesn't have parents

In the event the child's mother dies, custody can be established through court order.....Find out the process. I really don't know.

If I would have adopted Josiah.

JoJo will get to a point where he seeks information and under-standing for himself and he would approach his father asking, why didn't he make an effort to be in his life. His Father would more than likely respond, your parents didn't allow me to be a part of your life and pushed me out. JoJo can possibly develop resentment due to our actions, even if we felt it was in his best interest.

This is a great segway into the definition of "Dad." Dads come in all different forms, types, relationships and can be interchange-able for almost anyone providing support that uplifts positive change and growth. When my father wasn't around, coaches became father figures to me including men in the community that taught me fundamentals of manhood. When my father wasn't around, men in the community would hire me and my brother to pickup leaves. It probably was one of the worst jobs I've ever experienced but it built character and work ethic that I wouldn't trade for the world. There is a village that becomes available to instill the lessons children need to learn and the role of "dad" can often be spread throughout the village to ensure children learn fundamentals of life. This concept also applies when the dad is around. Everyone is limited on the amount of information we know. If someone excels in a certain area, send the child to exceed your own understanding as the future depends on our children being smarter and more skilled than us.

Confidence I'm a firm believer that what's for me is for me and no one can take it away. If something isn't for me, then it was only supposed to be in my life for a season and I'm fine.

Adoption

BEING OKAY WITH JoJo's biological dad coming into the picture. Studies show, 85% of blended familes are dysfunctional.While Drew and I were dating, she was very intentional not to allow me to play the dad role. She didn't want to scare me off or put responsibility on me before we had a chance to know if our relationship would last. Her family also assisted in our dating process. Their goal was to help Drew find the man of her dreams and would take JoJo so she could go out on dates. Well, that strategy worked! Drew and I went on a date that lasted 12hrs. Her family wasn't very happy when I brought her home at 4am. To no despair, we stayed in contact and she became my wife. I would ask Drew if I could take JoJo for ice cream or take him to the park while she was working if I felt she needed a helping hand so I could build a stronger bond with him. I knew if I married Drew, he would become my son. JoJo's biological father currently wasn't around and I knew JoJo needed a male influence to help him navigate the world, instill moral and values and grow into the man he would become. I had great expectations however I didn't know what a son or father figure meant from my wifes's eyes. My thought was once we were married, I would automatically take on the father role.

In our scenario, we got married extremely fast and Drew was pregnant 2mo after. We had a huge decision to make, where do we stay to raise the kids. At the time we were in LA and didn't feel like we had much support. We could either go to NJ to my family or Chicago with her family. I spoke with Drew's mom and she said I really can't help you if you stay in LA. Drew has a big family, her mom and dad and 4 sisters. It was a no brainer and we relocated to Chicago before Machai was born. I didn't have a chance to fully assume the "Dad" role as everything was moving fast. We were living under the same roof however Drew was making moves the way she programmed and without much involvement or opinion from my side. There were a few things that I didn't like entirely too much such as JoJo staying up until any time he wanted as if he was a little rockstar in a diaper and him sleeping in the same bed. Drew wasn't receptive to him staying up late and defended by saying she's an actress and her hours flucturate. To combat, I provided studies and reports on best practices for sleeping. I also provided a guidance for the tv staying on all night and she said her parents did it with them and everyone is okay so it's not that bad. I tried developing the "My House, My Rules" concept but it quickly fell on death ears as my concerns weren't enforced. Opposed to supporting, JoJo would cry and mom would come to the rescue. I began to see a common thread, where JoJo was also learning how to get his way and It then became an issue where it was Me vs. Them.

Boiling Point where I felt I couldn't parent

Due to JoJo not receiving adequate sleep, he struggled to get up for school in the morning. Being a man, I had my way of getting you to follow directions which was to place the fear of God in you because at the end of the day, I'm the parent. JoJo stood by the sink and didn't want to brush his teeth so I "acted" as if I was going to give him a pinch and he started crying, not because of pain but because of the act. His mother ran upstairs and grabbed JoJo, asking what happened. JoJo responded, daddy pinched me. Drew grabbed JoJo and repremanded me saying I

told you not to do that to him. I asked JoJo to demonstrate on his mother exactly how hard I pinched him and he barely touched his mother. I walked out the room as I felt emasculated and minimized below a child. I thought to myself if I wanted to stay in a relationship where I didn't have a parenting voice. Besides all that I've done and contributed, I should feel more respected. We ended up seeking out a marriage counselor that told us we're doing things all wrong. We didn't have a plan and it shows.

but she did ask for my thoughts to correct him sleeping in the bed.

Introduce Drew's mom, millinial

Support we had and lacked

Realistic / Unrealistic Expectations

It's either him or me

Village mindset, when JoJo's dad came home, Respect. Territorial. No this is my house.

Drew received a call from JoJo's biological dad that he came home from jail and wanted to see his son if possible. At the time Drew was still hurt by the lack of support and effort. Her perspective was, if you haven't been around or made an effort all this time, why now. JoJo doesn't need you. Besides she had me in her life which "filled" the void of JoJo's lack of a father figure. Once Drew brought the conversation and intention to my attention, I had a lot of thinking to do also. As a man or the other man in the situation, I had several thoughts run through my mind. As men, we can rightfully be territorial and protective of their castle. After I let my pride down, put myself in his shoes and think big picture, there were a few things I had to evaluate. Did JoJo's father approach the situation respectfully for my wife and also for me? Did he do anything to neglect the wellbeing and safety of JoJo? What is the intention? Is this relationship in the best interest for JoJo? I immediately thought of my father and our circumstances.

As a child, no one couldn't tell me that my father wasn't the best in the world and guess what, that's my perspective. If you

measured or quantified the value of our relationship, there would be large gaps in his presence, missed games and events, missed birthdays, missed growth and bonding opportunities. Yet, my father was still the best thing that could have ever happened to me. How could this be, the heart doesn't measure value in the way our minds do. Love is blind and that's what makes love beautiful, innocent and cherished. Without love, we would be robots, incapable of forgiving or giving someone an opportunity to succeed. If we were robotic in our heart, we would leave a baby that didn't learn to walk fast enough or talk. Sometimes the greatest lessons on earth is experiencing life.

Interesting enough, Initially I didn't speak with JoJo's biological father as Drew had to feel comfortable with the interaction first however I was always by her side supporting the process. Change is very hard especially on a child therefore she wanted to make sure he wanted to really be part of his life before introducing his Father and he deciding he didn't want that role. Consistency is important to know if you're in this for the long run or if it's a nice experience because you think you should do it. Drew put JoJo's father on a call schedule to slowly introduce JoJo to his Father. JoJo visited with him as a baby but it's been years since they spoke and as a child, they don't know what a father means. The first few interactions was awkward just as any person that walks into a child's life that doesn't have kids, there is a learning process.

Adoption Because JoJo's father wasn't around, people would ask if I would adopt him, which is a great question. These are my rules on adopting in a blended family:

The Father doesn't want to be in the child's life therefore the child is fatherless

The Father is deceased.

The child is in harm or danger, therefore it's an unfit home.

The child doesn't have parents

In the event the child's mother dies, custody can be established through court order......Find out the process. I really don't know.

If I would have adopted Josiah.

JoJo will get to a point where he seeks information and understanding for himself and he would approach his father asking, why didn't he make an effort to be in his life. His Father would more than likely respond, your parents didn't allow me to be a part of your life and pushed me out. JoJo can possibly develop resentment due to our actions, even if we felt it was in his best interest.

This is a great segway into the definition of "Dad." Dads come in all different forms, types, relationships and can be interchangeable for almost anyone providing support that uplifts positive change and growth. When my father wasn't around, coaches became father figures to me including men in the community that taught me fundamentals of manhood. When my father wasn't around, men in the community would hire me and my brother to pickup leaves. It probably was one of the worst jobs I've ever experienced but it built character and work ethic that I wouldn't trade for the world. There is a village that becomes available to instill the lessons children need to learn and the role of "dad" can often be spread throughout the village to ensure children learn fundamentals of life. This concept also applies when the dad is around. Everyone is limited on the amount of information we know. If someone excels in a certain area, send the child to exceed your own understanding as the future depends on our children being smarter and more skilled than us.

Confidence I'm a firm believer that what's for me is for me and no one can take it away. If something isn't for me, then it was only supposed to be in my life for a season and I'm fine.

Being okay with JoJo's biological dad coming into the picture Studies show, 85% of blended familes are dysfunctional. While Drew and I were dating, she was very intentional not to allow me to play the dad role. She didn't want to scare me off or put responsibility on me before we had a chance to know if our relationship would last. Her family also assisted in our dating process. Their goal was to help Drew find the man of her dreams

and would take JoJo so she could go out on dates. Well, that strategy worked! Drew and I went on a date that lasted 12hrs. Her family wasn't very happy when I brought her home at 4am. To no despair, we stayed in contact and she became my wife. I would ask Drew if I could take JoJo for ice cream or take him to the park while she was working if I felt she needed a helping hand so I could build a stronger bond with him. I knew if I married Drew, he would become my son. JoJo's biological father currently wasn't around and I knew JoJo needed a male influence to help him navigate the world, instill moral and values and grow into the man he would become. I had great expectations however I didn't know what a son or father figure meant from my wifes's eyes. My thought was once we were married, I would automatically take on the father role.

In our scenario, we got married extremely fast and Drew was pregnant 2mo after. We had a huge decision to make, where do we stay to raise the kids. At the time we were in LA and didn't feel like we had much support. We could either go to NJ to my family or Chicago with her family. I spoke with Drew's mom and she said I really can't help you if you stay in LA. Drew has a big family, her mom and dad and 4 sisters. It was a no brainer and we relocated to Chicago before Machai was born. I didn't have a chance to fully assume the "Dad" role as everything was moving fast. We were living under the same roof however Drew was making moves the way she programmed and without much involvement or opinion from my side. There were a few things that I didn't like entirely too much such as JoJo staying up until any time he wanted as if he was a little rockstar in a diaper and him sleeping in the same bed. Drew wasn't receptive to him staying up late and defended by saying she's an actress and her hours flucturate. To combat, I provided studies and reports on best practices for sleeping. I also provided a guidance for the tv staying on all night and she said her parents did it with them and everyone is okay so it's not that bad. I tried developing the "My House, My Rules" concept but it quickly fell on death ears as my

concerns weren't enforced. Opposed to supporting, JoJo would cry and mom would come to the rescue. I began to see a common thread, where JoJo was also learning how to get his way and It then became an issue where it was Me vs. Them.

Boiling Point where I felt I couldn't parent

Due to JoJo not receiving adequate sleep, he struggled to get up for school in the morning. Being a man, I had my way of getting you to follow directions which was to place the fear of God in you because at the end of the day, I'm the parent. JoJo stood by the sink and didn't want to brush his teeth so I "acted" as if I was going to give him a pinch and he started crying, not because of pain but because of the act. His mother ran upstairs and grabbed JoJo, asking what happened. JoJo responded, daddy pinched me. Drew grabbed JoJo and repremanded me saying I told you not to do that to him. I asked JoJo to demonstrate on his mother exactly how hard I pinched him and he barely touched his mother. I walked out the room as I felt emasculated and minimized below a child. I thought to myself if I wanted to stay in a relationship where I didn't have a parenting voice. Besides all that I've done and contributed, I should feel more respected. We ended up seeking out a marriage counselor that told us we're doing things all wrong. We didn't have a plan and it shows.

but she did ask for my thoughts to correct him sleeping in the bed.

Introduce Drew's mom, millinial

Support we had and lacked

Realistic / Unrealistic Expectations

It's either him or me

Village mindset, when JoJo's dad came home, Respect. Territorial. No this is my house.

Drew received a call from JoJo's biological dad that he came home from jail and wanted to see his son if possible. At the time Drew was still hurt by the lack of support and effort. Her perspective was, if you haven't been around or made an effort all this time, why now. JoJo doesn't need you. Besides she had me

in her life which "filled" the void of JoJo's lack of a father figure. Once Drew brought the conversation and intention to my attention, I had a lot of thinking to do also. As a man or the other man in the situation, I had several thoughts run through my mind. As men, we can rightfully be territorial and protective of their castle. After I let my pride down, put myself in his shoes and think big picture, there were a few things I had to evaluate. Did JoJo's father approach the situation respectfully for my wife and also for me? Did he do anything to neglect the wellbeing and safety of JoJo? What is the intention? Is this relationship in the best interest for JoJo? I immediately thought of my father and our circumstances.

As a child, no one couldn't tell me that my father wasn't the best in the world and guess what, that's my perspective. If you measured or quantified the value of our relationship, there would be large gaps in his presence, missed games and events, missed birthdays, missed growth and bonding opportunities. Yet, my father was still the best thing that could have ever happened to me. How could this be, the heart doesn't measure value in the way our minds do. Love is blind and that's what makes love beautiful, innocent and cherished. Without love, we would be robots, incapable of forgiving or giving someone an opportunity to succeed. If we were robotic in our heart, we would leave a baby that didn't learn to walk fast enough or talk. Sometimes the greatest lessons on earth is experiencing life.

Interesting enough, Initially I didn't speak with JoJo's biological father as Drew had to feel comfortable with the interaction first however I was always by her side supporting the process. Change is very hard especially on a child therefore she wanted to make sure he wanted to really be part of his life before introducing his Father and he deciding he didn't want that role. Consistency is important to know if you're in this for the long run or if it's a nice experience because you think you should do it. Drew put JoJo's father on a call schedule to slowly introduce JoJo to his Father. JoJo visited with him as a baby but it's been

years since they spoke and as a child, they don't know what a father means. The first few interactions was awkward just as any person that walks into a child's life that doesn't have kids, there is a learning process.

Adoption Because JoJo's father wasn't around, people would ask if I would adopt him, which is a great question. These are my rules on adopting in a blended family:

The Father doesn't want to be in the child's life therefore the child is fatherless

The Father is deceased.

The child is in harm or danger, therefore it's an unfit home.

The child doesn't have parents

In the event the child's mother dies, custody can be established through court order.....Find out the process. I really don't know.

If I would have adopted Josiah.

JoJo will get to a point where he seeks information and understanding for himself and he would approach his father asking, why didn't he make an effort to be in his life. His Father would more than likely respond, your parents didn't allow me to be a part of your life and pushed me out. JoJo can possibly develop resentment due to our actions, even if we felt it was in his best interest.

This is a great segway into the definition of "Dad." Dads come in all different forms, types, relationships and can be interchangeable for almost anyone providing support that uplifts positive change and growth. When my father wasn't around, coaches became father figures to me including men in the community that taught me fundamentals of manhood. When my father wasn't around, men in the community would hire me and my brother to pickup leaves. It probably was one of the worst jobs I've ever experienced but it built character and work ethic that I wouldn't trade for the world. There is a village that becomes available to instill the lessons children need to learn and the role of "dad" can often be spread throughout the village to ensure children learn fundamentals of life. This concept also applies when the

dad is around. Everyone is limited on the amount of information we know. If someone excels in a certain area, send the child to exceed your own understanding as the future depends on our children being smarter and more skilled than us.

Confidence I'm a firm believer that what's for me is for me and no one can take it away. If something isn't for me, then it was only supposed to be in my life for a season and I'm fine.

Being okay with JoJo's biological dad coming into the picture

Studies show, 85% of blended familes are dysfunctional. While Drew and I were dating, she was very intentional not to allow me to play the dad role. She didn't want to scare me off or put responsibility on me before we had a chance to know if our relationship would last. Her family also assisted in our dating process. Their goal was to help Drew find the man of her dreams and would take JoJo so she could go out on dates. Well, that strategy worked! Drew and I went on a date that lasted 12hrs. Her family wasn't very happy when I brought her home at 4am. To no despair, we stayed in contact and she became my wife. I would ask Drew if I could take JoJo for ice cream or take him to the park while she was working if I felt she needed a helping hand so I could build a stronger bond with him. I knew if I married Drew, he would become my son. JoJo's biological father currently wasn't around and I knew JoJo needed a male influence to help him navigate the world, instill moral and values and grow into the man he would become. I had great expectations however I didn't know what a son or father figure meant from my wifes's eyes. My thought was once we were married, I would automatically take on the father role.

In our scenario, we got married extremely fast and Drew was pregnant 2mo after. We had a huge decision to make, where do we stay to raise the kids. At the time we were in LA and didn't feel like we had much support. We could either go to NJ to my family or Chicago with her family. I spoke with Drew's mom and she said I really can't help you if you stay in LA. Drew has a big family, her mom and dad and 4 sisters. It was a no brainer and we relocated to Chicago before Machai was born. I didn't have a chance to fully assume the "Dad" role as everything was moving fast. We were living under the same roof however Drew was making moves the way she programmed and without much involvement or opinion from my side. There were a few things that I didn't like entirely too much such as JoJo staying up until any time he wanted as if he was a little rockstar in a diaper and him sleeping in the same bed. Drew wasn't receptive to him staying up late and defended by saying she's an actress and her hours flucturate. To combat, I provided studies and reports on best practices for sleeping. I also provided a guidance for the tv staying on all night and she said her parents did it with them and everyone is okay so it's not that bad. I tried developing the "My House, My Rules" concept but it quickly fell on death ears as my concerns weren't enforced. Opposed to supporting, JoJo would cry and mom would come to the rescue. I began to see a common thread, where JoJo was also learning how to get his way and It then became an issue where it was Me vs. Them.

Boiling Point where I felt I couldn't parent

Due to JoJo not receiving adequate sleep, he struggled to get up for school in the morning. Being a man, I had my way of getting you to follow directions which was to place the fear of God in you because at the end of the day, I'm the parent. JoJo stood by the sink and didn't want to brush his teeth so I "acted" as if I was going to give him a pinch and he started crying, not because of pain but because of the act. His mother ran upstairs and grabbed JoJo, asking what happened. JoJo responded, daddy pinched me. Drew grabbed JoJo and repremanded me saying I told you not to do that to him. I asked JoJo to demonstrate on his mother exactly how hard I pinched him and he barely touched his mother. I walked out the room as I felt emasculated and minimized below a child. I thought to myself if I wanted to stay in a relationship where I didn't have a parenting voice. Besides all that I've done and contributed, I should feel more respected. We

ended up seeking out a marriage counselor that told us we're doing things all wrong. We didn't have a plan and it shows.

but she did ask for my thoughts to correct him sleeping in the bed.

Introduce Drew's mom, millinial

Support we had and lacked

Realistic / Unrealistic Expectations

It's either him or me

Village mindset, when JoJo's dad came home, Respect. Territorial. No this is my house.

Drew received a call from JoJo's biological dad that he came home from jail and wanted to see his son if possible. At the time Drew was still hurt by the lack of support and effort. Her perspective was, if you haven't been around or made an effort all this time, why now. JoJo doesn't need you. Besides she had me in her life which "filled" the void of JoJo's lack of a father figure. Once Drew brought the conversation and intention to my attention, I had a lot of thinking to do also. As a man or the other man in the situation, I had several thoughts run through my mind. As men, we can rightfully be territorial and protective of their castle. After I let my pride down, put myself in his shoes and think big picture, there were a few things I had to evaluate. Did JoJo's father approach the situation respectfully for my wife and also for me? Did he do anything to neglect the wellbeing and safety of JoJo? What is the intention? Is this relationship in the best interest for JoJo? I immediately thought of my father and our circumstances.

As a child, no one couldn't tell me that my father wasn't the best in the world and guess what, that's my perspective. If you measured or quantified the value of our relationship, there would be large gaps in his presence, missed games and events, missed birthdays, missed growth and bonding opportunities. Yet, my father was still the best thing that could have ever happened to me. How could this be, the heart doesn't measure value in the way our minds do. Love is blind and that's what makes

love beautiful, innocent and cherished. Without love, we would be robots, incapable of forgiving or giving someone an opportunity to succeed. If we were robotic in our heart, we would leave a baby that didn't learn to walk fast enough or talk. Sometimes the greatest lessons on earth is experiencing life.

Interesting enough, Initially I didn't speak with JoJo's biological father as Drew had to feel comfortable with the interaction first however I was always by her side supporting the process. Change is very hard especially on a child therefore she wanted to make sure he wanted to really be part of his life before introducing his Father and he deciding he didn't want that role. Consistency is important to know if you're in this for the long run or if it's a nice experience because you think you should do it. Drew put JoJo's father on a call schedule to slowly introduce JoJo to his Father. JoJo visited with him as a baby but it's been years since they spoke and as a child, they don't know what a father means. The first few interactions was awkward just as any person that walks into a child's life that doesn't have kids, there is a learning process.

Adoption Because JoJo's father wasn't around, people would ask if I would adopt him, which is a great question. These are my rules on adopting in a blended family:

The Father doesn't want to be in the child's life therefore the child is fatherless

The Father is deceased.

The child is in harm or danger, therefore it's an unfit home.

The child doesn't have parents

In the event the child's mother dies, custody can be established through court order.....Find out the process. I really don't know.

If I would have adopted Josiah.

JoJo will get to a point where he seeks information and understanding for himself and he would approach his father asking, why didn't he make an effort to be in his life. His Father would more than likely respond, your parents didn't allow me to be a part of your life and pushed me out. JoJo can possibly develop

resentment due to our actions, even if we felt it was in his best interest.

This is a great segway into the definition of "Dad." Dads come in all different forms, types, relationships and can be interchangeable for almost anyone providing support that uplifts positive change and growth. When my father wasn't around, coaches became father figures to me including men in the community that taught me fundamentals of manhood. When my father wasn't around, men in the community would hire me and my brother to pickup leaves. It probably was one of the worst jobs I've ever experienced but it built character and work ethic that I wouldn't trade for the world. There is a village that becomes available to instill the lessons children need to learn and the role of "dad" can often be spread throughout the village to ensure children learn fundamentals of life. This concept also applies when the dad is around. Everyone is limited on the amount of information we know. If someone excels in a certain area, send the child to exceed your own understanding as the future depends on our children being smarter and more skilled than us.

Confidence I'm a firm believer that what's for me is for me and no one can take it away. If something isn't for me, then it was only supposed to be in my life for a season and I'm fine.

Being okay with JoJo's biological dad coming into the picture Studies show, 85% of blended familes are dysfunctional. While Drew and I were dating, she was very intentional not to allow me to play the dad role. She didn't want to scare me off or put responsibility on me before we had a chance to know if our relationship would last. Her family also assisted in our dating process. Their goal was to help Drew find the man of her dreams and would take JoJo so she could go out on dates. Well, that strategy worked! Drew and I went on a date that lasted 12hrs. Her family wasn't very happy when I brought her home at 4am. To no despair, we stayed in contact and she became my wife. I would ask Drew if I could take JoJo for ice cream or take him to the park while she was working if I felt she needed a helping hand

so I could build a stronger bond with him. I knew if I married Drew, he would become my son. JoJo's biological father currently wasn't around and I knew JoJo needed a male influence to help him navigate the world, instill moral and values and grow into the man he would become. I had great expectations however I didn't know what a son or father figure meant from my wifes's eyes. My thought was once we were married, I would automatically take on the father role.

In our scenario, we got married extremely fast and Drew was pregnant 2mo after. We had a huge decision to make, where do we stay to raise the kids. At the time we were in LA and didn't feel like we had much support. We could either go to NJ to my family or Chicago with her family. I spoke with Drew's mom and she said I really can't help you if you stay in LA. Drew has a big family, her mom and dad and 4 sisters. It was a no brainer and we relocated to Chicago before Machai was born. I didn't have a chance to fully assume the "Dad" role as everything was moving fast. We were living under the same roof however Drew was making moves the way she programmed and without much involvement or opinion from my side. There were a few things that I didn't like entirely too much such as JoJo staying up until any time he wanted as if he was a little rockstar in a diaper and him sleeping in the same bed. Drew wasn't receptive to him staying up late and defended by saying she's an actress and her hours flucturate. To combat, I provided studies and reports on best practices for sleeping. I also provided a guidance for the tv staying on all night and she said her parents did it with them and everyone is okay so it's not that bad. I tried developing the "My House, My Rules" concept but it quickly fell on death ears as my concerns weren't enforced. Opposed to supporting, JoJo would cry and mom would come to the rescue. I began to see a common thread, where JoJo was also learning how to get his way and It then became an issue where it was Me vs. Them.

Boiling Point where I felt I couldn't parent

Due to JoJo not receiving adequate sleep, he struggled to get up for school in the morning. Being a man, I had my way of getting you to follow directions which was to place the fear of God in you because at the end of the day, I'm the parent. JoJo stood by the sink and didn't want to brush his teeth so I "acted" as if I was going to give him a pinch and he started crying, not because of pain but because of the act. His mother ran upstairs and grabbed JoJo, asking what happened. JoJo responded, daddy pinched me. Drew grabbed JoJo and reprimanded me saying I told you not to do that to him. I asked JoJo to demonstrate on his mother exactly how hard I pinched him and he barely touched his mother. I walked out the room as I felt emasculated and minimized below a child. I thought to myself if I wanted to stay in a relationship where I didn't have a parenting voice. Besides all that I've done and contributed, I should feel more respected. We ended up seeking out a marriage counselor that told us we're doing things all wrong. We didn't have a plan and it shows.

but she did ask for my thoughts to correct him sleeping in the bed.

Introduce Drew's mom, millinial

Support we had and lacked

Realistic / Unrealistic Expectations

It's either him or me

Village mindset, when JoJo's dad came home, Respect. Territorial. No this is my house.

Drew received a call from JoJo's biological dad that he came home from jail and wanted to see his son if possible. At the time Drew was still hurt by the lack of support and effort. Her perspective was, if you haven't been around or made an effort all this time, why now. JoJo doesn't need you. Besides she had me in her life which "filled" the void of JoJo's lack of a father figure. Once Drew brought the conversation and intention to my attention, I had a lot of thinking to do also. As a man or the other man in the situation, I had several thoughts run through my mind. As men, we can rightfully be territorial and protective of their

castle. After I let my pride down, put myself in his shoes and think big picture, there were a few things I had to evaluate. Did JoJo's father approach the situation respectfully for my wife and also for me? Did he do anything to neglect the wellbeing and safety of JoJo? What is the intention? Is this relationship in the best interest for JoJo? I immediately thought of my father and our circumstances.

As a child, no one couldn't tell me that my father wasn't the best in the world and guess what, that's my perspective. If you measured or quantified the value of our relationship, there would be large gaps in his presence, missed games and events, missed birthdays, missed growth and bonding opportunities. Yet, my father was still the best thing that could have ever happened to me. How could this be, the heart doesn't measure value in the way our minds do. Love is blind and that's what makes love beautiful, innocent and cherished. Without love, we would be robots, incapable of forgiving or giving someone an opportunity to succeed. If we were robotic in our heart, we would leave a baby that didn't learn to walk fast enough or talk. Sometimes the greatest lessons on earth is experiencing life.

Interesting enough, Initially I didn't speak with JoJo's biological father as Drew had to feel comfortable with the interaction first however I was always by her side supporting the process. Change is very hard especially on a child therefore she wanted to make sure he wanted to really be part of his life before introducing his Father and he deciding he didn't want that role. Consistency is important to know if you're in this for the long run or if it's a nice experience because you think you should do it. Drew put JoJo's father on a call schedule to slowly introduce JoJo to his Father. JoJo visited with him as a baby but it's been years since they spoke and as a child, they don't know what a father means. The first few interactions was awkward just as any person that walks into a child's life that doesn't have kids, there is a learning process.

Adoption Because JoJo's father wasn't around, people would ask if I would adopt him, which is a great question. These are my rules on adopting in a blended family:

The Father doesn't want to be in the child's life therefore the child is fatherless

The Father is deceased.

The child is in harm or danger, therefore it's an unfit home.

The child doesn't have parents

In the event the child's mother dies, custody can be established through court order.....Find out the process. I really don't know.

If I would have adopted Josiah.

JoJo will get to a point where he seeks information and understanding for himself and he would approach his father asking, why didn't he make an effort to be in his life. His Father would more than likely respond, your parents didn't allow me to be a part of your life and pushed me out. JoJo can possibly develop resentment due to our actions, even if we felt it was in his best interest.

This is a great segway into the definition of "Dad." Dads come in all different forms, types, relationships and can be interchangeable for almost anyone providing support that uplifts positive change and growth. When my father wasn't around, coaches became father figures to me including men in the community that taught me fundamentals of manhood. When my father wasn't around, men in the community would hire me and my brother to pickup leaves. It probably was one of the worst jobs I've ever experienced but it built character and work ethic that I wouldn't trade for the world. There is a village that becomes available to instill the lessons children need to learn and the role of "dad" can often be spread throughout the village to ensure children learn fundamentals of life. This concept also applies when the dad is around. Everyone is limited on the amount of information we know. If someone excels in a certain area, send the child to exceed your own understanding as the future depends on our children being smarter and more skilled than us.

Confidence I'm a firm believer that what's for me is for me and no one can take it away. If something isn't for me, then it was only supposed to be in my life for a season and I'm fine.

Being okay with JoJo's biological dad coming into the picture Studies show, 85% of blended familes are dysfunctional. While Drew and I were dating, she was very intentional not to allow me to play the dad role. She didn't want to scare me off or put responsibility on me before we had a chance to know if our relationship would last. Her family also assisted in our dating process. Their goal was to help Drew find the man of her dreams and would take JoJo so she could go out on dates. Well, that strategy worked! Drew and I went on a date that lasted 12hrs. Her family wasn't very happy when I brought her home at 4am. To no despair, we stayed in contact and she became my wife. I would ask Drew if I could take JoJo for ice cream or take him to the park while she was working if I felt she needed a helping hand so I could build a stronger bond with him. I knew if I married Drew, he would become my son. JoJo's biological father currently wasn't around and I knew JoJo needed a male influence to help him navigate the world, instill moral and values and grow into the man he would become. I had great expectations however I didn't know what a son or father figure meant from my wifes's eyes. My thought was once we were married, I would automatically take on the father role.

In our scenario, we got married extremely fast and Drew was pregnant 2mo after. We had a huge decision to make, where do we stay to raise the kids. At the time we were in LA and didn't feel like we had much support. We could either go to NJ to my family or Chicago with her family. I spoke with Drew's mom and she said I really can't help you if you stay in LA. Drew has a big family, her mom and dad and 4 sisters. It was a no brainer and we relocated to Chicago before Machai was born. I didn't have a chance to fully assume the "Dad" role as everything was moving fast. We were living under the same roof however Drew was making moves the way she programmed and without much

involvement or opinion from my side. There were a few things that I didn't like entirely too much such as JoJo staying up until any time he wanted as if he was a little rockstar in a diaper and him sleeping in the same bed. Drew wasn't receptive to him staying up late and defended by saying she's an actress and her hours flucturate. To combat, I provided studies and reports on best practices for sleeping. I also provided a guidance for the tv staying on all night and she said her parents did it with them and everyone is okay so it's not that bad. I tried developing the "My House, My Rules" concept but it quickly fell on death ears as my concerns weren't enforced. Opposed to supporting, JoJo would cry and mom would come to the rescue. I began to see a common thread, where JoJo was also learning how to get his way and It then became an issue where it was Me vs. Them.

Boiling Point where I felt I couldn't parent

Due to JoJo not receiving adequate sleep, he struggled to get up for school in the morning. Being a man, I had my way of getting you to follow directions which was to place the fear of God in you because at the end of the day, I'm the parent. JoJo stood by the sink and didn't want to brush his teeth so I "acted" as if I was going to give him a pinch and he started crying, not because of pain but because of the act. His mother ran upstairs and grabbed JoJo, asking what happened. JoJo responded, daddy pinched me. Drew grabbed JoJo and repremanded me saying I told you not to do that to him. I asked JoJo to demonstrate on his mother exactly how hard I pinched him and he barely touched his mother. I walked out the room as I felt emasculated and minimized below a child. I thought to myself if I wanted to stay in a relationship where I didn't have a parenting voice. Besides all that I've done and contributed, I should feel more respected. We ended up seeking out a marriage counselor that told us we're doing things all wrong. We didn't have a plan and it shows.

but she did ask for my thoughts to correct him sleeping in the bed.

Introduce Drew's mom, millinial

Support we had and lacked

Realistic / Unrealistic Expectations

It's either him or me

Village mindset, when JoJo's dad came home, Respect. Territorial. No this is my house.

Drew received a call from JoJo's biological dad that he came home from jail and wanted to see his son if possible. At the time Drew was still hurt by the lack of support and effort. Her perspective was, if you haven't been around or made an effort all this time, why now. JoJo doesn't need you. Besides she had me in her life which "filled" the void of JoJo's lack of a father figure. Once Drew brought the conversation and intention to my attention, I had a lot of thinking to do also. As a man or the other man in the situation, I had several thoughts run through my mind. As men, we can rightfully be territorial and protective of their castle. After I let my pride down, put myself in his shoes and think big picture, there were a few things I had to evaluate. Did JoJo's father approach the situation respectfully for my wife and also for me? Did he do anything to neglect the wellbeing and safety of JoJo? What is the intention? Is this relationship in the best interest for JoJo? I immediately thought of my father and our circumstances.

As a child, no one couldn't tell me that my father wasn't the best in the world and guess what, that's my perspective. If you measured or quantified the value of our relationship, there would be large gaps in his presence, missed games and events, missed birthdays, missed growth and bonding opportunities. Yet, my father was still the best thing that could have ever happened to me. How could this be, the heart doesn't measure value in the way our minds do. Love is blind and that's what makes love beautiful, innocent and cherished. Without love, we would be robots, incapable of forgiving or giving someone an opportunity to succeed. If we were robotic in our heart, we would leave a baby that didn't learn to walk fast enough or talk. Sometimes the greatest lessons on earth is experiencing life.

Interesting enough, Initially I didn't speak with JoJo's biological father as Drew had to feel comfortable with the interaction first however I was always by her side supporting the process. Change is very hard especially on a child therefore she wanted to make sure he wanted to really be part of his life before introducing his Father and he deciding he didn't want that role. Consistency is important to know if you're in this for the long run or if it's a nice experience because you think you should do it. Drew put JoJo's father on a call schedule to slowly introduce JoJo to his Father. JoJo visited with him as a baby but it's been years since they spoke and as a child, they don't know what a father means. The first few interactions was awkward just as any person that walks into a child's life that doesn't have kids, there is a learning process.

Adoption Because JoJo's father wasn't around, people would ask if I would adopt him, which is a great question. These are my rules on adopting in a blended family:

The Father doesn't want to be in the child's life therefore the child is fatherless

The Father is deceased.

The child is in harm or danger, therefore it's an unfit home.

The child doesn't have parents

In the event the child's mother dies, custody can be established through court order.....Find out the process. I really don't know.

If I would have adopted Josiah.

JoJo will get to a point where he seeks information and understanding for himself and he would approach his father asking, why didn't he make an effort to be in his life. His Father would more than likely respond, your parents didn't allow me to be a part of your life and pushed me out. JoJo can possibly develop resentment due to our actions, even if we felt it was in his best interest.

This is a great segway into the definition of "Dad." Dads come in all different forms, types, relationships and can be interchangeable for almost anyone providing support that uplifts positive

change and growth. When my father wasn't around, coaches became father figures to me including men in the community that taught me fundamentals of manhood. When my father wasn't around, men in the community would hire me and my brother to pickup leaves. It probably was one of the worst jobs I've ever experienced but it built character and work ethic that I wouldn't trade for the world. There is a village that becomes available to instill the lessons children need to learn and the role of "dad" can often be spread throughout the village to ensure children learn fundamentals of life. This concept also applies when the dad is around. Everyone is limited on the amount of information we know. If someone excels in a certain area, send the child to exceed your own understanding as the future depends on our children being smarter and more skilled than us.

Confidence I'm a firm believer that what's for me is for me and no one can take it away. If something isn't for me, then it was only supposed to be in my life for a season and I'm fine.

Being okay with JoJo's biological dad coming into the picture Studies show, 85% of blended familes are dysfunctional. While Drew and I were dating, she was very intentional not to allow me to play the dad role. She didn't want to scare me off or put responsibility on me before we had a chance to know if our relationship would last. Her family also assisted in our dating process. Their goal was to help Drew find the man of her dreams and would take JoJo so she could go out on dates. Well, that strategy worked! Drew and I went on a date that lasted 12hrs. Her family wasn't very happy when I brought her home at 4am. To no despair, we stayed in contact and she became my wife. I would ask Drew if I could take JoJo for ice cream or take him to the park while she was working if I felt she needed a helping hand so I could build a stronger bond with him. I knew if I married Drew, he would become my son. JoJo's biological father currently wasn't around and I knew JoJo needed a male influence to help him navigate the world, instill moral and values and grow into the man he would become. I had great expectations however

I didn't know what a son or father figure meant from my wifes's eyes. My thought was once we were married, I would automatically take on the father role.

In our scenario, we got married extremely fast and Drew was pregnant 2mo after. We had a huge decision to make, where do we stay to raise the kids. At the time we were in LA and didn't feel like we had much support. We could either go to NJ to my family or Chicago with her family. I spoke with Drew's mom and she said I really can't help you if you stay in LA. Drew has a big family, her mom and dad and 4 sisters. It was a no brainer and we relocated to Chicago before Machai was born. I didn't have a chance to fully assume the "Dad" role as everything was moving fast. We were living under the same roof however Drew was making moves the way she programmed and without much involvement or opinion from my side. There were a few things that I didn't like entirely too much such as JoJo staying up until any time he wanted as if he was a little rockstar in a diaper and him sleeping in the same bed. Drew wasn't receptive to him staying up late and defended by saying she's an actress and her hours flucturate. To combat, I provided studies and reports on best practices for sleeping. I also provided a guidance for the tv staying on all night and she said her parents did it with them and everyone is okay so it's not that bad. I tried developing the "My House, My Rules" concept but it quickly fell on death ears as my concerns weren't enforced. Opposed to supporting, JoJo would cry and mom would come to the rescue. I began to see a common thread, where JoJo was also learning how to get his way and It then became an issue where it was Me vs. Them.

Boiling Point where I felt I couldn't parent

Due to JoJo not receiving adequate sleep, he struggled to get up for school in the morning. Being a man, I had my way of getting you to follow directions which was to place the fear of God in you because at the end of the day, I'm the parent. JoJo stood by the sink and didn't want to brush his teeth so I "acted" as if I was going to give him a pinch and he started crying, not because

of pain but because of the act. His mother ran upstairs and grabbed JoJo, asking what happened. JoJo responded, daddy pinched me. Drew grabbed JoJo and repremanded me saying I told you not to do that to him. I asked JoJo to demonstrate on his mother exactly how hard I pinched him and he barely touched his mother. I walked out the room as I felt emasculated and minimized below a child. I thought to myself if I wanted to stay in a relationship where I didn't have a parenting voice. Besides all that I've done and contributed, I should feel more respected. We ended up seeking out a marriage counselor that told us we're doing things all wrong. We didn't have a plan and it shows.

but she did ask for my thoughts to correct him sleeping in the bed.

Introduce Drew's mom, millinial

Support we had and lacked

Realistic / Unrealistic Expectations

It's either him or me

Village mindset, when JoJo's dad came home, Respect. Territorial. No this is my house.

Drew received a call from JoJo's biological dad that he came home from jail and wanted to see his son if possible. At the time Drew was still hurt by the lack of support and effort. Her perspective was, if you haven't been around or made an effort all this time, why now. JoJo doesn't need you. Besides she had me in her life which "filled" the void of JoJo's lack of a father figure. Once Drew brought the conversation and intention to my attention, I had a lot of thinking to do also. As a man or the other man in the situation, I had several thoughts run through my mind. As men, we can rightfully be territorial and protective of their castle. After I let my pride down, put myself in his shoes and think big picture, there were a few things I had to evaluate. Did JoJo's father approach the situation respectfully for my wife and also for me? Did he do anything to neglect the wellbeing and safety of JoJo? What is the intention? Is this relationship in the

best interest for JoJo? I immediately thought of my father and our circumstances.

As a child, no one couldn't tell me that my father wasn't the best in the world and guess what, that's my perspective. If you measured or quantified the value of our relationship, there would be large gaps in his presence, missed games and events, missed birthdays, missed growth and bonding opportunities. Yet, my father was still the best thing that could have ever happened to me. How could this be, the heart doesn't measure value in the way our minds do. Love is blind and that's what makes love beautiful, innocent and cherished. Without love, we would be robots, incapable of forgiving or giving someone an opportunity to succeed. If we were robotic in our heart, we would leave a baby that didn't learn to walk fast enough or talk. Sometimes the greatest lessons on earth is experiencing life.

Interesting enough, Initially I didn't speak with JoJo's biological father as Drew had to feel comfortable with the interaction first however I was always by her side supporting the process. Change is very hard especially on a child therefore she wanted to make sure he wanted to really be part of his life before introducing his Father and he deciding he didn't want that role. Consistency is important to know if you're in this for the long run or if it's a nice experience because you think you should do it. Drew put JoJo's father on a call schedule to slowly introduce JoJo to his Father. JoJo visited with him as a baby but it's been years since they spoke and as a child, they don't know what a father means. The first few interactions was awkward just as any person that walks into a child's life that doesn't have kids, there is a learning process.

Adoption Because JoJo's father wasn't around, people would ask if I would adopt him, which is a great question. These are my rules on adopting in a blended family:

The Father doesn't want to be in the child's life therefore the child is fatherless

The Father is deceased.

The child is in harm or danger, therefore it's an unfit home.

The child doesn't have parents

In the event the child's mother dies, custody can be established through court order.....Find out the process. I really don't know.

If I would have adopted Josiah.

JoJo will get to a point where he seeks information and understanding for himself and he would approach his father asking, why didn't he make an effort to be in his life. His Father would more than likely respond, your parents didn't allow me to be a part of your life and pushed me out. JoJo can possibly develop resentment due to our actions, even if we felt it was in his best interest.

This is a great segway into the definition of "Dad." Dads come in all different forms, types, relationships and can be interchangeable for almost anyone providing support that uplifts positive change and growth. When my father wasn't around, coaches became father figures to me including men in the community that taught me fundamentals of manhood. When my father wasn't around, men in the community would hire me and my brother to pickup leaves. It probably was one of the worst jobs I've ever experienced but it built character and work ethic that I wouldn't trade for the world. There is a village that becomes available to instill the lessons children need to learn and the role of "dad" can often be spread throughout the village to ensure children learn fundamentals of life. This concept also applies when the dad is around. Everyone is limited on the amount of information we know. If someone excels in a certain area, send the child to exceed your own understanding as the future depends on our children being smarter and more skilled than us.

Confidence I'm a firm believer that what's for me is for me and no one can take it away. If something isn't for me, then it was only supposed to be in my life for a season and I'm fine.

Being okay with JoJo's biological dad coming into the picture

Studies show, 85% of blended familes are dysfunctional. While Drew and I were dating, she was very intentional not to

allow me to play the dad role. She didn't want to scare me off or put responsibility on me before we had a chance to know if our relationship would last. Her family also assisted in our dating process. Their goal was to help Drew find the man of her dreams and would take JoJo so she could go out on dates. Well, that strategy worked! Drew and I went on a date that lasted 12hrs. Her family wasn't very happy when I brought her home at 4am. To no despair, we stayed in contact and she became my wife. I would ask Drew if I could take JoJo for ice cream or take him to the park while she was working if I felt she needed a helping hand so I could build a stronger bond with him. I knew if I married Drew, he would become my son. JoJo's biological father currently wasn't around and I knew JoJo needed a male influence to help him navigate the world, instill moral and values and grow into the man he would become. I had great expectations however I didn't know what a son or father figure meant from my wifes's eyes. My thought was once we were married, I would automatically take on the father role.

In our scenario, we got married extremely fast and Drew was pregnant 2mo after. We had a huge decision to make, where do we stay to raise the kids. At the time we were in LA and didn't feel like we had much support. We could either go to NJ to my family or Chicago with her family. I spoke with Drew's mom and she said I really can't help you if you stay in LA. Drew has a big family, her mom and dad and 4 sisters. It was a no brainer and we relocated to Chicago before Machai was born. I didn't have a chance to fully assume the "Dad" role as everything was moving fast. We were living under the same roof however Drew was making moves the way she programmed and without much involvement or opinion from my side. There were a few things that I didn't like entirely too much such as JoJo staying up until any time he wanted as if he was a little rockstar in a diaper and him sleeping in the same bed. Drew wasn't receptive to him staying up late and defended by saying she's an actress and her hours flucturate. To combat, I provided studies and reports on

best practices for sleeping. I also provided a guidance for the tv staying on all night and she said her parents did it with them and everyone is okay so it's not that bad. I tried developing the "My House, My Rules" concept but it quickly fell on death ears as my concerns weren't enforced. Opposed to supporting, JoJo would cry and mom would come to the rescue. I began to see a common thread, where JoJo was also learning how to get his way and It then became an issue where it was Me vs. Them.

Boiling Point where I felt I couldn't parent

Due to JoJo not receiving adequate sleep, he struggled to get up for school in the morning. Being a man, I had my way of getting you to follow directions which was to place the fear of God in you because at the end of the day, I'm the parent. JoJo stood by the sink and didn't want to brush his teeth so I "acted" as if I was going to give him a pinch and he started crying, not because of pain but because of the act. His mother ran upstairs and grabbed JoJo, asking what happened. JoJo responded, daddy pinched me. Drew grabbed JoJo and repremanded me saying I told you not to do that to him. I asked JoJo to demonstrate on his mother exactly how hard I pinched him and he barely touched his mother. I walked out the room as I felt emasculated and minimized below a child. I thought to myself if I wanted to stay in a relationship where I didn't have a parenting voice. Besides all that I've done and contributed, I should feel more respected. We ended up seeking out a marriage counselor that told us we're doing things all wrong. We didn't have a plan and it shows.

but she did ask for my thoughts to correct him sleeping in the bed.

Introduce Drew's mom, millinial

Support we had and lacked

Realistic / Unrealistic Expectations

It's either him or me

Village mindset, when JoJo's dad came home, Respect. Territorial. No this is my house.

Drew received a call from JoJo's biological dad that he came home from jail and wanted to see his son if possible. At the time Drew was still hurt by the lack of support and effort. Her perspective was, if you haven't been around or made an effort all this time, why now. JoJo doesn't need you. Besides she had me in her life which "filled" the void of JoJo's lack of a father figure. Once Drew brought the conversation and intention to my attention, I had a lot of thinking to do also. As a man or the other man in the situation, I had several thoughts run through my mind. As men, we can rightfully be territorial and protective of their castle. After I let my pride down, put myself in his shoes and think big picture, there were a few things I had to evaluate. Did JoJo's father approach the situation respectfully for my wife and also for me? Did he do anything to neglect the wellbeing and safety of JoJo? What is the intention? Is this relationship in the best interest for JoJo? I immediately thought of my father and our circumstances.

As a child, no one couldn't tell me that my father wasn't the best in the world and guess what, that's my perspective. If you measured or quantified the value of our relationship, there would be large gaps in his presence, missed games and events, missed birthdays, missed growth and bonding opportunities. Yet, my father was still the best thing that could have ever happened to me. How could this be, the heart doesn't measure value in the way our minds do. Love is blind and that's what makes love beautiful, innocent and cherished. Without love, we would be robots, incapable of forgiving or giving someone an opportunity to succeed. If we were robotic in our heart, we would leave a baby that didn't learn to walk fast enough or talk. Sometimes the greatest lessons on earth is experiencing life.

Interesting enough, Initially I didn't speak with JoJo's biological father as Drew had to feel comfortable with the interaction first however I was always by her side supporting the process. Change is very hard especially on a child therefore she wanted to make sure he wanted to really be part of his life before

introducing his Father and he deciding he didn't want that role. Consistency is important to know if you're in this for the long run or if it's a nice experience because you think you should do it. Drew put JoJo's father on a call schedule to slowly introduce JoJo to his Father. JoJo visited with him as a baby but it's been years since they spoke and as a child, they don't know what a father means. The first few interactions was awkward just as any person that walks into a child's life that doesn't have kids, there is a learning process.

Adoption Because JoJo's father wasn't around, people would ask if I would adopt him, which is a great question. These are my rules on adopting in a blended family:

The Father doesn't want to be in the child's life therefore the child is fatherless

The Father is deceased.

The child is in harm or danger, therefore it's an unfit home.

The child doesn't have parents

In the event the child's mother dies, custody can be established through court order.....Find out the process. I really don't know.

If I would have adopted Josiah.

JoJo will get to a point where he seeks information and understanding for himself and he would approach his father asking, why didn't he make an effort to be in his life. His Father would more than likely respond, your parents didn't allow me to be a part of your life and pushed me out. JoJo can possibly develop resentment due to our actions, even if we felt it was in his best interest.

This is a great segway into the definition of "Dad." Dads come in all different forms, types, relationships and can be interchangeable for almost anyone providing support that uplifts positive change and growth. When my father wasn't around, coaches became father figures to me including men in the community that taught me fundamentals of manhood. When my father wasn't around, men in the community would hire me and my brother to pickup leaves. It probably was one of the worst jobs I've ever

experienced but it built character and work ethic that I wouldn't trade for the world. There is a village that becomes available to instill the lessons children need to learn and the role of "dad" can often be spread throughout the village to ensure children learn fundamentals of life. This concept also applies when the dad is around. Everyone is limited on the amount of information we know. If someone excels in a certain area, send the child to exceed your own understanding as the future depends on our children being smarter and more skilled than us.

Confidence I'm a firm believer that what's for me is for me and no one can take it away. If something isn't for me, then it was only supposed to be in my life for a season and I'm fine.

Being okay with JoJo's biological dad coming into the picture

Studies show, 85% of blended familes are dysfunctional. While Drew and I were dating, she was very intentional not to allow me to play the dad role. She didn't want to scare me off or put responsibility on me before we had a chance to know if our relationship would last. Her family also assisted in our dating process. Their goal was to help Drew find the man of her dreams and would take JoJo so she could go out on dates. Well, that strategy worked! Drew and I went on a date that lasted 12hrs. Her family wasn't very happy when I brought her home at 4am. To no despair, we stayed in contact and she became my wife. I would ask Drew if I could take JoJo for ice cream or take him to the park while she was working if I felt she needed a helping hand so I could build a stronger bond with him. I knew if I married Drew, he would become my son. JoJo's biological father currently wasn't around and I knew JoJo needed a male influence to help him navigate the world, instill moral and values and grow into the man he would become. I had great expectations however I didn't know what a son or father figure meant from my wifes's eyes. My thought was once we were married, I would automatically take on the father role.

In our scenario, we got married extremely fast and Drew was pregnant 2mo after. We had a huge decision to make, where do

we stay to raise the kids. At the time we were in LA and didn't feel like we had much support. We could either go to NJ to my family or Chicago with her family. I spoke with Drew's mom and she said I really can't help you if you stay in LA. Drew has a big family, her mom and dad and 4 sisters. It was a no brainer and we relocated to Chicago before Machai was born. I didn't have a chance to fully assume the "Dad" role as everything was moving fast. We were living under the same roof however Drew was making moves the way she programmed and without much involvement or opinion from my side. There were a few things that I didn't like entirely too much such as JoJo staying up until any time he wanted as if he was a little rockstar in a diaper and him sleeping in the same bed. Drew wasn't receptive to him staying up late and defended by saying she's an actress and her hours flucturate. To combat, I provided studies and reports on best practices for sleeping. I also provided a guidance for the tv staying on all night and she said her parents did it with them and everyone is okay so it's not that bad. I tried developing the "My House, My Rules" concept but it quickly fell on death ears as my concerns weren't enforced. Opposed to supporting, JoJo would cry and mom would come to the rescue. I began to see a common thread, where JoJo was also learning how to get his way and It then became an issue where it was Me vs. Them.

Boiling Point where I felt I couldn't parent

Due to JoJo not receiving adequate sleep, he struggled to get up for school in the morning. Being a man, I had my way of getting you to follow directions which was to place the fear of God in you because at the end of the day, I'm the parent. JoJo stood by the sink and didn't want to brush his teeth so I "acted" as if I was going to give him a pinch and he started crying, not because of pain but because of the act. His mother ran upstairs and grabbed JoJo, asking what happened. JoJo responded, daddy pinched me. Drew grabbed JoJo and reprimanded me saying I told you not to do that to him. I asked JoJo to demonstrate on his mother exactly how hard I pinched him and he barely touched

his mother. I walked out the room as I felt emasculated and minimized below a child. I thought to myself if I wanted to stay in a relationship where I didn't have a parenting voice. Besides all that I've done and contributed, I should feel more respected. We ended up seeking out a marriage counselor that told us we're doing things all wrong. We didn't have a plan and it shows.

but she did ask for my thoughts to correct him sleeping in the bed.

Introduce Drew's mom, millinial

Support we had and lacked

Realistic / Unrealistic Expectations

It's either him or me

Village mindset, when JoJo's dad came home, Respect. Territorial. No this is my house.

Drew received a call from JoJo's biological dad that he came home from jail and wanted to see his son if possible. At the time Drew was still hurt by the lack of support and effort. Her perspective was, if you haven't been around or made an effort all this time, why now. JoJo doesn't need you. Besides she had me in her life which "filled" the void of JoJo's lack of a father figure. Once Drew brought the conversation and intention to my attention, I had a lot of thinking to do also. As a man or the other man in the situation, I had several thoughts run through my mind. As men, we can rightfully be territorial and protective of their castle. After I let my pride down, put myself in his shoes and think big picture, there were a few things I had to evaluate. Did JoJo's father approach the situation respectfully for my wife and also for me? Did he do anything to neglect the wellbeing and safety of JoJo? What is the intention? Is this relationship in the best interest for JoJo? I immediately thought of my father and our circumstances.

As a child, no one couldn't tell me that my father wasn't the best in the world and guess what, that's my perspective. If you measured or quantified the value of our relationship, there would be large gaps in his presence, missed games and events,

missed birthdays, missed growth and bonding opportunities. Yet, my father was still the best thing that could have ever happened to me. How could this be, the heart doesn't measure value in the way our minds do. Love is blind and that's what makes love beautiful, innocent and cherished. Without love, we would be robots, incapable of forgiving or giving someone an opportunity to succeed. If we were robotic in our heart, we would leave a baby that didn't learn to walk fast enough or talk. Sometimes the greatest lessons on earth is experiencing life.

Interesting enough, Initially I didn't speak with JoJo's biological father as Drew had to feel comfortable with the interaction first however I was always by her side supporting the process. Change is very hard especially on a child therefore she wanted to make sure he wanted to really be part of his life before introducing his Father and he deciding he didn't want that role. Consistency is important to know if you're in this for the long run or if it's a nice experience because you think you should do it. Drew put JoJo's father on a call schedule to slowly introduce JoJo to his Father. JoJo visited with him as a baby but it's been years since they spoke and as a child, they don't know what a father means. The first few interactions was awkward just as any person that walks into a child's life that doesn't have kids, there is a learning process.

Adoption Because JoJo's father wasn't around, people would ask if I would adopt him, which is a great question. These are my rules on adopting in a blended family:

The Father doesn't want to be in the child's life therefore the child is fatherless

The Father is deceased.

The child is in harm or danger, therefore it's an unfit home.

The child doesn't have parents

In the event the child's mother dies, custody can be established through court order.....Find out the process. I really don't know.

If I would have adopted Josiah.

JoJo will get to a point where he seeks information and understanding for himself and he would approach his father asking, why didn't he make an effort to be in his life. His Father would more than likely respond, your parents didn't allow me to be a part of your life and pushed me out. JoJo can possibly develop resentment due to our actions, even if we felt it was in his best interest.

This is a great segway into the definition of "Dad." Dads come in all different forms, types, relationships and can be interchangeable for almost anyone providing support that uplifts positive change and growth. When my father wasn't around, coaches became father figures to me including men in the community that taught me fundamentals of manhood. When my father wasn't around, men in the community would hire me and my brother to pickup leaves. It probably was one of the worst jobs I've ever experienced but it built character and work ethic that I wouldn't trade for the world. There is a village that becomes available to instill the lessons children need to learn and the role of "dad" can often be spread throughout the village to ensure children learn fundamentals of life. This concept also applies when the dad is around. Everyone is limited on the amount of information we know. If someone excels in a certain area, send the child to exceed your own understanding as the future depends on our children being smarter and more skilled than us.

Confidence I'm a firm believer that what's for me is for me and no one can take it away. If something isn't for me, then it was only supposed to be in my life for a season and I'm fine.

Being okay with JoJo's biological dad coming into the picture Studies show, 85% of blended familes are dysfunctional. While Drew and I were dating, she was very intentional not to allow me to play the dad role. She didn't want to scare me off or put responsibility on me before we had a chance to know if our relationship would last. Her family also assisted in our dating process. Their goal was to help Drew find the man of her dreams and would take JoJo so she could go out on dates. Well, that

strategy worked! Drew and I went on a date that lasted 12hrs. Her family wasn't very happy when I brought her home at 4am. To no despair, we stayed in contact and she became my wife. I would ask Drew if I could take JoJo for ice cream or take him to the park while she was working if I felt she needed a helping hand so I could build a stronger bond with him. I knew if I married Drew, he would become my son. JoJo's biological father currently wasn't around and I knew JoJo needed a male influence to help him navigate the world, instill moral and values and grow into the man he would become. I had great expectations however I didn't know what a son or father figure meant from my wifes's eyes. My thought was once we were married, I would automatically take on the father role.

In our scenario, we got married extremely fast and Drew was pregnant 2mo after. We had a huge decision to make, where do we stay to raise the kids. At the time we were in LA and didn't feel like we had much support. We could either go to NJ to my family or Chicago with her family. I spoke with Drew's mom and she said I really can't help you if you stay in LA. Drew has a big family, her mom and dad and 4 sisters. It was a no brainer and we relocated to Chicago before Machai was born. I didn't have a chance to fully assume the "Dad" role as everything was moving fast. We were living under the same roof however Drew was making moves the way she programmed and without much involvement or opinion from my side. There were a few things that I didn't like entirely too much such as JoJo staying up until any time he wanted as if he was a little rockstar in a diaper and him sleeping in the same bed. Drew wasn't receptive to him staying up late and defended by saying she's an actress and her hours flucturate. To combat, I provided studies and reports on best practices for sleeping. I also provided a guidance for the tv staying on all night and she said her parents did it with them and everyone is okay so it's not that bad. I tried developing the "My House, My Rules" concept but it quickly fell on death ears as my concerns weren't enforced. Opposed to supporting, JoJo would

cry and mom would come to the rescue. I began to see a common thread, where JoJo was also learning how to get his way and It then became an issue where it was Me vs. Them.

Boiling Point where I felt I couldn't parent

Due to JoJo not receiving adequate sleep, he struggled to get up for school in the morning. Being a man, I had my way of getting you to follow directions which was to place the fear of God in you because at the end of the day, I'm the parent. JoJo stood by the sink and didn't want to brush his teeth so I "acted" as if I was going to give him a pinch and he started crying, not because of pain but because of the act. His mother ran upstairs and grabbed JoJo, asking what happened. JoJo responded, daddy pinched me. Drew grabbed JoJo and repremanded me saying I told you not to do that to him. I asked JoJo to demonstrate on his mother exactly how hard I pinched him and he barely touched his mother. I walked out the room as I felt emasculated and minimized below a child. I thought to myself if I wanted to stay in a relationship where I didn't have a parenting voice. Besides all that I've done and contributed, I should feel more respected. We ended up seeking out a marriage counselor that told us we're doing things all wrong. We didn't have a plan and it shows.

but she did ask for my thoughts to correct him sleeping in the bed.

Introduce Drew's mom, millinial

Support we had and lacked

Realistic / Unrealistic Expectations

It's either him or me

Village mindset, when JoJo's dad came home, Respect. Territorial. No this is my house.

Drew received a call from JoJo's biological dad that he came home from jail and wanted to see his son if possible. At the time Drew was still hurt by the lack of support and effort. Her perspective was, if you haven't been around or made an effort all this time, why now. JoJo doesn't need you. Besides she had me in her life which "filled" the void of JoJo's lack of a father figure.

Once Drew brought the conversation and intention to my attention, I had a lot of thinking to do also. As a man or the other man in the situation, I had several thoughts run through my mind. As men, we can rightfully be territorial and protective of their castle. After I let my pride down, put myself in his shoes and think big picture, there were a few things I had to evaluate. Did JoJo's father approach the situation respectfully for my wife and also for me? Did he do anything to neglect the wellbeing and safety of JoJo? What is the intention? Is this relationship in the best interest for JoJo? I immediately thought of my father and our circumstances.

Love is Blind

AS A CHILD, no one couldn't tell me that my father wasn't the best in the world and guess what, that's my perspective. If you measured or quantified the value of our relationship, there would be large gaps in his presence, missed games and events, missed birthdays, missed growth and bonding opportunities. Yet, my father was still the best thing that could have ever happened to me. How could this be, the heart doesn't measure value in the way our minds do. Love is blind and that's what makes love beautiful, innocent and cherished. Without love, we would be robots, incapable of forgiving or giving someone an opportunity to succeed. If we were robotic in our heart, we would leave a baby that didn't learn to walk fast enough or talk. Sometimes the greatest lessons on earth is experiencing life.

Interesting enough, Initially I didn't speak with JoJo's biological father as Drew had to feel comfortable with the interaction first however I was always by her side supporting the process. Change is very hard especially on a child therefore she wanted to make sure he wanted to really be part of his life before introducing his Father and he deciding he didn't want that role. Consistency is important to know if you're in this for the long run or if it's a nice experience because you think you should do

it. Drew put JoJo's father on a call schedule to slowly introduce JoJo to his Father. JoJo visited with him as a baby but it's been years since they spoke and as a child, they don't know what a father means. The first few interactions was awkward just as any person that walks into a child's life that doesn't have kids, there is a learning process.

Adoption Because JoJo's father wasn't around, people would ask if I would adopt him, which is a great question. These are my rules on adopting in a blended family:

The Father doesn't want to be in the child's life therefore the child is fatherless

The Father is deceased.

The child is in harm or danger, therefore it's an unfit home.

The child doesn't have parents

In the event the child's mother dies, custody can be established through court order.....Find out the process. I really don't know.

If I would have adopted Josiah.

JoJo will get to a point where he seeks information and understanding for himself and he would approach his father asking, why didn't he make an effort to be in his life. His Father would more than likely respond, your parents didn't allow me to be a part of your life and pushed me out. JoJo can possibly develop resentment due to our actions, even if we felt it was in his best interest.

This is a great segway into the definition of "Dad." Dads come in all different forms, types, relationships and can be interchangeable for almost anyone providing support that uplifts positive change and growth. When my father wasn't around, coaches became father figures to me including men in the community that taught me fundamentals of manhood. When my father wasn't around, men in the community would hire me and my brother to pickup leaves. It probably was one of the worst jobs I've ever experienced but it built character and work ethic that I wouldn't trade for the world. There is a village that becomes available to instill the lessons children need to learn and the role of "dad"

can often be spread throughout the village to ensure children learn fundamentals of life. This concept also applies when the dad is around. Everyone is limited on the amount of information we know. If someone excels in a certain area, send the child to exceed your own understanding as the future depends on our children being smarter and more skilled than us.

Confidence I'm a firm believer that what's for me is for me and no one can take it away. If something isn't for me, then it was only supposed to be in my life for a season and I'm fine.

Being okay with JoJo's biological dad coming into the picture Studies show, 85% of blended familes are dysfunctional. While Drew and I were dating, she was very intentional not to allow me to play the dad role. She didn't want to scare me off or put responsibility on me before we had a chance to know if our relationship would last. Her family also assisted in our dating process. Their goal was to help Drew find the man of her dreams and would take JoJo so she could go out on dates. Well, that strategy worked! Drew and I went on a date that lasted 12hrs. Her family wasn't very happy when I brought her home at 4am. To no despair, we stayed in contact and she became my wife. I would ask Drew if I could take JoJo for ice cream or take him to the park while she was working if I felt she needed a helping hand so I could build a stronger bond with him. I knew if I married Drew, he would become my son. JoJo's biological father currently wasn't around and I knew JoJo needed a male influence to help him navigate the world, instill moral and values and grow into the man he would become. I had great expectations however I didn't know what a son or father figure meant from my wifes's eyes. My thought was once we were married, I would automatically take on the father role.

In our scenario, we got married extremely fast and Drew was pregnant 2mo after. We had a huge decision to make, where do we stay to raise the kids. At the time we were in LA and didn't feel like we had much support. We could either go to NJ to my family or Chicago with her family. I spoke with Drew's mom

and she said I really can't help you if you stay in LA. Drew has a big family, her mom and dad and 4 sisters. It was a no brainer and we relocated to Chicago before Machai was born. I didn't have a chance to fully assume the "Dad" role as everything was moving fast. We were living under the same roof however Drew was making moves the way she programmed and without much involvement or opinion from my side. There were a few things that I didn't like entirely too much such as JoJo staying up until any time he wanted as if he was a little rockstar in a diaper and him sleeping in the same bed. Drew wasn't receptive to him staying up late and defended by saying she's an actress and her hours flucturate. To combat, I provided studies and reports on best practices for sleeping. I also provided a guidance for the tv staying on all night and she said her parents did it with them and everyone is okay so it's not that bad. I tried developing the "My House, My Rules" concept but it quickly fell on death ears as my concerns weren't enforced. Opposed to supporting, JoJo would cry and mom would come to the rescue. I began to see a common thread, where JoJo was also learning how to get his way and It then became an issue where it was Me vs. Them.

Boiling Point where I felt I couldn't parent

Due to JoJo not receiving adequate sleep, he struggled to get up for school in the morning. Being a man, I had my way of getting you to follow directions which was to place the fear of God in you because at the end of the day, I'm the parent. JoJo stood by the sink and didn't want to brush his teeth so I "acted" as if I was going to give him a pinch and he started crying, not because of pain but because of the act. His mother ran upstairs and grabbed JoJo, asking what happened. JoJo responded, daddy pinched me. Drew grabbed JoJo and reprimanded me saying I told you not to do that to him. I asked JoJo to demonstrate on his mother exactly how hard I pinched him and he barely touched his mother. I walked out the room as I felt emasculated and minimized below a child. I thought to myself if I wanted to stay in a relationship where I didn't have a parenting voice. Besides all

that I've done and contributed, I should feel more respected. We ended up seeking out a marriage counselor that told us we're doing things all wrong. We didn't have a plan and it shows.

but she did ask for my thoughts to correct him sleeping in the bed.

Introduce Drew's mom, millinial

Support we had and lacked

Realistic / Unrealistic Expectations

It's either him or me

Village mindset, when JoJo's dad came home, Respect. Territorial. No this is my house.

Drew received a call from JoJo's biological dad that he came home from jail and wanted to see his son if possible. At the time Drew was still hurt by the lack of support and effort. Her perspective was, if you haven't been around or made an effort all this time, why now. JoJo doesn't need you. Besides she had me in her life which "filled" the void of JoJo's lack of a father figure. Once Drew brought the conversation and intention to my attention, I had a lot of thinking to do also. As a man or the other man in the situation, I had several thoughts run through my mind. As men, we can rightfully be territorial and protective of their castle. After I let my pride down, put myself in his shoes and think big picture, there were a few things I had to evaluate. Did JoJo's father approach the situation respectfully for my wife and also for me? Did he do anything to neglect the wellbeing and safety of JoJo? What is the intention? Is this relationship in the best interest for JoJo? I immediately thought of my father and our circumstances.

As a child, no one couldn't tell me that my father wasn't the best in the world and guess what, that's my perspective. If you measured or quantified the value of our relationship, there would be large gaps in his presence, missed games and events, missed birthdays, missed growth and bonding opportunities. Yet, my father was still the best thing that could have ever happened to me. How could this be, the heart doesn't measure value

in the way our minds do. Love is blind and that's what makes love beautiful, innocent and cherished. Without love, we would be robots, incapable of forgiving or giving someone an opportunity to succeed. If we were robotic in our heart, we would leave a baby that didn't learn to walk fast enough or talk. Sometimes the greatest lessons on earth is experiencing life.

Interesting enough, Initially I didn't speak with JoJo's biological father as Drew had to feel comfortable with the interaction first however I was always by her side supporting the process. Change is very hard especially on a child therefore she wanted to make sure he wanted to really be part of his life before introducing his Father and he deciding he didn't want that role. Consistency is important to know if you're in this for the long run or if it's a nice experience because you think you should do it. Drew put JoJo's father on a call schedule to slowly introduce JoJo to his Father. JoJo visited with him as a baby but it's been years since they spoke and as a child, they don't know what a father means. The first few interactions was awkward just as any person that walks into a child's life that doesn't have kids, there is a learning process.

Adoption Because JoJo's father wasn't around, people would ask if I would adopt him, which is a great question. These are my rules on adopting in a blended family:

The Father doesn't want to be in the child's life therefore the child is fatherless

The Father is deceased.

The child is in harm or danger, therefore it's an unfit home.

The child doesn't have parents

In the event the child's mother dies, custody can be established through court order.....Find out the process. I really don't know.

If I would have adopted Josiah.

JoJo will get to a point where he seeks information and understanding for himself and he would approach his father asking, why didn't he make an effort to be in his life. His Father would more than likely respond, your parents didn't allow me to be a

part of your life and pushed me out. JoJo can possibly develop resentment due to our actions, even if we felt it was in his best interest.

This is a great segway into the definition of "Dad." Dads come in all different forms, types, relationships and can be interchangeable for almost anyone providing support that uplifts positive change and growth. When my father wasn't around, coaches became father figures to me including men in the community that taught me fundamentals of manhood. When my father wasn't around, men in the community would hire me and my brother to pickup leaves. It probably was one of the worst jobs I've ever experienced but it built character and work ethic that I wouldn't trade for the world. There is a village that becomes available to instill the lessons children need to learn and the role of "dad" can often be spread throughout the village to ensure children learn fundamentals of life. This concept also applies when the dad is around. Everyone is limited on the amount of information we know. If someone excels in a certain area, send the child to exceed your own understanding as the future depends on our children being smarter and more skilled than us.

Confidence I'm a firm believer that what's for me is for me and no one can take it away. If something isn't for me, then it was only supposed to be in my life for a season and I'm fine.

Being okay with JoJo's biological dad coming into the picture

Studies show, 85% of blended familes are dysfunctional. While Drew and I were dating, she was very intentional not to allow me to play the dad role. She didn't want to scare me off or put responsibility on me before we had a chance to know if our relationship would last. Her family also assisted in our dating process. Their goal was to help Drew find the man of her dreams and would take JoJo so she could go out on dates. Well, that strategy worked! Drew and I went on a date that lasted 12hrs. Her family wasn't very happy when I brought her home at 4am. To no despair, we stayed in contact and she became my wife. I would ask Drew if I could take JoJo for ice cream or take him to the

park while she was working if I felt she needed a helping hand so I could build a stronger bond with him. I knew if I married Drew, he would become my son. JoJo's biological father currently wasn't around and I knew JoJo needed a male influence to help him navigate the world, instill moral and values and grow into the man he would become. I had great expectations however I didn't know what a son or father figure meant from my wifes's eyes. My thought was once we were married, I would automatically take on the father role.

In our scenario, we got married extremely fast and Drew was pregnant 2mo after. We had a huge decision to make, where do we stay to raise the kids. At the time we were in LA and didn't feel like we had much support. We could either go to NJ to my family or Chicago with her family. I spoke with Drew's mom and she said I really can't help you if you stay in LA. Drew has a big family, her mom and dad and 4 sisters. It was a no brainer and we relocated to Chicago before Machai was born. I didn't have a chance to fully assume the "Dad" role as everything was moving fast. We were living under the same roof however Drew was making moves the way she programmed and without much involvement or opinion from my side. There were a few things that I didn't like entirely too much such as JoJo staying up until any time he wanted as if he was a little rockstar in a diaper and him sleeping in the same bed. Drew wasn't receptive to him staying up late and defended by saying she's an actress and her hours flucturate. To combat, I provided studies and reports on best practices for sleeping. I also provided a guidance for the tv staying on all night and she said her parents did it with them and everyone is okay so it's not that bad. I tried developing the "My House, My Rules" concept but it quickly fell on death ears as my concerns weren't enforced. Opposed to supporting, JoJo would cry and mom would come to the rescue. I began to see a common thread, where JoJo was also learning how to get his way and It then became an issue where it was Me vs. Them.

Boiling Point where I felt I couldn't parent

Due to JoJo not receiving adequate sleep, he struggled to get up for school in the morning. Being a man, I had my way of getting you to follow directions which was to place the fear of God in you because at the end of the day, I'm the parent. JoJo stood by the sink and didn't want to brush his teeth so I "acted" as if I was going to give him a pinch and he started crying, not because of pain but because of the act. His mother ran upstairs and grabbed JoJo, asking what happened. JoJo responded, daddy pinched me. Drew grabbed JoJo and repremanded me saying I told you not to do that to him. I asked JoJo to demonstrate on his mother exactly how hard I pinched him and he barely touched his mother. I walked out the room as I felt emasculated and minimized below a child. I thought to myself if I wanted to stay in a relationship where I didn't have a parenting voice. Besides all that I've done and contributed, I should feel more respected. We ended up seeking out a marriage counselor that told us we're doing things all wrong. We didn't have a plan and it shows.

but she did ask for my thoughts to correct him sleeping in the bed.

Introduce Drew's mom, millinial

Support we had and lacked

Realistic / Unrealistic Expectations

It's either him or me

Village mindset, when JoJo's dad came home, Respect. Territorial. No this is my house.

Drew received a call from JoJo's biological dad that he came home from jail and wanted to see his son if possible. At the time Drew was still hurt by the lack of support and effort. Her perspective was, if you haven't been around or made an effort all this time, why now. JoJo doesn't need you. Besides she had me in her life which "filled" the void of JoJo's lack of a father figure. Once Drew brought the conversation and intention to my attention, I had a lot of thinking to do also. As a man or the other man in the situation, I had several thoughts run through my mind. As men, we can rightfully be territorial and protective of their

castle. After I let my pride down, put myself in his shoes and think big picture, there were a few things I had to evaluate. Did JoJo's father approach the situation respectfully for my wife and also for me? Did he do anything to neglect the wellbeing and safety of JoJo? What is the intention? Is this relationship in the best interest for JoJo? I immediately thought of my father and our circumstances.

As a child, no one couldn't tell me that my father wasn't the best in the world and guess what, that's my perspective. If you measured or quantified the value of our relationship, there would be large gaps in his presence, missed games and events, missed birthdays, missed growth and bonding opportunities. Yet, my father was still the best thing that could have ever happened to me. How could this be, the heart doesn't measure value in the way our minds do. Love is blind and that's what makes love beautiful, innocent and cherished. Without love, we would be robots, incapable of forgiving or giving someone an opportunity to succeed. If we were robotic in our heart, we would leave a baby that didn't learn to walk fast enough or talk. Sometimes the greatest lessons on earth is experiencing life.

Interesting enough, Initially I didn't speak with JoJo's biological father as Drew had to feel comfortable with the interaction first however I was always by her side supporting the process. Change is very hard especially on a child therefore she wanted to make sure he wanted to really be part of his life before introducing his Father and he deciding he didn't want that role. Consistency is important to know if you're in this for the long run or if it's a nice experience because you think you should do it. Drew put JoJo's father on a call schedule to slowly introduce JoJo to his Father. JoJo visited with him as a baby but it's been years since they spoke and as a child, they don't know what a father means. The first few interactions was awkward just as any person that walks into a child's life that doesn't have kids, there is a learning process.

Adoption Because JoJo's father wasn't around, people would ask if I would adopt him, which is a great question. These are my rules on adopting in a blended family:

The Father doesn't want to be in the child's life therefore the child is fatherless

The Father is deceased.

The child is in harm or danger, therefore it's an unfit home.

The child doesn't have parents

In the event the child's mother dies, custody can be established through court order.....Find out the process. I really don't know.

If I would have adopted Josiah.

JoJo will get to a point where he seeks information and understanding for himself and he would approach his father asking, why didn't he make an effort to be in his life. His Father would more than likely respond, your parents didn't allow me to be a part of your life and pushed me out. JoJo can possibly develop resentment due to our actions, even if we felt it was in his best interest.

This is a great segway into the definition of "Dad." Dads come in all different forms, types, relationships and can be interchangeable for almost anyone providing support that uplifts positive change and growth. When my father wasn't around, coaches became father figures to me including men in the community that taught me fundamentals of manhood. When my father wasn't around, men in the community would hire me and my brother to pickup leaves. It probably was one of the worst jobs I've ever experienced but it built character and work ethic that I wouldn't trade for the world. There is a village that becomes available to instill the lessons children need to learn and the role of "dad" can often be spread throughout the village to ensure children learn fundamentals of life. This concept also applies when the dad is around. Everyone is limited on the amount of information we know. If someone excels in a certain area, send the child to exceed your own understanding as the future depends on our children being smarter and more skilled than us.

Confidence I'm a firm believer that what's for me is for me and no one can take it away. If something isn't for me, then it was only supposed to be in my life for a season and I'm fine.

Being okay with JoJo's biological dad coming into the picture Studies show, 85% of blended familes are dysfunctional. While Drew and I were dating, she was very intentional not to allow me to play the dad role. She didn't want to scare me off or put responsibility on me before we had a chance to know if our relationship would last. Her family also assisted in our dating process. Their goal was to help Drew find the man of her dreams and would take JoJo so she could go out on dates. Well, that strategy worked! Drew and I went on a date that lasted 12hrs. Her family wasn't very happy when I brought her home at 4am. To no despair, we stayed in contact and she became my wife. I would ask Drew if I could take JoJo for ice cream or take him to the park while she was working if I felt she needed a helping hand so I could build a stronger bond with him. I knew if I married Drew, he would become my son. JoJo's biological father currently wasn't around and I knew JoJo needed a male influence to help him navigate the world, instill moral and values and grow into the man he would become. I had great expectations however I didn't know what a son or father figure meant from my wifes's eyes. My thought was once we were married, I would automatically take on the father role.

In our scenario, we got married extremely fast and Drew was pregnant 2mo after. We had a huge decision to make, where do we stay to raise the kids. At the time we were in LA and didn't feel like we had much support. We could either go to NJ to my family or Chicago with her family. I spoke with Drew's mom and she said I really can't help you if you stay in LA. Drew has a big family, her mom and dad and 4 sisters. It was a no brainer and we relocated to Chicago before Machai was born. I didn't have a chance to fully assume the "Dad" role as everything was moving fast. We were living under the same roof however Drew was making moves the way she programmed and without much

involvement or opinion from my side. There were a few things that I didn't like entirely too much such as JoJo staying up until any time he wanted as if he was a little rockstar in a diaper and him sleeping in the same bed. Drew wasn't receptive to him staying up late and defended by saying she's an actress and her hours flucturate. To combat, I provided studies and reports on best practices for sleeping. I also provided a guidance for the tv staying on all night and she said her parents did it with them and everyone is okay so it's not that bad. I tried developing the "My House, My Rules" concept but it quickly fell on death ears as my concerns weren't enforced. Opposed to supporting, JoJo would cry and mom would come to the rescue. I began to see a common thread, where JoJo was also learning how to get his way and It then became an issue where it was Me vs. Them.

Boiling Point where I felt I couldn't parent

Due to JoJo not receiving adequate sleep, he struggled to get up for school in the morning. Being a man, I had my way of getting you to follow directions which was to place the fear of God in you because at the end of the day, I'm the parent. JoJo stood by the sink and didn't want to brush his teeth so I "acted" as if I was going to give him a pinch and he started crying, not because of pain but because of the act. His mother ran upstairs and grabbed JoJo, asking what happened. JoJo responded, daddy pinched me. Drew grabbed JoJo and repremanded me saying I told you not to do that to him. I asked JoJo to demonstrate on his mother exactly how hard I pinched him and he barely touched his mother. I walked out the room as I felt emasculated and minimized below a child. I thought to myself if I wanted to stay in a relationship where I didn't have a parenting voice. Besides all that I've done and contributed, I should feel more respected. We ended up seeking out a marriage counselor that told us we're doing things all wrong. We didn't have a plan and it shows.

but she did ask for my thoughts to correct him sleeping in the bed.

Introduce Drew's mom, millinial

Support we had and lacked
Realistic / Unrealistic Expectations
It's either him or me
Village mindset, when JoJo's dad came home, Respect. Territorial. No this is my house.

Drew received a call from JoJo's biological dad that he came home from jail and wanted to see his son if possible. At the time Drew was still hurt by the lack of support and effort. Her perspective was, if you haven't been around or made an effort all this time, why now. JoJo doesn't need you. Besides she had me in her life which "filled" the void of JoJo's lack of a father figure. Once Drew brought the conversation and intention to my attention, I had a lot of thinking to do also. As a man or the other man in the situation, I had several thoughts run through my mind. As men, we can rightfully be territorial and protective of their castle. After I let my pride down, put myself in his shoes and think big picture, there were a few things I had to evaluate. Did JoJo's father approach the situation respectfully for my wife and also for me? Did he do anything to neglect the wellbeing and safety of JoJo? What is the intention? Is this relationship in the best interest for JoJo? I immediately thought of my father and our circumstances.

As a child, no one couldn't tell me that my father wasn't the best in the world and guess what, that's my perspective. If you measured or quantified the value of our relationship, there would be large gaps in his presence, missed games and events, missed birthdays, missed growth and bonding opportunities. Yet, my father was still the best thing that could have ever happened to me. How could this be, the heart doesn't measure value in the way our minds do. Love is blind and that's what makes love beautiful, innocent and cherished. Without love, we would be robots, incapable of forgiving or giving someone an opportunity to succeed. If we were robotic in our heart, we would leave a baby that didn't learn to walk fast enough or talk. Sometimes the greatest lessons on earth is experiencing life.

Interesting enough, Initially I didn't speak with JoJo's biological father as Drew had to feel comfortable with the interaction first however I was always by her side supporting the process. Change is very hard especially on a child therefore she wanted to make sure he wanted to really be part of his life before introducing his Father and he deciding he didn't want that role. Consistency is important to know if you're in this for the long run or if it's a nice experience because you think you should do it. Drew put JoJo's father on a call schedule to slowly introduce JoJo to his Father. JoJo visited with him as a baby but it's been years since they spoke and as a child, they don't know what a father means. The first few interactions was awkward just as any person that walks into a child's life that doesn't have kids, there is a learning process.

Adoption Because JoJo's father wasn't around, people would ask if I would adopt him, which is a great question. These are my rules on adopting in a blended family:

The Father doesn't want to be in the child's life therefore the child is fatherless

The Father is deceased.

The child is in harm or danger, therefore it's an unfit home.

The child doesn't have parents

In the event the child's mother dies, custody can be established through court order.....Find out the process. I really don't know.

If I would have adopted Josiah.

JoJo will get to a point where he seeks information and understanding for himself and he would approach his father asking, why didn't he make an effort to be in his life. His Father would more than likely respond, your parents didn't allow me to be a part of your life and pushed me out. JoJo can possibly develop resentment due to our actions, even if we felt it was in his best interest.

This is a great segway into the definition of "Dad." Dads come in all different forms, types, relationships and can be interchangeable for almost anyone providing support that uplifts positive

change and growth. When my father wasn't around, coaches became father figures to me including men in the community that taught me fundamentals of manhood. When my father wasn't around, men in the community would hire me and my brother to pickup leaves. It probably was one of the worst jobs I've ever experienced but it built character and work ethic that I wouldn't trade for the world. There is a village that becomes available to instill the lessons children need to learn and the role of "dad" can often be spread throughout the village to ensure children learn fundamentals of life. This concept also applies when the dad is around. Everyone is limited on the amount of information we know. If someone excels in a certain area, send the child to exceed your own understanding as the future depends on our children being smarter and more skilled than us.

Confidence I'm a firm believer that what's for me is for me and no one can take it away. If something isn't for me, then it was only supposed to be in my life for a season and I'm fine.

Being okay with JoJo's biological dad coming into the picture Studies show, 85% of blended familes are dysfunctional. While Drew and I were dating, she was very intentional not to allow me to play the dad role. She didn't want to scare me off or put responsibility on me before we had a chance to know if our relationship would last. Her family also assisted in our dating process. Their goal was to help Drew find the man of her dreams and would take JoJo so she could go out on dates. Well, that strategy worked! Drew and I went on a date that lasted 12hrs. Her family wasn't very happy when I brought her home at 4am. To no despair, we stayed in contact and she became my wife. I would ask Drew if I could take JoJo for ice cream or take him to the park while she was working if I felt she needed a helping hand so I could build a stronger bond with him. I knew if I married Drew, he would become my son. JoJo's biological father currently wasn't around and I knew JoJo needed a male influence to help him navigate the world, instill moral and values and grow into the man he would become. I had great expectations however

I didn't know what a son or father figure meant from my wifes's eyes. My thought was once we were married, I would automatically take on the father role.

In our scenario, we got married extremely fast and Drew was pregnant 2mo after. We had a huge decision to make, where do we stay to raise the kids. At the time we were in LA and didn't feel like we had much support. We could either go to NJ to my family or Chicago with her family. I spoke with Drew's mom and she said I really can't help you if you stay in LA. Drew has a big family, her mom and dad and 4 sisters. It was a no brainer and we relocated to Chicago before Machai was born. I didn't have a chance to fully assume the "Dad" role as everything was moving fast. We were living under the same roof however Drew was making moves the way she programmed and without much involvement or opinion from my side. There were a few things that I didn't like entirely too much such as JoJo staying up until any time he wanted as if he was a little rockstar in a diaper and him sleeping in the same bed. Drew wasn't receptive to him staying up late and defended by saying she's an actress and her hours flucturate. To combat, I provided studies and reports on best practices for sleeping. I also provided a guidance for the tv staying on all night and she said her parents did it with them and everyone is okay so it's not that bad. I tried developing the "My House, My Rules" concept but it quickly fell on death ears as my concerns weren't enforced. Opposed to supporting, JoJo would cry and mom would come to the rescue. I began to see a common thread, where JoJo was also learning how to get his way and It then became an issue where it was Me vs. Them.

Boiling Point where I felt I couldn't parent

Due to JoJo not receiving adequate sleep, he struggled to get up for school in the morning. Being a man, I had my way of getting you to follow directions which was to place the fear of God in you because at the end of the day, I'm the parent. JoJo stood by the sink and didn't want to brush his teeth so I "acted" as if I was going to give him a pinch and he started crying, not because

of pain but because of the act. His mother ran upstairs and grabbed JoJo, asking what happened. JoJo responded, daddy pinched me. Drew grabbed JoJo and reprimanded me saying I told you not to do that to him. I asked JoJo to demonstrate on his mother exactly how hard I pinched him and he barely touched his mother. I walked out the room as I felt emasculated and minimized below a child. I thought to myself if I wanted to stay in a relationship where I didn't have a parenting voice. Besides all that I've done and contributed, I should feel more respected. We ended up seeking out a marriage counselor that told us we're doing things all wrong. We didn't have a plan and it shows.

but she did ask for my thoughts to correct him sleeping in the bed.

Introduce Drew's mom, millinial

Support we had and lacked

Realistic / Unrealistic Expectations

It's either him or me

Village mindset, when JoJo's dad came home, Respect. Territorial. No this is my house.

Drew received a call from JoJo's biological dad that he came home from jail and wanted to see his son if possible. At the time Drew was still hurt by the lack of support and effort. Her perspective was, if you haven't been around or made an effort all this time, why now. JoJo doesn't need you. Besides she had me in her life which "filled" the void of JoJo's lack of a father figure. Once Drew brought the conversation and intention to my attention, I had a lot of thinking to do also. As a man or the other man in the situation, I had several thoughts run through my mind. As men, we can rightfully be territorial and protective of their castle. After I let my pride down, put myself in his shoes and think big picture, there were a few things I had to evaluate. Did JoJo's father approach the situation respectfully for my wife and also for me? Did he do anything to neglect the wellbeing and safety of JoJo? What is the intention? Is this relationship in the

best interest for JoJo? I immediately thought of my father and our circumstances.

JoJo will get to a point where he seeks information and understanding for himself and he would approach his father asking, why didn't he make an effort to be in his life. His Father would more than likely respond, your parents didn't allow me to be a part of your life and pushed me out. JoJo can possibly develop resentment due to our actions, even if we felt it was in his best interest.

This is a great segway into the definition of "Dad." Dads come in all different forms, types, relationships and can be interchangeable for almost anyone providing support that uplifts positive change and growth. When my father wasn't around, coaches became father figures to me including men in the community that taught me fundamentals of manhood. When my father wasn't around, men in the community would hire me and my brother to pickup leaves. It probably was one of the worst jobs I've ever experienced but it built character and work ethic that I wouldn't trade for the world. There is a village that becomes available to instill the lessons children need to learn and the role of "dad" can often be spread throughout the village to ensure children learn fundamentals of life. This concept also applies when the dad is around. Everyone is limited on the amount of information we know. If someone excels in a certain area, send the child to exceed your own understanding as the future depends on our children being smarter and more skilled than us.

Confidence I'm a firm believer that what's for me is for me and no one can take it away. If something isn't for me, then it was only supposed to be in my life for a season and I'm fine.

Being okay with JoJo's biological dad coming into the picture Studies show, 85% of blended familes are dysfunctional. While Drew and I were dating, she was very intentional not to allow me to play the dad role. She didn't want to scare me off or put responsibility on me before we had a chance to know if our relationship would last. Her family also assisted in our dating process. Their goal was to help Drew find the man of her dreams and would take JoJo so she could go out on dates. Well, that strategy worked! Drew and I went on a date that lasted 12hrs. Her family wasn't very happy when I brought her home at 4am. To no despair, we stayed in contact and she became my wife. I would ask Drew if I could take JoJo for ice cream or take him to the park while she was working if I felt she needed a helping hand so I could build a stronger bond with him. I knew if I married Drew, he would become my son. JoJo's biological father currently wasn't around and I knew JoJo needed a male influence to help him navigate the world, instill moral and values and grow into the man he would become. I had great expectations however I didn't know what a son or father figure meant from my wifes's eyes. My thought was once we were married, I would automatically take on the father role.

In our scenario, we got married extremely fast and Drew was pregnant 2mo after. We had a huge decision to make, where do we stay to raise the kids. At the time we were in LA and didn't feel like we had much support. We could either go to NJ to my family or Chicago with her family. I spoke with Drew's mom and she said I really can't help you if you stay in LA. Drew has a big family, her mom and dad and 4 sisters. It was a no brainer and we relocated to Chicago before Machai was born. I didn't have a chance to fully assume the "Dad" role as everything was moving fast. We were living under the same roof however Drew was making moves the way she programmed and without much involvement or opinion from my side. There were a few things that I didn't like entirely too much such as JoJo staying up until any time he wanted as if he was a little rockstar in a diaper and him sleeping in the same bed. Drew wasn't receptive to him staying up late and defended by saying she's an actress and her hours flucturate. To combat, I provided studies and reports on best practices for sleeping. I also provided a guidance for the tv staying on all night and she said her parents did it with them and everyone is okay so it's not that bad. I tried developing the "My

House, My Rules" concept but it quickly fell on death ears as my concerns weren't enforced. Opposed to supporting, JoJo would cry and mom would come to the rescue. I began to see a common thread, where JoJo was also learning how to get his way and It then became an issue where it was Me vs. Them.

JoJo will get to a point where he seeks information and understanding for himself and he would approach his father asking, why didn't he make an effort to be in his life. His Father would more than likely respond, your parents didn't allow me to be a part of your life and pushed me out. JoJo can possibly develop resentment due to our actions, even if we felt it was in his best interest.

This is a great segway into the definition of "Dad." Dads come in all different forms, types, relationships and can be interchangeable for almost anyone providing support that uplifts positive change and growth. When my father wasn't around, coaches became father figures to me including men in the community that taught me fundamentals of manhood. When my father wasn't around, men in the community would hire me and my brother to pickup leaves. It probably was one of the worst jobs I've ever experienced but it built character and work ethic that I wouldn't trade for the world. There is a village that becomes available to instill the lessons children need to learn and the role of "dad" can often be spread throughout the village to ensure children learn fundamentals of life. This concept also applies when the dad is around. Everyone is limited on the amount of information we know. If someone excels in a certain area, send the child to exceed your own understanding as the future depends on our children being smarter and more skilled than us.

Confidence I'm a firm believer that what's for me is for me and no one can take it away. If something isn't for me, then it was only supposed to be in my life for a season and I'm fine.

Being okay with JoJo's biological dad coming into the picture

Studies show, 85% of blended familes are dysfunctional. While Drew and I were dating, she was very intentional not to

allow me to play the dad role. She didn't want to scare me off or put responsibility on me before we had a chance to know if our relationship would last. Her family also assisted in our dating process. Their goal was to help Drew find the man of her dreams and would take JoJo so she could go out on dates. Well, that strategy worked! Drew and I went on a date that lasted 12hrs. Her family wasn't very happy when I brought her home at 4am. To no despair, we stayed in contact and she became my wife. I would ask Drew if I could take JoJo for ice cream or take him to the park while she was working if I felt she needed a helping hand so I could build a stronger bond with him. I knew if I married Drew, he would become my son. JoJo's biological father currently wasn't around and I knew JoJo needed a male influence to help him navigate the world, instill moral and values and grow into the man he would become. I had great expectations however I didn't know what a son or father figure meant from my wifes's eyes. My thought was once we were married, I would automatically take on the father role.

In our scenario, we got married extremely fast and Drew was pregnant 2mo after. We had a huge decision to make, where do we stay to raise the kids. At the time we were in LA and didn't feel like we had much support. We could either go to NJ to my family or Chicago with her family. I spoke with Drew's mom and she said I really can't help you if you stay in LA. Drew has a big family, her mom and dad and 4 sisters. It was a no brainer and we relocated to Chicago before Machai was born. I didn't have a chance to fully assume the "Dad" role as everything was moving fast. We were living under the same roof however Drew was making moves the way she programmed and without much involvement or opinion from my side. There were a few things that I didn't like entirely too much such as JoJo staying up until any time he wanted as if he was a little rockstar in a diaper and him sleeping in the same bed. Drew wasn't receptive to him staying up late and defended by saying she's an actress and her hours flucturate. To combat, I provided studies and reports on

best practices for sleeping. I also provided a guidance for the tv staying on all night and she said her parents did it with them and everyone is okay so it's not that bad. I tried developing the "My House, My Rules" concept but it quickly fell on death ears as my concerns weren't enforced. Opposed to supporting, JoJo would cry and mom would come to the rescue. I began to see a common thread, where JoJo was also learning how to get his way and It then became an issue where it was Me vs. Them.

JoJo will get to a point where he seeks information and understanding for himself and he would approach his father asking, why didn't he make an effort to be in his life. His Father would more than likely respond, your parents didn't allow me to be a part of your life and pushed me out. JoJo can possibly develop resentment due to our actions, even if we felt it was in his best interest.

This is a great segway into the definition of "Dad." Dads come in all different forms, types, relationships and can be interchangeable for almost anyone providing support that uplifts positive change and growth. When my father wasn't around, coaches became father figures to me including men in the community that taught me fundamentals of manhood. When my father wasn't around, men in the community would hire me and my brother to pickup leaves. It probably was one of the worst jobs I've ever experienced but it built character and work ethic that I wouldn't trade for the world. There is a village that becomes available to instill the lessons children need to learn and the role of "dad" can often be spread throughout the village to ensure children learn fundamentals of life. This concept also applies when the dad is around. Everyone is limited on the amount of information we know. If someone excels in a certain area, send the child to exceed your own understanding as the future depends on our children being smarter and more skilled than us.

Confidence I'm a firm believer that what's for me is for me and no one can take it away. If something isn't for me, then it was only supposed to be in my life for a season and I'm fine.

Being okay with JoJo's biological dad coming into the picture

Studies show, 85% of blended familes are dysfunctional. While Drew and I were dating, she was very intentional not to allow me to play the dad role. She didn't want to scare me off or put responsibility on me before we had a chance to know if our relationship would last. Her family also assisted in our dating process. Their goal was to help Drew find the man of her dreams and would take JoJo so she could go out on dates. Well, that strategy worked! Drew and I went on a date that lasted 12hrs. Her family wasn't very happy when I brought her home at 4am. To no despair, we stayed in contact and she became my wife. I would ask Drew if I could take JoJo for ice cream or take him to the park while she was working if I felt she needed a helping hand so I could build a stronger bond with him. I knew if I married Drew, he would become my son. JoJo's biological father currently wasn't around and I knew JoJo needed a male influence to help him navigate the world, instill moral and values and grow into the man he would become. I had great expectations however I didn't know what a son or father figure meant from my wifes's eyes. My thought was once we were married, I would automatically take on the father role.

In our scenario, we got married extremely fast and Drew was pregnant 2mo after. We had a huge decision to make, where do we stay to raise the kids. At the time we were in LA and didn't feel like we had much support. We could either go to NJ to my family or Chicago with her family. I spoke with Drew's mom and she said I really can't help you if you stay in LA. Drew has a big family, her mom and dad and 4 sisters. It was a no brainer and we relocated to Chicago before Machai was born. I didn't have a chance to fully assume the "Dad" role as everything was moving fast. We were living under the same roof however Drew was making moves the way she programmed and without much involvement or opinion from my side. There were a few things that I didn't like entirely too much such as JoJo staying up until any time he wanted as if he was a little rockstar in a diaper and

him sleeping in the same bed. Drew wasn't receptive to him staying up late and defended by saying she's an actress and her hours flucturate. To combat, I provided studies and reports on best practices for sleeping. I also provided a guidance for the tv staying on all night and she said her parents did it with them and everyone is okay so it's not that bad. I tried developing the "My House, My Rules" concept but it quickly fell on death ears as my concerns weren't enforced. Opposed to supporting, JoJo would cry and mom would come to the rescue. I began to see a common thread, where JoJo was also learning how to get his way and It then became an issue where it was Me vs. Them.

JoJo will get to a point where he seeks information and understanding for himself and he would approach his father asking, why didn't he make an effort to be in his life. His Father would more than likely respond, your parents didn't allow me to be a part of your life and pushed me out. JoJo can possibly develop resentment due to our actions, even if we felt it was in his best interest.

This is a great segway into the definition of "Dad." Dads come in all different forms, types, relationships and can be interchangeable for almost anyone providing support that uplifts positive change and growth. When my father wasn't around, coaches became father figures to me including men in the community that taught me fundamentals of manhood. When my father wasn't around, men in the community would hire me and my brother to pickup leaves. It probably was one of the worst jobs I've ever experienced but it built character and work ethic that I wouldn't trade for the world. There is a village that becomes available to instill the lessons children need to learn and the role of "dad" can often be spread throughout the village to ensure children learn fundamentals of life. This concept also applies when the dad is around. Everyone is limited on the amount of information we know. If someone excels in a certain area, send the child to exceed your own understanding as the future depends on our children being smarter and more skilled than us.

Confidence I'm a firm believer that what's for me is for me and no one can take it away. If something isn't for me, then it was only supposed to be in my life for a season and I'm fine.

Being okay with JoJo's biological dad coming into the picture Studies show, 85% of blended familes are dysfunctional. While Drew and I were dating, she was very intentional not to allow me to play the dad role. She didn't want to scare me off or put responsibility on me before we had a chance to know if our relationship would last. Her family also assisted in our dating process. Their goal was to help Drew find the man of her dreams and would take JoJo so she could go out on dates. Well, that strategy worked! Drew and I went on a date that lasted 12hrs. Her family wasn't very happy when I brought her home at 4am. To no despair, we stayed in contact and she became my wife. I would ask Drew if I could take JoJo for ice cream or take him to the park while she was working if I felt she needed a helping hand so I could build a stronger bond with him. I knew if I married Drew, he would become my son. JoJo's biological father currently wasn't around and I knew JoJo needed a male influence to help him navigate the world, instill moral and values and grow into the man he would become. I had great expectations however I didn't know what a son or father figure meant from my wifes's eyes. My thought was once we were married, I would automatically take on the father role.

In our scenario, we got married extremely fast and Drew was pregnant 2mo after. We had a huge decision to make, where do we stay to raise the kids. At the time we were in LA and didn't feel like we had much support. We could either go to NJ to my family or Chicago with her family. I spoke with Drew's mom and she said I really can't help you if you stay in LA. Drew has a big family, her mom and dad and 4 sisters. It was a no brainer and we relocated to Chicago before Machai was born. I didn't have a chance to fully assume the "Dad" role as everything was moving fast. We were living under the same roof however Drew was making moves the way she programmed and without much

involvement or opinion from my side. There were a few things that I didn't like entirely too much such as JoJo staying up until any time he wanted as if he was a little rockstar in a diaper and him sleeping in the same bed. Drew wasn't receptive to him staying up late and defended by saying she's an actress and her hours flucturate. To combat, I provided studies and reports on best practices for sleeping. I also provided a guidance for the tv staying on all night and she said her parents did it with them and everyone is okay so it's not that bad. I tried developing the "My House, My Rules" concept but it quickly fell on death ears as my concerns weren't enforced. Opposed to supporting, JoJo would cry and mom would come to the rescue. I began to see a common thread, where JoJo was also learning how to get his way and It then became an issue where it was Me vs. Them.

JoJo will get to a point where he seeks information and understanding for himself and he would approach his father asking, why didn't he make an effort to be in his life. His Father would more than likely respond, your parents didn't allow me to be a part of your life and pushed me out. JoJo can possibly develop resentment due to our actions, even if we felt it was in his best interest.

This is a great segway into the definition of "Dad." Dads come in all different forms, types, relationships and can be interchangeable for almost anyone providing support that uplifts positive change and growth. When my father wasn't around, coaches became father figures to me including men in the community that taught me fundamentals of manhood. When my father wasn't around, men in the community would hire me and my brother to pickup leaves. It probably was one of the worst jobs I've ever experienced but it built character and work ethic that I wouldn't trade for the world. There is a village that becomes available to instill the lessons children need to learn and the role of "dad" can often be spread throughout the village to ensure children learn fundamentals of life. This concept also applies when the dad is around. Everyone is limited on the amount of information

we know. If someone excels in a certain area, send the child to exceed your own understanding as the future depends on our children being smarter and more skilled than us.

Confidence I'm a firm believer that what's for me is for me and no one can take it away. If something isn't for me, then it was only supposed to be in my life for a season and I'm fine.

Being okay with JoJo's biological dad coming into the picture Studies show, 85% of blended familes are dysfunctional. While Drew and I were dating, she was very intentional not to allow me to play the dad role. She didn't want to scare me off or put responsibility on me before we had a chance to know if our relationship would last. Her family also assisted in our dating process. Their goal was to help Drew find the man of her dreams and would take JoJo so she could go out on dates. Well, that strategy worked! Drew and I went on a date that lasted 12hrs. Her family wasn't very happy when I brought her home at 4am. To no despair, we stayed in contact and she became my wife. I would ask Drew if I could take JoJo for ice cream or take him to the park while she was working if I felt she needed a helping hand so I could build a stronger bond with him. I knew if I married Drew, he would become my son. JoJo's biological father currently wasn't around and I knew JoJo needed a male influence to help him navigate the world, instill moral and values and grow into the man he would become. I had great expectations however I didn't know what a son or father figure meant from my wifes's eyes. My thought was once we were married, I would automatically take on the father role.

In our scenario, we got married extremely fast and Drew was pregnant 2mo after. We had a huge decision to make, where do we stay to raise the kids. At the time we were in LA and didn't feel like we had much support. We could either go to NJ to my family or Chicago with her family. I spoke with Drew's mom and she said I really can't help you if you stay in LA. Drew has a big family, her mom and dad and 4 sisters. It was a no brainer and we relocated to Chicago before Machai was born. I didn't

have a chance to fully assume the "Dad" role as everything was moving fast. We were living under the same roof however Drew was making moves the way she programmed and without much involvement or opinion from my side. There were a few things that I didn't like entirely too much such as JoJo staying up until any time he wanted as if he was a little rockstar in a diaper and him sleeping in the same bed. Drew wasn't receptive to him staying up late and defended by saying she's an actress and her hours flucturate. To combat, I provided studies and reports on best practices for sleeping. I also provided a guidance for the tv staying on all night and she said her parents did it with them and everyone is okay so it's not that bad. I tried developing the "My House, My Rules" concept but it quickly fell on death ears as my concerns weren't enforced. Opposed to supporting, JoJo would cry and mom would come to the rescue. I began to see a common thread, where JoJo was also learning how to get his way and It then became an issue where it was Me vs. Them.

As a child, no one couldn't tell me that my father wasn't the best in the world and guess what, that's my perspective. If you measured or quantified the value of our relationship, there would be large gaps in his presence, missed games and events, missed birthdays, missed growth and bonding opportunities. Yet, my father was still the best thing that could have ever happened to me. How could this be, the heart doesn't measure value in the way our minds do. Love is blind and that's what makes love beautiful, innocent and cherished. Without love, we would be robots, incapable of forgiving or giving someone an opportunity to succeed. If we were robotic in our heart, we would leave a baby that didn't learn to walk fast enough or talk. Sometimes the greatest lessons on earth is experiencing life.

Interesting enough, Initially I didn't speak with JoJo's biological father as Drew had to feel comfortable with the interaction first however I was always by her side supporting the process. Change is very hard especially on a child therefore she wanted to make sure he wanted to really be part of his life before

introducing his Father and he deciding he didn't want that role. Consistency is important to know if you're in this for the long run or if it's a nice experience because you think you should do it. Drew put JoJo's father on a call schedule to slowly introduce JoJo to his Father. JoJo visited with him as a baby but it's been years since they spoke and as a child, they don't know what a father means. The first few interactions was awkward just as any person that walks into a child's life that doesn't have kids, there is a learning process.

Adoption Because JoJo's father wasn't around, people would ask if I would adopt him, which is a great question. These are my rules on adopting in a blended family:

The Father doesn't want to be in the child's life therefore the child is fatherless

The Father is deceased.

The child is in harm or danger, therefore it's an unfit home.

The child doesn't have parents

In the event the child's mother dies, custody can be established through court order.....Find out the process. I really don't know.

If I would have adopted Josiah.

JoJo will get to a point where he seeks information and understanding for himself and he would approach his father asking, why didn't he make an effort to be in his life. His Father would more than likely respond, your parents didn't allow me to be a part of your life and pushed me out. JoJo can possibly develop resentment due to our actions, even if we felt it was in his best interest.

JoJo will get to a point where he seeks information and understanding for himself and he would approach his father asking, why didn't he make an effort to be in his life. His Father would more than likely respond, your parents didn't allow me to be a part of your life and pushed me out. JoJo can possibly develop resentment due to our actions, even if we felt it was in his best interest.

This is a great segway into the definition of "Dad." Dads come in all different forms, types, relationships and can be interchangeable for almost anyone providing support that uplifts positive change and growth. When my father wasn't around, coaches became father figures to me including men in the community that taught me fundamentals of manhood. When my father wasn't around, men in the community would hire me and my brother to pickup leaves. It probably was one of the worst jobs I've ever experienced but it built character and work ethic that I wouldn't trade for the world. There is a village that becomes available to instill the lessons children need to learn and the role of "dad" can often be spread throughout the village to ensure children learn fundamentals of life. This concept also applies when the dad is around. Everyone is limited on the amount of information we know. If someone excels in a certain area, send the child to exceed your own understanding as the future depends on our children being smarter and more skilled than us.

Confidence I'm a firm believer that what's for me is for me and no one can take it away. If something isn't for me, then it was only supposed to be in my life for a season and I'm fine.

Being okay with JoJo's biological dad coming into the picture Studies show, 85% of blended familes are dysfunctional. While Drew and I were dating, she was very intentional not to allow me to play the dad role. She didn't want to scare me off or put responsibility on me before we had a chance to know if our relationship would last. Her family also assisted in our dating process. Their goal was to help Drew find the man of her dreams and would take JoJo so she could go out on dates. Well, that strategy worked! Drew and I went on a date that lasted 12hrs. Her family wasn't very happy when I brought her home at 4am. To no despair, we stayed in contact and she became my wife. I would ask Drew if I could take JoJo for ice cream or take him to the park while she was working if I felt she needed a helping hand so I could build a stronger bond with him. I knew if I married Drew, he would become my son. JoJo's biological father currently

wasn't around and I knew JoJo needed a male influence to help him navigate the world, instill moral and values and grow into the man he would become. I had great expectations however I didn't know what a son or father figure meant from my wifes's eyes. My thought was once we were married, I would automatically take on the father role.

In our scenario, we got married extremely fast and Drew was pregnant 2mo after. We had a huge decision to make, where do we stay to raise the kids. At the time we were in LA and didn't feel like we had much support. We could either go to NJ to my family or Chicago with her family. I spoke with Drew's mom and she said I really can't help you if you stay in LA. Drew has a big family, her mom and dad and 4 sisters. It was a no brainer and we relocated to Chicago before Machai was born. I didn't have a chance to fully assume the "Dad" role as everything was moving fast. We were living under the same roof however Drew was making moves the way she programmed and without much involvement or opinion from my side. There were a few things that I didn't like entirely too much such as JoJo staying up until any time he wanted as if he was a little rockstar in a diaper and him sleeping in the same bed. Drew wasn't receptive to him staying up late and defended by saying she's an actress and her hours flucturate. To combat, I provided studies and reports on best practices for sleeping. I also provided a guidance for the tv staying on all night and she said her parents did it with them and everyone is okay so it's not that bad. I tried developing the "My House, My Rules" concept but it quickly fell on death ears as my concerns weren't enforced. Opposed to supporting, JoJo would cry and mom would come to the rescue. I began to see a common thread, where JoJo was also learning how to get his way and It then became an issue where it was Me vs. Them.

This is a great segway into the definition of "Dad." Dads come in all different forms, types, relationships and can be interchangeable for almost anyone providing support that uplifts positive change and growth. When my father wasn't around, coaches became father figures to me including men in the community that taught me fundamentals of manhood. When my father wasn't around, men in the community would hire me and my brother to pickup leaves. It probably was one of the worst jobs I've ever experienced but it built character and work ethic that I wouldn't trade for the world. There is a village that becomes available to instill the lessons children need to learn and the role of "dad" can often be spread throughout the village to ensure children learn fundamentals of life. This concept also applies when the dad is around. Everyone is limited on the amount of information we know. If someone excels in a certain area, send the child to exceed your own understanding as the future depends on our children being smarter and more skilled than us.

Confidence I'm a firm believer that what's for me is for me and no one can take it away. If something isn't for me, then it was only supposed to be in my life for a season and I'm fine.

Being okay with JoJo's biological dad coming into the picture Studies show, 85% of blended familes are dysfunctional. While Drew and I were dating, she was very intentional not to allow me to play the dad role. She didn't want to scare me off or put responsibility on me before we had a chance to know if our relationship would last. Her family also assisted in our dating process. Their goal was to help Drew find the man of her dreams and would take JoJo so she could go out on dates. Well, that strategy worked! Drew and I went on a date that lasted 12hrs. Her family wasn't very happy when I brought her home at 4am. To no despair, we stayed in contact and she became my wife. I would ask Drew if I could take JoJo for ice cream or take him to the park while she was working if I felt she needed a helping hand so I could build a stronger bond with him. I knew if I married Drew, he would become my son. JoJo's biological father currently wasn't around and I knew JoJo needed a male influence to help him navigate the world, instill moral and values and grow into the man he would become. I had great expectations however I didn't know what a son or father figure meant from my wifes's eyes. My thought was once we were married, I would automatically take on the father role.

In our scenario, we got married extremely fast and Drew was pregnant 2mo after. We had a huge decision to make, where do we stay to raise the kids. At the time we were in LA and didn't feel like we had much support. We could either go to NJ to my family or Chicago with her family. I spoke with Drew's mom and she said I really can't help you if you stay in LA. Drew has a big family, her mom and dad and 4 sisters. It was a no brainer and we relocated to Chicago before Machai was born. I didn't have a chance to fully assume the "Dad" role as everything was moving fast. We were living under the same roof however Drew was making moves the way she programmed and without much involvement or opinion from my side. There were a few things that I didn't like entirely too much such as JoJo staying up until any time he wanted as if he was a little rockstar in a diaper and him sleeping in the same bed. Drew wasn't receptive to him staying up late and defended by saying she's an actress and her hours flucturate. To combat, I provided studies and reports on best practices for sleeping. I also provided a guidance for the tv staying on all night and she said her parents did it with them and everyone is okay so it's not that bad. I tried developing the "My House, My Rules" concept but it quickly fell on death ears as my concerns weren't enforced. Opposed to supporting, JoJo would cry and mom would come to the rescue. I began to see a common thread, where JoJo was also learning how to get his way and It then became an issue where it was Me vs. Them.

Boiling Point where I felt I couldn't parent

Due to JoJo not receiving adequate sleep, he struggled to get up for school in the morning. Being a man, I had my way of getting you to follow directions which was to place the fear of God in you because at the end of the day, I'm the parent. JoJo stood by the sink and didn't want to brush his teeth so I "acted" as if I was going to give him a pinch and he started crying, not because of pain but because of the act. His mother ran upstairs and grabbed JoJo, asking what happened. JoJo responded, daddy pinched me. Drew grabbed JoJo and reprimanded me saying I told you not to do that to him. I asked JoJo to demonstrate on his mother exactly how hard I pinched him and he barely touched his mother. I walked out the room as I felt emasculated and minimized below a child. I thought to myself if I wanted to stay in a relationship where I didn't have a parenting voice. Besides all that I've done and contributed, I should feel more respected. We ended up seeking out a marriage counselor that told us we're doing things all wrong. We didn't have a plan and it shows.

but she did ask for my thoughts to correct him sleeping in the bed.

Introduce Drew's mom, millinial

Support we had and lacked

Realistic / Unrealistic Expectations

It's either him or me

Village mindset, when JoJo's dad came home, Respect. Territorial. No this is my house.

Drew received a call from JoJo's biological dad that he came home from jail and wanted to see his son if possible. At the time Drew was still hurt by the lack of support and effort. Her perspective was, if you haven't been around or made an effort all this time, why now. JoJo doesn't need you. Besides she had me in her life which "filled" the void of JoJo's lack of a father figure. Once Drew brought the conversation and intention to my attention, I had a lot of thinking to do also. As a man or the other man in the situation, I had several thoughts run through my mind. As men, we can rightfully be territorial and protective of their castle. After I let my pride down, put myself in his shoes and think big picture, there were a few things I had to evaluate. Did JoJo's father approach the situation respectfully for my wife and also for me? Did he do anything to neglect the wellbeing and safety of JoJo? What is the intention? Is this relationship in the best interest for JoJo? I immediately thought of my father and our circumstances.

As a child, no one couldn't tell me that my father wasn't the best in the world and guess what, that's my perspective. If you measured or quantified the value of our relationship, there would be large gaps in his presence, missed games and events, missed birthdays, missed growth and bonding opportunities. Yet, my father was still the best thing that could have ever happened to me. How could this be, the heart doesn't measure value in the way our minds do. Love is blind and that's what makes love beautiful, innocent and cherished. Without love, we would be robots, incapable of forgiving or giving someone an opportunity to succeed. If we were robotic in our heart, we would leave a baby that didn't learn to walk fast enough or talk. Sometimes the greatest lessons on earth is experiencing life.

Interesting enough, Initially I didn't speak with JoJo's biological father as Drew had to feel comfortable with the interaction first however I was always by her side supporting the process. Change is very hard especially on a child therefore she wanted to make sure he wanted to really be part of his life before introducing his Father and he deciding he didn't want that role. Consistency is important to know if you're in this for the long run or if it's a nice experience because you think you should do it. Drew put JoJo's father on a call schedule to slowly introduce JoJo to his Father. JoJo visited with him as a baby but it's been years since they spoke and as a child, they don't know what a father means. The first few interactions was awkward just as any person that walks into a child's life that doesn't have kids, there is a learning process.

Adoption Because JoJo's father wasn't around, people would ask if I would adopt him, which is a great question. These are my rules on adopting in a blended family:

The Father doesn't want to be in the child's life therefore the child is fatherless

The Father is deceased.

The child is in harm or danger, therefore it's an unfit home.

The child doesn't have parents

In the event the child's mother dies, custody can be established through court order......Find out the process. I really don't know.

If I would have adopted Josiah.

JoJo will get to a point where he seeks information and understanding for himself and he would approach his father asking, why didn't he make an effort to be in his life. His Father would more than likely respond, your parents didn't allow me to be a part of your life and pushed me out. JoJo can possibly develop resentment due to our actions, even if we felt it was in his best interest.

This is a great segway into the definition of "Dad." Dads come in all different forms, types, relationships and can be interchangeable for almost anyone providing support that uplifts positive change and growth. When my father wasn't around, coaches became father figures to me including men in the community that taught me fundamentals of manhood. When my father wasn't around, men in the community would hire me and my brother to pickup leaves. It probably was one of the worst jobs I've ever experienced but it built character and work ethic that I wouldn't trade for the world. There is a village that becomes available to instill the lessons children need to learn and the role of "dad" can often be spread throughout the village to ensure children learn fundamentals of life. This concept also applies when the dad is around. Everyone is limited on the amount of information we know. If someone excels in a certain area, send the child to exceed your own understanding as the future depends on our children being smarter and more skilled than us.

Confidence I'm a firm believer that what's for me is for me and no one can take it away. If something isn't for me, then it was only supposed to be in my life for a season and I'm fine.

Being okay with JoJo's biological dad coming into the picture

Studies show, 85% of blended familes are dysfunctional. While Drew and I were dating, she was very intentional not to allow me to play the dad role. She didn't want to scare me off or put responsibility on me before we had a chance to know if

our relationship would last. Her family also assisted in our dating process. Their goal was to help Drew find the man of her dreams and would take JoJo so she could go out on dates. Well, that strategy worked! Drew and I went on a date that lasted 12hrs. Her family wasn't very happy when I brought her home at 4am. To no despair, we stayed in contact and she became my wife. I would ask Drew if I could take JoJo for ice cream or take him to the park while she was working if I felt she needed a helping hand so I could build a stronger bond with him. I knew if I married Drew, he would become my son. JoJo's biological father currently wasn't around and I knew JoJo needed a male influence to help him navigate the world, instill moral and values and grow into the man he would become. I had great expectations however I didn't know what a son or father figure meant from my wifes's eyes. My thought was once we were married, I would automatically take on the father role.

Blended Family

IN OUR SCENARIO, we got married extremely fast and Drew was pregnant 2mo after. We had a huge decision to make, where do we stay to raise the kids. At the time we were in LA and didn't feel like we had much support. We could either go to NJ to my family or Chicago with her family. I spoke with Drew's mom and she said I really can't help you if you stay in LA. Drew has a big family, her mom and dad and 4 sisters. It was a no brainer and we relocated to Chicago before Machai was born. I didn't have a chance to fully assume the "Dad" role as everything was moving fast. We were living under the same roof however Drew was making moves the way she programmed and without much involvement or opinion from my side. There were a few things that I didn't like entirely too much such as JoJo staying up until any time he wanted as if he was a little rockstar in a diaper and him sleeping in the same bed. Drew wasn't receptive to him staying up late and defended by saying she's an actress and her hours flucturate. To combat, I provided studies and reports on best practices for sleeping. I also provided a guidance for the tv staying on all night and she said her parents did it with them and everyone is okay so it's not that bad. I tried developing the "My House, My Rules" concept but it quickly fell on death ears as my concerns weren't enforced. Opposed to supporting, JoJo would

cry and mom would come to the rescue. I began to see a common thread, where JoJo was also learning how to get his way and It then became an issue where it was Me vs. Them.

Boiling Point where I felt I couldn't parent

Due to JoJo not receiving adequate sleep, he struggled to get up for school in the morning. Being a man, I had my way of getting you to follow directions which was to place the fear of God in you because at the end of the day, I'm the parent. JoJo stood by the sink and didn't want to brush his teeth so I "acted" as if I was going to give him a pinch and he started crying, not because of pain but because of the act. His mother ran upstairs and grabbed JoJo, asking what happened. JoJo responded, daddy pinched me. Drew grabbed JoJo and reprimanded me saying I told you not to do that to him. I asked JoJo to demonstrate on his mother exactly how hard I pinched him and he barely touched his mother. I walked out the room as I felt emasculated and minimized below a child. I thought to myself if I wanted to stay in a relationship where I didn't have a parenting voice. Besides all that I've done and contributed, I should feel more respected. We ended up seeking out a marriage counselor that told us we're doing things all wrong. We didn't have a plan and it shows.

but she did ask for my thoughts to correct him sleeping in the bed.

Introduce Drew's mom, millinial

Support we had and lacked

Realistic / Unrealistic Expectations

It's either him or me

Village mindset, when JoJo's dad came home, Respect. Territorial. No this is my house.

Drew received a call from JoJo's biological dad that he came home from jail and wanted to see his son if possible. At the time Drew was still hurt by the lack of support and effort. Her perspective was, if you haven't been around or made an effort all this time, why now. JoJo doesn't need you. Besides she had me in her life which "filled" the void of JoJo's lack of a father figure.

Once Drew brought the conversation and intention to my attention, I had a lot of thinking to do also. As a man or the other man in the situation, I had several thoughts run through my mind. As men, we can rightfully be territorial and protective of their castle. After I let my pride down, put myself in his shoes and think big picture, there were a few things I had to evaluate. Did JoJo's father approach the situation respectfully for my wife and also for me? Did he do anything to neglect the wellbeing and safety of JoJo? What is the intention? Is this relationship in the best interest for JoJo? I immediately thought of my father and our circumstances.

As a child, no one couldn't tell me that my father wasn't the best in the world and guess what, that's my perspective. If you measured or quantified the value of our relationship, there would be large gaps in his presence, missed games and events, missed birthdays, missed growth and bonding opportunities. Yet, my father was still the best thing that could have ever happened to me. How could this be, the heart doesn't measure value in the way our minds do. Love is blind and that's what makes love beautiful, innocent and cherished. Without love, we would be robots, incapable of forgiving or giving someone an opportunity to succeed. If we were robotic in our heart, we would leave a baby that didn't learn to walk fast enough or talk. Sometimes the greatest lessons on earth is experiencing life.

Interesting enough, Initially I didn't speak with JoJo's biological father as Drew had to feel comfortable with the interaction first however I was always by her side supporting the process. Change is very hard especially on a child therefore she wanted to make sure he wanted to really be part of his life before introducing his Father and he deciding he didn't want that role. Consistency is important to know if you're in this for the long run or if it's a nice experience because you think you should do it. Drew put JoJo's father on a call schedule to slowly introduce JoJo to his Father. JoJo visited with him as a baby but it's been years since they spoke and as a child, they don't know what a

father means. The first few interactions was awkward just as any person that walks into a child's life that doesn't have kids, there is a learning process.

Adoption Because JoJo's father wasn't around, people would ask if I would adopt him, which is a great question. These are my rules on adopting in a blended family:

The Father doesn't want to be in the child's life therefore the child is fatherless

The Father is deceased.

The child is in harm or danger, therefore it's an unfit home.

The child doesn't have parents

In the event the child's mother dies, custody can be established through court order.....Find out the process. I really don't know.

If I would have adopted Josiah.

JoJo will get to a point where he seeks information and understanding for himself and he would approach his father asking, why didn't he make an effort to be in his life. His Father would more than likely respond, your parents didn't allow me to be a part of your life and pushed me out. JoJo can possibly develop resentment due to our actions, even if we felt it was in his best interest.

This is a great segway into the definition of "Dad." Dads come in all different forms, types, relationships and can be interchangeable for almost anyone providing support that uplifts positive change and growth. When my father wasn't around, coaches became father figures to me including men in the community that taught me fundamentals of manhood. When my father wasn't around, men in the community would hire me and my brother to pickup leaves. It probably was one of the worst jobs I've ever experienced but it built character and work ethic that I wouldn't trade for the world. There is a village that becomes available to instill the lessons children need to learn and the role of "dad" can often be spread throughout the village to ensure children learn fundamentals of life. This concept also applies when the dad is around. Everyone is limited on the amount of information

we know. If someone excels in a certain area, send the child to exceed your own understanding as the future depends on our children being smarter and more skilled than us.

Confidence I'm a firm believer that what's for me is for me and no one can take it away. If something isn't for me, then it was only supposed to be in my life for a season and I'm fine.

Being okay with JoJo's biological dad coming into the picture Studies show, 85% of blended familes are dysfunctional. While Drew and I were dating, she was very intentional not to allow me to play the dad role. She didn't want to scare me off or put responsibility on me before we had a chance to know if our relationship would last. Her family also assisted in our dating process. Their goal was to help Drew find the man of her dreams and would take JoJo so she could go out on dates. Well, that strategy worked! Drew and I went on a date that lasted 12hrs. Her family wasn't very happy when I brought her home at 4am. To no despair, we stayed in contact and she became my wife. I would ask Drew if I could take JoJo for ice cream or take him to the park while she was working if I felt she needed a helping hand so I could build a stronger bond with him. I knew if I married Drew, he would become my son. JoJo's biological father currently wasn't around and I knew JoJo needed a male influence to help him navigate the world, instill moral and values and grow into the man he would become. I had great expectations however I didn't know what a son or father figure meant from my wifes's eyes. My thought was once we were married, I would automatically take on the father role.

In our scenario, we got married extremely fast and Drew was pregnant 2mo after. We had a huge decision to make, where do we stay to raise the kids. At the time we were in LA and didn't feel like we had much support. We could either go to NJ to my family or Chicago with her family. I spoke with Drew's mom and she said I really can't help you if you stay in LA. Drew has a big family, her mom and dad and 4 sisters. It was a no brainer and we relocated to Chicago before Machai was born. I didn't

have a chance to fully assume the "Dad" role as everything was moving fast. We were living under the same roof however Drew was making moves the way she programmed and without much involvement or opinion from my side. There were a few things that I didn't like entirely too much such as JoJo staying up until any time he wanted as if he was a little rockstar in a diaper and him sleeping in the same bed. Drew wasn't receptive to him staying up late and defended by saying she's an actress and her hours flucturate. To combat, I provided studies and reports on best practices for sleeping. I also provided a guidance for the tv staying on all night and she said her parents did it with them and everyone is okay so it's not that bad. I tried developing the "My House, My Rules" concept but it quickly fell on death ears as my concerns weren't enforced. Opposed to supporting, JoJo would cry and mom would come to the rescue. I began to see a common thread, where JoJo was also learning how to get his way and It then became an issue where it was Me vs. Them.

Boiling Point where I felt I couldn't parent

Due to JoJo not receiving adequate sleep, he struggled to get up for school in the morning. Being a man, I had my way of getting you to follow directions which was to place the fear of God in you because at the end of the day, I'm the parent. JoJo stood by the sink and didn't want to brush his teeth so I "acted" as if I was going to give him a pinch and he started crying, not because of pain but because of the act. His mother ran upstairs and grabbed JoJo, asking what happened. JoJo responded, daddy pinched me. Drew grabbed JoJo and reprimanded me saying I told you not to do that to him. I asked JoJo to demonstrate on his mother exactly how hard I pinched him and he barely touched his mother. I walked out the room as I felt emasculated and minimized below a child. I thought to myself if I wanted to stay in a relationship where I didn't have a parenting voice. Besides all that I've done and contributed, I should feel more respected. We ended up seeking out a marriage counselor that told us we're doing things all wrong. We didn't have a plan and it shows.

but she did ask for my thoughts to correct him sleeping in the bed.

Introduce Drew's mom, millinial

Support we had and lacked

Realistic / Unrealistic Expectations

It's either him or me

Village mindset, when JoJo's dad came home, Respect. Territorial. No this is my house.

Drew received a call from JoJo's biological dad that he came home from jail and wanted to see his son if possible. At the time Drew was still hurt by the lack of support and effort. Her perspective was, if you haven't been around or made an effort all this time, why now. JoJo doesn't need you. Besides she had me in her life which "filled" the void of JoJo's lack of a father figure. Once Drew brought the conversation and intention to my attention, I had a lot of thinking to do also. As a man or the other man in the situation, I had several thoughts run through my mind. As men, we can rightfully be territorial and protective of their castle. After I let my pride down, put myself in his shoes and think big picture, there were a few things I had to evaluate. Did JoJo's father approach the situation respectfully for my wife and also for me? Did he do anything to neglect the wellbeing and safety of JoJo? What is the intention? Is this relationship in the best interest for JoJo? I immediately thought of my father and our circumstances.

As a child, no one couldn't tell me that my father wasn't the best in the world and guess what, that's my perspective. If you measured or quantified the value of our relationship, there would be large gaps in his presence, missed games and events, missed birthdays, missed growth and bonding opportunities. Yet, my father was still the best thing that could have ever happened to me. How could this be, the heart doesn't measure value in the way our minds do. Love is blind and that's what makes love beautiful, innocent and cherished. Without love, we would be robots, incapable of forgiving or giving someone an opportunity to succeed.

If we were robotic in our heart, we would leave a baby that didn't learn to walk fast enough or talk. Sometimes the greatest lessons on earth is experiencing life.

Interesting enough, Initially I didn't speak with JoJo's biological father as Drew had to feel comfortable with the interaction first however I was always by her side supporting the process. Change is very hard especially on a child therefore she wanted to make sure he wanted to really be part of his life before introducing his Father and he deciding he didn't want that role. Consistency is important to know if you're in this for the long run or if it's a nice experience because you think you should do it. Drew put JoJo's father on a call schedule to slowly introduce JoJo to his Father. JoJo visited with him as a baby but it's been years since they spoke and as a child, they don't know what a father means. The first few interactions was awkward just as any person that walks into a child's life that doesn't have kids, there is a learning process.

Adoption Because JoJo's father wasn't around, people would ask if I would adopt him, which is a great question. These are my rules on adopting in a blended family:

The Father doesn't want to be in the child's life therefore the child is fatherless

The Father is deceased.

The child is in harm or danger, therefore it's an unfit home.

The child doesn't have parents

In the event the child's mother dies, custody can be established through court order.....Find out the process. I really don't know.

If I would have adopted Josiah.

JoJo will get to a point where he seeks information and understanding for himself and he would approach his father asking, why didn't he make an effort to be in his life. His Father would more than likely respond, your parents didn't allow me to be a part of your life and pushed me out. JoJo can possibly develop resentment due to our actions, even if we felt it was in his best interest.

This is a great segway into the definition of "Dad." Dads come in all different forms, types, relationships and can be interchangeable for almost anyone providing support that uplifts positive change and growth. When my father wasn't around, coaches became father figures to me including men in the community that taught me fundamentals of manhood. When my father wasn't around, men in the community would hire me and my brother to pickup leaves. It probably was one of the worst jobs I've ever experienced but it built character and work ethic that I wouldn't trade for the world. There is a village that becomes available to instill the lessons children need to learn and the role of "dad" can often be spread throughout the village to ensure children learn fundamentals of life. This concept also applies when the dad is around. Everyone is limited on the amount of information we know. If someone excels in a certain area, send the child to exceed your own understanding as the future depends on our children being smarter and more skilled than us.

Confidence I'm a firm believer that what's for me is for me and no one can take it away. If something isn't for me, then it was only supposed to be in my life for a season and I'm fine.

Being okay with JoJo's biological dad coming into the picture Studies show, 85% of blended familes are dysfunctional. While Drew and I were dating, she was very intentional not to allow me to play the dad role. She didn't want to scare me off or put responsibility on me before we had a chance to know if our relationship would last. Her family also assisted in our dating process. Their goal was to help Drew find the man of her dreams and would take JoJo so she could go out on dates. Well, that strategy worked! Drew and I went on a date that lasted 12hrs. Her family wasn't very happy when I brought her home at 4am. To no despair, we stayed in contact and she became my wife. I would ask Drew if I could take JoJo for ice cream or take him to the park while she was working if I felt she needed a helping hand so I could build a stronger bond with him. I knew if I married Drew, he would become my son. JoJo's biological father currently

wasn't around and I knew JoJo needed a male influence to help him navigate the world, instill moral and values and grow into the man he would become. I had great expectations however I didn't know what a son or father figure meant from my wifes's eyes. My thought was once we were married, I would automatically take on the father role.

In our scenario, we got married extremely fast and Drew was pregnant 2mo after. We had a huge decision to make, where do we stay to raise the kids. At the time we were in LA and didn't feel like we had much support. We could either go to NJ to my family or Chicago with her family. I spoke with Drew's mom and she said I really can't help you if you stay in LA. Drew has a big family, her mom and dad and 4 sisters. It was a no brainer and we relocated to Chicago before Machai was born. I didn't have a chance to fully assume the "Dad" role as everything was moving fast. We were living under the same roof however Drew was making moves the way she programmed and without much involvement or opinion from my side. There were a few things that I didn't like entirely too much such as JoJo staying up until any time he wanted as if he was a little rockstar in a diaper and him sleeping in the same bed. Drew wasn't receptive to him staying up late and defended by saying she's an actress and her hours flucturate. To combat, I provided studies and reports on best practices for sleeping. I also provided a guidance for the tv staying on all night and she said her parents did it with them and everyone is okay so it's not that bad. I tried developing the "My House, My Rules" concept but it quickly fell on death ears as my concerns weren't enforced. Opposed to supporting, JoJo would cry and mom would come to the rescue. I began to see a common thread, where JoJo was also learning how to get his way and It then became an issue where it was Me vs. Them.

Boiling Point where I felt I couldn't parent

Due to JoJo not receiving adequate sleep, he struggled to get up for school in the morning. Being a man, I had my way of getting you to follow directions which was to place the fear of God

in you because at the end of the day, I'm the parent. JoJo stood by the sink and didn't want to brush his teeth so I "acted" as if I was going to give him a pinch and he started crying, not because of pain but because of the act. His mother ran upstairs and grabbed JoJo, asking what happened. JoJo responded, daddy pinched me. Drew grabbed JoJo and repremanded me saying I told you not to do that to him. I asked JoJo to demonstrate on his mother exactly how hard I pinched him and he barely touched his mother. I walked out the room as I felt emasculated and minimized below a child. I thought to myself if I wanted to stay in a relationship where I didn't have a parenting voice. Besides all that I've done and contributed, I should feel more respected. We ended up seeking out a marriage counselor that told us we're doing things all wrong. We didn't have a plan and it shows.

but she did ask for my thoughts to correct him sleeping in the bed.

Introduce Drew's mom, millinial

Support we had and lacked

Realistic / Unrealistic Expectations

It's either him or me

Village mindset, when JoJo's dad came home, Respect. Territorial. No this is my house.

Drew received a call from JoJo's biological dad that he came home from jail and wanted to see his son if possible. At the time Drew was still hurt by the lack of support and effort. Her perspective was, if you haven't been around or made an effort all this time, why now. JoJo doesn't need you. Besides she had me in her life which "filled" the void of JoJo's lack of a father figure. Once Drew brought the conversation and intention to my attention, I had a lot of thinking to do also. As a man or the other man in the situation, I had several thoughts run through my mind. As men, we can rightfully be territorial and protective of their castle. After I let my pride down, put myself in his shoes and think big picture, there were a few things I had to evaluate. Did JoJo's father approach the situation respectfully for my wife and

also for me? Did he do anything to neglect the wellbeing and safety of JoJo? What is the intention? Is this relationship in the best interest for JoJo? I immediately thought of my father and our circumstances.

As a child, no one couldn't tell me that my father wasn't the best in the world and guess what, that's my perspective. If you measured or quantified the value of our relationship, there would be large gaps in his presence, missed games and events, missed birthdays, missed growth and bonding opportunities. Yet, my father was still the best thing that could have ever happened to me. How could this be, the heart doesn't measure value in the way our minds do. Love is blind and that's what makes love beautiful, innocent and cherished. Without love, we would be robots, incapable of forgiving or giving someone an opportunity to succeed. If we were robotic in our heart, we would leave a baby that didn't learn to walk fast enough or talk. Sometimes the greatest lessons on earth is experiencing life.

Interesting enough, Initially I didn't speak with JoJo's biological father as Drew had to feel comfortable with the interaction first however I was always by her side supporting the process. Change is very hard especially on a child therefore she wanted to make sure he wanted to really be part of his life before introducing his Father and he deciding he didn't want that role. Consistency is important to know if you're in this for the long run or if it's a nice experience because you think you should do it. Drew put JoJo's father on a call schedule to slowly introduce JoJo to his Father. JoJo visited with him as a baby but it's been years since they spoke and as a child, they don't know what a father means. The first few interactions was awkward just as any person that walks into a child's life that doesn't have kids, there is a learning process.

Adoption Because JoJo's father wasn't around, people would ask if I would adopt him, which is a great question. These are my rules on adopting in a blended family:

The Father doesn't want to be in the child's life therefore the child is fatherless

The Father is deceased.

The child is in harm or danger, therefore it's an unfit home.

The child doesn't have parents

In the event the child's mother dies, custody can be established through court order.....Find out the process. I really don't know.

If I would have adopted Josiah.

JoJo will get to a point where he seeks information and understanding for himself and he would approach his father asking, why didn't he make an effort to be in his life. His Father would more than likely respond, your parents didn't allow me to be a part of your life and pushed me out. JoJo can possibly develop resentment due to our actions, even if we felt it was in his best interest.

This is a great segway into the definition of "Dad." Dads come in all different forms, types, relationships and can be interchangeable for almost anyone providing support that uplifts positive change and growth. When my father wasn't around, coaches became father figures to me including men in the community that taught me fundamentals of manhood. When my father wasn't around, men in the community would hire me and my brother to pickup leaves. It probably was one of the worst jobs I've ever experienced but it built character and work ethic that I wouldn't trade for the world. There is a village that becomes available to instill the lessons children need to learn and the role of "dad" can often be spread throughout the village to ensure children learn fundamentals of life. This concept also applies when the dad is around. Everyone is limited on the amount of information we know. If someone excels in a certain area, send the child to exceed your own understanding as the future depends on our children being smarter and more skilled than us.

Confidence I'm a firm believer that what's for me is for me and no one can take it away. If something isn't for me, then it was only supposed to be in my life for a season and I'm fine.

Being okay with JoJo's biological dad coming into the picture
Studies show, 85% of blended familes are dysfunctional.
While Drew and I were dating, she was very intentional not to
allow me to play the dad role. She didn't want to scare me off
or put responsibility on me before we had a chance to know if
our relationship would last. Her family also assisted in our dating
process. Their goal was to help Drew find the man of her dreams
and would take JoJo so she could go out on dates. Well, that strategy worked! Drew and I went on a date that lasted 12hrs. Her
family wasn't very happy when I brought her home at 4am. To
no despair, we stayed in contact and she became my wife. I would
ask Drew if I could take JoJo for ice cream or take him to the
park while she was working if I felt she needed a helping hand
so I could build a stronger bond with him. I knew if I married
Drew, he would become my son. JoJo's biological father currently wasn't around and I knew JoJo needed a male influence to
help him navigate the world, instill moral and values and grow
into the man he would become. I had great expectations however
I didn't know what a son or father figure meant from my wifes's
eyes. My thought was once we were married, I would automatically take on the father role.

In our scenario, we got married extremely fast and Drew was
pregnant 2mo after. We had a huge decision to make, where do
we stay to raise the kids. At the time we were in LA and didn't
feel like we had much support. We could either go to NJ to my
family or Chicago with her family. I spoke with Drew's mom
and she said I really can't help you if you stay in LA. Drew has
a big family, her mom and dad and 4 sisters. It was a no brainer
and we relocated to Chicago before Machai was born. I didn't
have a chance to fully assume the "Dad" role as everything was
moving fast. We were living under the same roof however Drew
was making moves the way she programmed and without much
involvement or opinion from my side. There were a few things
that I didn't like entirely too much such as JoJo staying up until
any time he wanted as if he was a little rockstar in a diaper and

231

him sleeping in the same bed. Drew wasn't receptive to him staying up late and defended by saying she's an actress and her hours flucturate. To combat, I provided studies and reports on best practices for sleeping. I also provided a guidance for the tv staying on all night and she said her parents did it with them and everyone is okay so it's not that bad. I tried developing the "My House, My Rules" concept but it quickly fell on death ears as my concerns weren't enforced. Opposed to supporting, JoJo would cry and mom would come to the rescue. I began to see a common thread, where JoJo was also learning how to get his way and It then became an issue where it was Me vs. Them.

Boiling Point where I felt I couldn't parent

Due to JoJo not receiving adequate sleep, he struggled to get up for school in the morning. Being a man, I had my way of getting you to follow directions which was to place the fear of God in you because at the end of the day, I'm the parent. JoJo stood by the sink and didn't want to brush his teeth so I "acted" as if I was going to give him a pinch and he started crying, not because of pain but because of the act. His mother ran upstairs and grabbed JoJo, asking what happened. JoJo responded, daddy pinched me. Drew grabbed JoJo and repremanded me saying I told you not to do that to him. I asked JoJo to demonstrate on his mother exactly how hard I pinched him and he barely touched his mother. I walked out the room as I felt emasculated and minimized below a child. I thought to myself if I wanted to stay in a relationship where I didn't have a parenting voice. Besides all that I've done and contributed, I should feel more respected. We ended up seeking out a marriage counselor that told us we're doing things all wrong. We didn't have a plan and it shows.

but she did ask for my thoughts to correct him sleeping in the bed.

Introduce Drew's mom, millinial

Support we had and lacked

Realistic / Unrealistic Expectations

It's either him or me

Village mindset, when JoJo's dad came home, Respect. Territorial. No this is my house.

Drew received a call from JoJo's biological dad that he came home from jail and wanted to see his son if possible. At the time Drew was still hurt by the lack of support and effort. Her perspective was, if you haven't been around or made an effort all this time, why now. JoJo doesn't need you. Besides she had me in her life which "filled" the void of JoJo's lack of a father figure. Once Drew brought the conversation and intention to my attention, I had a lot of thinking to do also. As a man or the other man in the situation, I had several thoughts run through my mind. As men, we can rightfully be territorial and protective of their castle. After I let my pride down, put myself in his shoes and think big picture, there were a few things I had to evaluate. Did JoJo's father approach the situation respectfully for my wife and also for me? Did he do anything to neglect the wellbeing and safety of JoJo? What is the intention? Is this relationship in the best interest for JoJo? I immediately thought of my father and our circumstances.

As a child, no one couldn't tell me that my father wasn't the best in the world and guess what, that's my perspective. If you measured or quantified the value of our relationship, there would be large gaps in his presence, missed games and events, missed birthdays, missed growth and bonding opportunities. Yet, my father was still the best thing that could have ever happened to me. How could this be, the heart doesn't measure value in the way our minds do. Love is blind and that's what makes love beautiful, innocent and cherished. Without love, we would be robots, incapable of forgiving or giving someone an opportunity to succeed. If we were robotic in our heart, we would leave a baby that didn't learn to walk fast enough or talk. Sometimes the greatest lessons on earth is experiencing life.

Interesting enough, Initially I didn't speak with JoJo's biological father as Drew had to feel comfortable with the interaction first however I was always by her side supporting the process.

Change is very hard especially on a child therefore she wanted to make sure he wanted to really be part of his life before introducing his Father and he deciding he didn't want that role. Consistency is important to know if you're in this for the long run or if it's a nice experience because you think you should do it. Drew put JoJo's father on a call schedule to slowly introduce JoJo to his Father. JoJo visited with him as a baby but it's been years since they spoke and as a child, they don't know what a father means. The first few interactions was awkward just as any person that walks into a child's life that doesn't have kids, there is a learning process.

Adoption Because JoJo's father wasn't around, people would ask if I would adopt him, which is a great question. These are my rules on adopting in a blended family:

The Father doesn't want to be in the child's life therefore the child is fatherless

The Father is deceased.

The child is in harm or danger, therefore it's an unfit home.

The child doesn't have parents

In the event the child's mother dies, custody can be established through court order.....Find out the process. I really don't know.

If I would have adopted Josiah.

JoJo will get to a point where he seeks information and understanding for himself and he would approach his father asking, why didn't he make an effort to be in his life. His Father would more than likely respond, your parents didn't allow me to be a part of your life and pushed me out. JoJo can possibly develop resentment due to our actions, even if we felt it was in his best interest.

This is a great segway into the definition of "Dad." Dads come in all different forms, types, relationships and can be interchangeable for almost anyone providing support that uplifts positive change and growth. When my father wasn't around, coaches became father figures to me including men in the community that taught me fundamentals of manhood. When my father wasn't

around, men in the community would hire me and my brother to pickup leaves. It probably was one of the worst jobs I've ever experienced but it built character and work ethic that I wouldn't trade for the world. There is a village that becomes available to instill the lessons children need to learn and the role of "dad" can often be spread throughout the village to ensure children learn fundamentals of life. This concept also applies when the dad is around. Everyone is limited on the amount of information we know. If someone excels in a certain area, send the child to exceed your own understanding as the future depends on our children being smarter and more skilled than us.

Confidence I'm a firm believer that what's for me is for me and no one can take it away. If something isn't for me, then it was only supposed to be in my life for a season and I'm fine.

Being okay with JoJo's biological dad coming into the picture Studies show, 85% of blended familes are dysfunctional. While Drew and I were dating, she was very intentional not to allow me to play the dad role. She didn't want to scare me off or put responsibility on me before we had a chance to know if our relationship would last. Her family also assisted in our dating process. Their goal was to help Drew find the man of her dreams and would take JoJo so she could go out on dates. Well, that strategy worked! Drew and I went on a date that lasted 12hrs. Her family wasn't very happy when I brought her home at 4am. To no despair, we stayed in contact and she became my wife. I would ask Drew if I could take JoJo for ice cream or take him to the park while she was working if I felt she needed a helping hand so I could build a stronger bond with him. I knew if I married Drew, he would become my son. JoJo's biological father currently wasn't around and I knew JoJo needed a male influence to help him navigate the world, instill moral and values and grow into the man he would become. I had great expectations however I didn't know what a son or father figure meant from my wifes's eyes. My thought was once we were married, I would automatically take on the father role.

In our scenario, we got married extremely fast and Drew was pregnant 2mo after. We had a huge decision to make, where do we stay to raise the kids. At the time we were in LA and didn't feel like we had much support. We could either go to NJ to my family or Chicago with her family. I spoke with Drew's mom and she said I really can't help you if you stay in LA. Drew has a big family, her mom and dad and 4 sisters. It was a no brainer and we relocated to Chicago before Machai was born. I didn't have a chance to fully assume the "Dad" role as everything was moving fast. We were living under the same roof however Drew was making moves the way she programmed and without much involvement or opinion from my side. There were a few things that I didn't like entirely too much such as JoJo staying up until any time he wanted as if he was a little rockstar in a diaper and him sleeping in the same bed. Drew wasn't receptive to him staying up late and defended by saying she's an actress and her hours flucturate. To combat, I provided studies and reports on best practices for sleeping. I also provided a guidance for the tv staying on all night and she said her parents did it with them and everyone is okay so it's not that bad. I tried developing the "My House, My Rules" concept but it quickly fell on death ears as my concerns weren't enforced. Opposed to supporting, JoJo would cry and mom would come to the rescue. I began to see a common thread, where JoJo was also learning how to get his way and It then became an issue where it was Me vs. Them.

Boiling Point where I felt I couldn't parent

Due to JoJo not receiving adequate sleep, he struggled to get up for school in the morning. Being a man, I had my way of getting you to follow directions which was to place the fear of God in you because at the end of the day, I'm the parent. JoJo stood by the sink and didn't want to brush his teeth so I "acted" as if I was going to give him a pinch and he started crying, not because of pain but because of the act. His mother ran upstairs and grabbed JoJo, asking what happened. JoJo responded, daddy pinched me. Drew grabbed JoJo and repremanded me saying I

told you not to do that to him. I asked JoJo to demonstrate on his mother exactly how hard I pinched him and he barely touched his mother. I walked out the room as I felt emasculated and minimized below a child. I thought to myself if I wanted to stay in a relationship where I didn't have a parenting voice. Besides all that I've done and contributed, I should feel more respected. We ended up seeking out a marriage counselor that told us we're doing things all wrong. We didn't have a plan and it shows.

but she did ask for my thoughts to correct him sleeping in the bed.

Introduce Drew's mom, millinial

Support we had and lacked

Realistic / Unrealistic Expectations

It's either him or me

Village mindset, when JoJo's dad came home, Respect. Territorial. No this is my house.

Drew received a call from JoJo's biological dad that he came home from jail and wanted to see his son if possible. At the time Drew was still hurt by the lack of support and effort. Her perspective was, if you haven't been around or made an effort all this time, why now. JoJo doesn't need you. Besides she had me in her life which "filled" the void of JoJo's lack of a father figure. Once Drew brought the conversation and intention to my attention, I had a lot of thinking to do also. As a man or the other man in the situation, I had several thoughts run through my mind. As men, we can rightfully be territorial and protective of their castle. After I let my pride down, put myself in his shoes and think big picture, there were a few things I had to evaluate. Did JoJo's father approach the situation respectfully for my wife and also for me? Did he do anything to neglect the wellbeing and safety of JoJo? What is the intention? Is this relationship in the best interest for JoJo? I immediately thought of my father and our circumstances.

As a child, no one couldn't tell me that my father wasn't the best in the world and guess what, that's my perspective. If you

measured or quantified the value of our relationship, there would be large gaps in his presence, missed games and events, missed birthdays, missed growth and bonding opportunities. Yet, my father was still the best thing that could have ever happened to me. How could this be, the heart doesn't measure value in the way our minds do. Love is blind and that's what makes love beautiful, innocent and cherished. Without love, we would be robots, incapable of forgiving or giving someone an opportunity to succeed. If we were robotic in our heart, we would leave a baby that didn't learn to walk fast enough or talk. Sometimes the greatest lessons on earth is experiencing life.

Interesting enough, Initially I didn't speak with JoJo's biological father as Drew had to feel comfortable with the interaction first however I was always by her side supporting the process. Change is very hard especially on a child therefore she wanted to make sure he wanted to really be part of his life before introducing his Father and he deciding he didn't want that role. Consistency is important to know if you're in this for the long run or if it's a nice experience because you think you should do it. Drew put JoJo's father on a call schedule to slowly introduce JoJo to his Father. JoJo visited with him as a baby but it's been years since they spoke and as a child, they don't know what a father means. The first few interactions was awkward just as any person that walks into a child's life that doesn't have kids, there is a learning process.

Adoption Because JoJo's father wasn't around, people would ask if I would adopt him, which is a great question. These are my rules on adopting in a blended family:

The Father doesn't want to be in the child's life therefore the child is fatherless

The Father is deceased.

The child is in harm or danger, therefore it's an unfit home.

The child doesn't have parents

In the event the child's mother dies, custody can be established through court order.....Find out the process. I really don't know.

If I would have adopted Josiah.

JoJo will get to a point where he seeks information and under-standing for himself and he would approach his father asking, why didn't he make an effort to be in his life. His Father would more than likely respond, your parents didn't allow me to be a part of your life and pushed me out. JoJo can possibly develop resentment due to our actions, even if we felt it was in his best interest.

This is a great segway into the definition of "Dad." Dads come in all different forms, types, relationships and can be interchange-able for almost anyone providing support that uplifts positive change and growth. When my father wasn't around, coaches became father figures to me including men in the community that taught me fundamentals of manhood. When my father wasn't around, men in the community would hire me and my brother to pickup leaves. It probably was one of the worst jobs I've ever experienced but it built character and work ethic that I wouldn't trade for the world. There is a village that becomes available to instill the lessons children need to learn and the role of "dad" can often be spread throughout the village to ensure children learn fundamentals of life. This concept also applies when the dad is around. Everyone is limited on the amount of information we know. If someone excels in a certain area, send the child to exceed your own understanding as the future depends on our children being smarter and more skilled than us.

Confidence I'm a firm believer that what's for me is for me and no one can take it away. If something isn't for me, then it was only supposed to be in my life for a season and I'm fine.

Being okay with JoJo's biological dad coming into the picture Studies show, 85% of blended familes are dysfunctional. While Drew and I were dating, she was very intentional not to allow me to play the dad role. She didn't want to scare me off or put responsibility on me before we had a chance to know if our relationship would last. Her family also assisted in our dating process. Their goal was to help Drew find the man of her dreams

and would take JoJo so she could go out on dates. Well, that strategy worked! Drew and I went on a date that lasted 12hrs. Her family wasn't very happy when I brought her home at 4am. To no despair, we stayed in contact and she became my wife. I would ask Drew if I could take JoJo for ice cream or take him to the park while she was working if I felt she needed a helping hand so I could build a stronger bond with him. I knew if I married Drew, he would become my son. JoJo's biological father currently wasn't around and I knew JoJo needed a male influence to help him navigate the world, instill moral and values and grow into the man he would become. I had great expectations however I didn't know what a son or father figure meant from my wifes's eyes. My thought was once we were married, I would automatically take on the father role.

In our scenario, we got married extremely fast and Drew was pregnant 2mo after. We had a huge decision to make, where do we stay to raise the kids. At the time we were in LA and didn't feel like we had much support. We could either go to NJ to my family or Chicago with her family. I spoke with Drew's mom and she said I really can't help you if you stay in LA. Drew has a big family, her mom and dad and 4 sisters. It was a no brainer and we relocated to Chicago before Machai was born. I didn't have a chance to fully assume the "Dad" role as everything was moving fast. We were living under the same roof however Drew was making moves the way she programmed and without much involvement or opinion from my side. There were a few things that I didn't like entirely too much such as JoJo staying up until any time he wanted as if he was a little rockstar in a diaper and him sleeping in the same bed. Drew wasn't receptive to him staying up late and defended by saying she's an actress and her hours flucturate. To combat, I provided studies and reports on best practices for sleeping. I also provided a guidance for the tv staying on all night and she said her parents did it with them and everyone is okay so it's not that bad. I tried developing the "My House, My Rules" concept but it quickly fell on death ears as my

concerns weren't enforced. Opposed to supporting, JoJo would cry and mom would come to the rescue. I began to see a common thread, where JoJo was also learning how to get his way and It then became an issue where it was Me vs. Them.

Boiling Point where I felt I couldn't parent

Due to JoJo not receiving adequate sleep, he struggled to get up for school in the morning. Being a man, I had my way of getting you to follow directions which was to place the fear of God in you because at the end of the day, I'm the parent. JoJo stood by the sink and didn't want to brush his teeth so I "acted" as if I was going to give him a pinch and he started crying, not because of pain but because of the act. His mother ran upstairs and grabbed JoJo, asking what happened. JoJo responded, daddy pinched me. Drew grabbed JoJo and repremanded me saying I told you not to do that to him. I asked JoJo to demonstrate on his mother exactly how hard I pinched him and he barely touched his mother. I walked out the room as I felt emasculated and minimized below a child. I thought to myself if I wanted to stay in a relationship where I didn't have a parenting voice. Besides all that I've done and contributed, I should feel more respected. We ended up seeking out a marriage counselor that told us we're doing things all wrong. We didn't have a plan and it shows.

but she did ask for my thoughts to correct him sleeping in the bed.

Introduce Drew's mom, millinial

Support we had and lacked

Realistic / Unrealistic Expectations

It's either him or me

Village mindset, when JoJo's dad came home, Respect. Territorial. No this is my house.

Drew received a call from JoJo's biological dad that he came home from jail and wanted to see his son if possible. At the time Drew was still hurt by the lack of support and effort. Her perspective was, if you haven't been around or made an effort all this time, why now. JoJo doesn't need you. Besides she had me

in her life which "filled" the void of JoJo's lack of a father figure. Once Drew brought the conversation and intention to my attention, I had a lot of thinking to do also. As a man or the other man in the situation, I had several thoughts run through my mind. As men, we can rightfully be territorial and protective of their castle. After I let my pride down, put myself in his shoes and think big picture, there were a few things I had to evaluate. Did JoJo's father approach the situation respectfully for my wife and also for me? Did he do anything to neglect the wellbeing and safety of JoJo? What is the intention? Is this relationship in the best interest for JoJo? I immediately thought of my father and our circumstances.

As a child, no one couldn't tell me that my father wasn't the best in the world and guess what, that's my perspective. If you measured or quantified the value of our relationship, there would be large gaps in his presence, missed games and events, missed birthdays, missed growth and bonding opportunities. Yet, my father was still the best thing that could have ever happened to me. How could this be, the heart doesn't measure value in the way our minds do. Love is blind and that's what makes love beautiful, innocent and cherished. Without love, we would be robots, incapable of forgiving or giving someone an opportunity to succeed. If we were robotic in our heart, we would leave a baby that didn't learn to walk fast enough or talk. Sometimes the greatest lessons on earth is experiencing life.

Interesting enough, Initially I didn't speak with JoJo's biological father as Drew had to feel comfortable with the interaction first however I was always by her side supporting the process. Change is very hard especially on a child therefore she wanted to make sure he wanted to really be part of his life before introducing his Father and he deciding he didn't want that role. Consistency is important to know if you're in this for the long run or if it's a nice experience because you think you should do it. Drew put JoJo's father on a call schedule to slowly introduce JoJo to his Father. JoJo visited with him as a baby but it's been

years since they spoke and as a child, they don't know what a father means. The first few interactions was awkward just as any person that walks into a child's life that doesn't have kids, there is a learning process.

Adoption Because JoJo's father wasn't around, people would ask if I would adopt him, which is a great question. These are my rules on adopting in a blended family:

The Father doesn't want to be in the child's life therefore the child is fatherless

The Father is deceased.

The child is in harm or danger, therefore it's an unfit home.

The child doesn't have parents

In the event the child's mother dies, custody can be established through court order......Find out the process. I really don't know.

If I would have adopted Josiah.

JoJo will get to a point where he seeks information and understanding for himself and he would approach his father asking, why didn't he make an effort to be in his life. His Father would more than likely respond, your parents didn't allow me to be a part of your life and pushed me out. JoJo can possibly develop resentment due to our actions, even if we felt it was in his best interest.

This is a great segway into the definition of "Dad." Dads come in all different forms, types, relationships and can be interchangeable for almost anyone providing support that uplifts positive change and growth. When my father wasn't around, coaches became father figures to me including men in the community that taught me fundamentals of manhood. When my father wasn't around, men in the community would hire me and my brother to pickup leaves. It probably was one of the worst jobs I've ever experienced but it built character and work ethic that I wouldn't trade for the world. There is a village that becomes available to instill the lessons children need to learn and the role of "dad" can often be spread throughout the village to ensure children learn fundamentals of life. This concept also applies when the

dad is around. Everyone is limited on the amount of information we know. If someone excels in a certain area, send the child to exceed your own understanding as the future depends on our children being smarter and more skilled than us.

Confidence I'm a firm believer that what's for me is for me and no one can take it away. If something isn't for me, then it was only supposed to be in my life for a season and I'm fine.

Being okay with JoJo's biological dad coming into the picture Studies show, 85% of blended familes are dysfunctional.

In our scenario, we got married extremely fast and Drew was pregnant 2mo after. We had a huge decision to make, where do we stay to raise the kids. At the time we were in LA and didn't feel like we had much support. We could either go to NJ to my family or Chicago with her family. I spoke with Drew's mom and she said I really can't help you if you stay in LA. Drew has a big family, her mom and dad and 4 sisters. It was a no brainer and we relocated to Chicago before Machai was born. I didn't have a chance to fully assume the "Dad" role as everything was moving fast. We were living under the same roof however Drew was making moves the way she programmed and without much involvement or opinion from my side. There were a few things that I didn't like entirely too much such as JoJo staying up until any time he wanted as if he was a little rockstar in a diaper and him sleeping in the same bed. Drew wasn't receptive to him staying up late and defended by saying she's an actress and her hours flucturate. To combat, I provided studies and reports on best practices for sleeping. I also provided a guidance for the tv staying on all night and she said her parents did it with them and everyone is okay so it's not that bad. I tried developing the "My House, My Rules" concept but it quickly fell on death ears as my concerns weren't enforced. Opposed to supporting, JoJo would cry and mom would come to the rescue. I began to see a common thread, where JoJo was also learning how to get his way and It then became an issue where it was Me vs. Them.

Boiling Point where I felt I couldn't parent

Due to JoJo not receiving adequate sleep, he struggled to get up for school in the morning. Being a man, I had my way of getting you to follow directions which was to place the fear of God in you because at the end of the day, I'm the parent. JoJo stood by the sink and didn't want to brush his teeth so I "acted" as if I was going to give him a pinch and he started crying, not because of pain but because of the act. His mother ran upstairs and grabbed JoJo, asking what happened. JoJo responded, daddy pinched me. Drew grabbed JoJo and reprimanded me saying I told you not to do that to him. I asked JoJo to demonstrate on his mother exactly how hard I pinched him and he barely touched his mother. I walked out the room as I felt emasculated and minimized below a child. I thought to myself if I wanted to stay in a relationship where I didn't have a parenting voice. Besides all that I've done and contributed, I should feel more respected. We ended up seeking out a marriage counselor that told us we're doing things all wrong. We didn't have a plan and it shows.

but she did ask for my thoughts to correct him sleeping in the bed.

Introduce Drew's mom, millinial

Support we had and lacked

Realistic / Unrealistic Expectations

It's either him or me

Village mindset, when JoJo's dad came home, Respect. Territorial. No this is my house.

Drew received a call from JoJo's biological dad that he came home from jail and wanted to see his son if possible. At the time Drew was still hurt by the lack of support and effort. Her perspective was, if you haven't been around or made an effort all this time, why now. JoJo doesn't need you. Besides she had me in her life which "filled" the void of JoJo's lack of a father figure. Once Drew brought the conversation and intention to my attention, I had a lot of thinking to do also. As a man or the other man in the situation, I had several thoughts run through my mind. As men, we can rightfully be territorial and protective of their

castle. After I let my pride down, put myself in his shoes and think big picture, there were a few things I had to evaluate. Did JoJo's father approach the situation respectfully for my wife and also for me? Did he do anything to neglect the wellbeing and safety of JoJo? What is the intention? Is this relationship in the best interest for JoJo? I immediately thought of my father and our circumstances.

As a child, no one couldn't tell me that my father wasn't the best in the world and guess what, that's my perspective. If you measured or quantified the value of our relationship, there would be large gaps in his presence, missed games and events, missed birthdays, missed growth and bonding opportunities. Yet, my father was still the best thing that could have ever happened to me. How could this be, the heart doesn't measure value in the way our minds do. Love is blind and that's what makes love beautiful, innocent and cherished. Without love, we would be robots, incapable of forgiving or giving someone an opportunity to succeed. If we were robotic in our heart, we would leave a baby that didn't learn to walk fast enough or talk. Sometimes the greatest lessons on earth is experiencing life.

Interesting enough, Initially I didn't speak with JoJo's biological father as Drew had to feel comfortable with the interaction first however I was always by her side supporting the process. Change is very hard especially on a child therefore she wanted to make sure he wanted to really be part of his life before introducing his Father and he deciding he didn't want that role. Consistency is important to know if you're in this for the long run or if it's a nice experience because you think you should do it. Drew put JoJo's father on a call schedule to slowly introduce JoJo to his Father. JoJo visited with him as a baby but it's been years since they spoke and as a child, they don't know what a father means. The first few interactions was awkward just as any person that walks into a child's life that doesn't have kids, there is a learning process.

Adoption Because JoJo's father wasn't around, people would ask if I would adopt him, which is a great question. These are my rules on adopting in a blended family:

The Father doesn't want to be in the child's life therefore the child is fatherless

The Father is deceased.

The child is in harm or danger, therefore it's an unfit home.

The child doesn't have parents

In the event the child's mother dies, custody can be established through court order.....Find out the process. I really don't know.

If I would have adopted Josiah.

JoJo will get to a point where he seeks information and understanding for himself and he would approach his father asking, why didn't he make an effort to be in his life. His Father would more than likely respond, your parents didn't allow me to be a part of your life and pushed me out. JoJo can possibly develop resentment due to our actions, even if we felt it was in his best interest.

This is a great segway into the definition of "Dad." Dads come in all different forms, types, relationships and can be interchangeable for almost anyone providing support that uplifts positive change and growth. When my father wasn't around, coaches became father figures to me including men in the community that taught me fundamentals of manhood. When my father wasn't around, men in the community would hire me and my brother to pickup leaves. It probably was one of the worst jobs I've ever experienced but it built character and work ethic that I wouldn't trade for the world. There is a village that becomes available to instill the lessons children need to learn and the role of "dad" can often be spread throughout the village to ensure children learn fundamentals of life. This concept also applies when the dad is around. Everyone is limited on the amount of information we know. If someone excels in a certain area, send the child to exceed your own understanding as the future depends on our children being smarter and more skilled than us.

Confidence I'm a firm believer that what's for me is for me and no one can take it away. If something isn't for me, then it was only supposed to be in my life for a season and I'm fine.

Being okay with JoJo's biological dad coming into the picture Studies show, 85% of blended familes are dysfunctional. While Drew and I were dating, she was very intentional not to allow me to play the dad role. She didn't want to scare me off or put responsibility on me before we had a chance to know if our relationship would last. Her family also assisted in our dating process. Their goal was to help Drew find the man of her dreams and would take JoJo so she could go out on dates. Well, that strategy worked! Drew and I went on a date that lasted 12hrs. Her family wasn't very happy when I brought her home at 4am. To no despair, we stayed in contact and she became my wife. I would ask Drew if I could take JoJo for ice cream or take him to the park while she was working if I felt she needed a helping hand so I could build a stronger bond with him. I knew if I married Drew, he would become my son. JoJo's biological father currently wasn't around and I knew JoJo needed a male influence to help him navigate the world, instill moral and values and grow into the man he would become. I had great expectations however I didn't know what a son or father figure meant from my wifes's eyes. My thought was once we were married, I would automatically take on the father role.

In our scenario, we got married extremely fast and Drew was pregnant 2mo after. We had a huge decision to make, where do we stay to raise the kids. At the time we were in LA and didn't feel like we had much support. We could either go to NJ to my family or Chicago with her family. I spoke with Drew's mom and she said I really can't help you if you stay in LA. Drew has a big family, her mom and dad and 4 sisters. It was a no brainer and we relocated to Chicago before Machai was born. I didn't have a chance to fully assume the "Dad" role as everything was moving fast. We were living under the same roof however Drew was making moves the way she programmed and without much

involvement or opinion from my side. There were a few things that I didn't like entirely too much such as JoJo staying up until any time he wanted as if he was a little rockstar in a diaper and him sleeping in the same bed. Drew wasn't receptive to him staying up late and defended by saying she's an actress and her hours flucturate. To combat, I provided studies and reports on best practices for sleeping. I also provided a guidance for the tv staying on all night and she said her parents did it with them and everyone is okay so it's not that bad. I tried developing the "My House, My Rules" concept but it quickly fell on death ears as my concerns weren't enforced. Opposed to supporting, JoJo would cry and mom would come to the rescue. I began to see a common thread, where JoJo was also learning how to get his way and It then became an issue where it was Me vs. Them.

Boiling Point where I felt I couldn't parent

Due to JoJo not receiving adequate sleep, he struggled to get up for school in the morning. Being a man, I had my way of getting you to follow directions which was to place the fear of God in you because at the end of the day, I'm the parent. JoJo stood by the sink and didn't want to brush his teeth so I "acted" as if I was going to give him a pinch and he started crying, not because of pain but because of the act. His mother ran upstairs and grabbed JoJo, asking what happened. JoJo responded, daddy pinched me. Drew grabbed JoJo and repremanded me saying I told you not to do that to him. I asked JoJo to demonstrate on his mother exactly how hard I pinched him and he barely touched his mother. I walked out the room as I felt emasculated and minimized below a child. I thought to myself if I wanted to stay in a relationship where I didn't have a parenting voice. Besides all that I've done and contributed, I should feel more respected. We ended up seeking out a marriage counselor that told us we're doing things all wrong. We didn't have a plan and it shows.

but she did ask for my thoughts to correct him sleeping in the bed.

Introduce Drew's mom, millinial

Support we had and lacked
Realistic / Unrealistic Expectations
It's either him or me
Village mindset, when JoJo's dad came home, Respect. Territorial. No this is my house.

Drew received a call from JoJo's biological dad that he came home from jail and wanted to see his son if possible. At the time Drew was still hurt by the lack of support and effort. Her perspective was, if you haven't been around or made an effort all this time, why now. JoJo doesn't need you. Besides she had me in her life which "filled" the void of JoJo's lack of a father figure. Once Drew brought the conversation and intention to my attention, I had a lot of thinking to do also. As a man or the other man in the situation, I had several thoughts run through my mind. As men, we can rightfully be territorial and protective of their castle. After I let my pride down, put myself in his shoes and think big picture, there were a few things I had to evaluate. Did JoJo's father approach the situation respectfully for my wife and also for me? Did he do anything to neglect the wellbeing and safety of JoJo? What is the intention? Is this relationship in the best interest for JoJo? I immediately thought of my father and our circumstances.

As a child, no one couldn't tell me that my father wasn't the best in the world and guess what, that's my perspective. If you measured or quantified the value of our relationship, there would be large gaps in his presence, missed games and events, missed birthdays, missed growth and bonding opportunities. Yet, my father was still the best thing that could have ever happened to me. How could this be, the heart doesn't measure value in the way our minds do. Love is blind and that's what makes love beautiful, innocent and cherished. Without love, we would be robots, incapable of forgiving or giving someone an opportunity to succeed. If we were robotic in our heart, we would leave a baby that didn't learn to walk fast enough or talk. Sometimes the greatest lessons on earth is experiencing life.

Interesting enough, Initially I didn't speak with JoJo's biological father as Drew had to feel comfortable with the interaction first however I was always by her side supporting the process. Change is very hard especially on a child therefore she wanted to make sure he wanted to really be part of his life before introducing his Father and he deciding he didn't want that role. Consistency is important to know if you're in this for the long run or if it's a nice experience because you think you should do it. Drew put JoJo's father on a call schedule to slowly introduce JoJo to his Father. JoJo visited with him as a baby but it's been years since they spoke and as a child, they don't know what a father means. The first few interactions was awkward just as any person that walks into a child's life that doesn't have kids, there is a learning process.

Adoption Because JoJo's father wasn't around, people would ask if I would adopt him, which is a great question. These are my rules on adopting in a blended family:

The Father doesn't want to be in the child's life therefore the child is fatherless

The Father is deceased.

The child is in harm or danger, therefore it's an unfit home.

The child doesn't have parents

In the event the child's mother dies, custody can be established through court order.....Find out the process. I really don't know.

If I would have adopted Josiah.

JoJo will get to a point where he seeks information and understanding for himself and he would approach his father asking, why didn't he make an effort to be in his life. His Father would more than likely respond, your parents didn't allow me to be a part of your life and pushed me out. JoJo can possibly develop resentment due to our actions, even if we felt it was in his best interest.

This is a great segway into the definition of "Dad." Dads come in all different forms, types, relationships and can be interchangeable for almost anyone providing support that uplifts positive

251

change and growth. When my father wasn't around, coaches became father figures to me including men in the community that taught me fundamentals of manhood. When my father wasn't around, men in the community would hire me and my brother to pickup leaves. It probably was one of the worst jobs I've ever experienced but it built character and work ethic that I wouldn't trade for the world. There is a village that becomes available to instill the lessons children need to learn and the role of "dad" can often be spread throughout the village to ensure children learn fundamentals of life. This concept also applies when the dad is around. Everyone is limited on the amount of information we know. If someone excels in a certain area, send the child to exceed your own understanding as the future depends on our children being smarter and more skilled than us.

Confidence I'm a firm believer that what's for me is for me and no one can take it away. If something isn't for me, then it was only supposed to be in my life for a season and I'm fine.

Being okay with JoJo's biological dad coming into the picture Studies show, 85% of blended familes are dysfunctional.

In our scenario, we got married extremely fast and Drew was pregnant 2mo after. We had a huge decision to make, where do we stay to raise the kids. At the time we were in LA and didn't feel like we had much support. We could either go to NJ to my family or Chicago with her family. I spoke with Drew's mom and she said I really can't help you if you stay in LA. Drew has a big family, her mom and dad and 4 sisters. It was a no brainer and we relocated to Chicago before Machai was born. I didn't have a chance to fully assume the "Dad" role as everything was moving fast. We were living under the same roof however Drew was making moves the way she programmed and without much involvement or opinion from my side. There were a few things that I didn't like entirely too much such as JoJo staying up until any time he wanted as if he was a little rockstar in a diaper and him sleeping in the same bed. Drew wasn't receptive to him staying up late and defended by saying she's an actress and her hours flucturate. To combat, I provided studies and reports on best practices for sleeping. I also provided a guidance for the tv staying on all night and she said her parents did it with them and everyone is okay so it's not that bad. I tried developing the "My House, My Rules" concept but it quickly fell on death ears as my concerns weren't enforced. Opposed to supporting, JoJo would cry and mom would come to the rescue. I began to see a common thread, where JoJo was also learning how to get his way and It then became an issue where it was Me vs. Them.

Boiling Point where I felt I couldn't parent

Due to JoJo not receiving adequate sleep, he struggled to get up for school in the morning. Being a man, I had my way of getting you to follow directions which was to place the fear of God in you because at the end of the day, I'm the parent. JoJo stood by the sink and didn't want to brush his teeth so I "acted" as if I was going to give him a pinch and he started crying, not because of pain but because of the act. His mother ran upstairs and grabbed JoJo, asking what happened. JoJo responded, daddy pinched me. Drew grabbed JoJo and repremanded me saying I told you not to do that to him. I asked JoJo to demonstrate on his mother exactly how hard I pinched him and he barely touched his mother. I walked out the room as I felt emasculated and minimized below a child. I thought to myself if I wanted to stay in a relationship where I didn't have a parenting voice. Besides all that I've done and contributed, I should feel more respected. We ended up seeking out a marriage counselor that told us we're doing things all wrong. We didn't have a plan and it shows.

but she did ask for my thoughts to correct him sleeping in the bed.

Introduce Drew's mom, millinial

Support we had and lacked

Realistic / Unrealistic Expectations

It's either him or me

Village mindset, when JoJo's dad came home, Respect. Territorial. No this is my house.

Drew received a call from JoJo's biological dad that he came home from jail and wanted to see his son if possible. At the time Drew was still hurt by the lack of support and effort. Her perspective was, if you haven't been around or made an effort all this time, why now. JoJo doesn't need you. Besides she had me in her life which "filled" the void of JoJo's lack of a father figure. Once Drew brought the conversation and intention to my attention, I had a lot of thinking to do also. As a man or the other man in the situation, I had several thoughts run through my mind. As men, we can rightfully be territorial and protective of their castle. After I let my pride down, put myself in his shoes and think big picture, there were a few things I had to evaluate. Did JoJo's father approach the situation respectfully for my wife and also for me? Did he do anything to neglect the wellbeing and safety of JoJo? What is the intention? Is this relationship in the best interest for JoJo? I immediately thought of my father and our circumstances.

As a child, no one couldn't tell me that my father wasn't the best in the world and guess what, that's my perspective. If you measured or quantified the value of our relationship, there would be large gaps in his presence, missed games and events, missed birthdays, missed growth and bonding opportunities. Yet, my father was still the best thing that could have ever happened to me. How could this be, the heart doesn't measure value in the way our minds do. Love is blind and that's what makes love beautiful, innocent and cherished. Without love, we would be robots, incapable of forgiving or giving someone an opportunity to succeed. If we were robotic in our heart, we would leave a baby that didn't learn to walk fast enough or talk. Sometimes the greatest lessons on earth is experiencing life.

Interesting enough, Initially I didn't speak with JoJo's biological father as Drew had to feel comfortable with the interaction first however I was always by her side supporting the process. Change is very hard especially on a child therefore she wanted to make sure he wanted to really be part of his life before

introducing his Father and he deciding he didn't want that role. Consistency is important to know if you're in this for the long run or if it's a nice experience because you think you should do it. Drew put JoJo's father on a call schedule to slowly introduce JoJo to his Father. JoJo visited with him as a baby but it's been years since they spoke and as a child, they don't know what a father means. The first few interactions was awkward just as any person that walks into a child's life that doesn't have kids, there is a learning process.

Adoption Because JoJo's father wasn't around, people would ask if I would adopt him, which is a great question. These are my rules on adopting in a blended family:

The Father doesn't want to be in the child's life therefore the child is fatherless

The Father is deceased.

The child is in harm or danger, therefore it's an unfit home.

The child doesn't have parents

In the event the child's mother dies, custody can be established through court order......Find out the process. I really don't know.

If I would have adopted Josiah.

JoJo will get to a point where he seeks information and understanding for himself and he would approach his father asking, why didn't he make an effort to be in his life. His Father would more than likely respond, your parents didn't allow me to be a part of your life and pushed me out. JoJo can possibly develop resentment due to our actions, even if we felt it was in his best interest.

This is a great segway into the definition of "Dad." Dads come in all different forms, types, relationships and can be interchangeable for almost anyone providing support that uplifts positive change and growth. When my father wasn't around, coaches became father figures to me including men in the community that taught me fundamentals of manhood. When my father wasn't around, men in the community would hire me and my brother to pickup leaves. It probably was one of the worst jobs I've ever

experienced but it built character and work ethic that I wouldn't trade for the world. There is a village that becomes available to instill the lessons children need to learn and the role of "dad" can often be spread throughout the village to ensure children learn fundamentals of life. This concept also applies when the dad is around. Everyone is limited on the amount of information we know. If someone excels in a certain area, send the child to exceed your own understanding as the future depends on our children being smarter and more skilled than us.

Confidence I'm a firm believer that what's for me is for me and no one can take it away. If something isn't for me, then it was only supposed to be in my life for a season and I'm fine.

Being okay with JoJo's biological dad coming into the picture Studies show, 85% of blended familes are dysfunctional. While Drew and I were dating, she was very intentional not to allow me to play the dad role. She didn't want to scare me off or put responsibility on me before we had a chance to know if our relationship would last. Her family also assisted in our dating process. Their goal was to help Drew find the man of her dreams and would take JoJo so she could go out on dates. Well, that strategy worked! Drew and I went on a date that lasted 12hrs. Her family wasn't very happy when I brought her home at 4am. To no despair, we stayed in contact and she became my wife. I would ask Drew if I could take JoJo for ice cream or take him to the park while she was working if I felt she needed a helping hand so I could build a stronger bond with him. I knew if I married Drew, he would become my son. JoJo's biological father currently wasn't around and I knew JoJo needed a male influence to help him navigate the world, instill moral and values and grow into the man he would become. I had great expectations however I didn't know what a son or father figure meant from my wifes's eyes. My thought was once we were married, I would automatically take on the father role.

In our scenario, we got married extremely fast and Drew was pregnant 2mo after. We had a huge decision to make, where do

we stay to raise the kids. At the time we were in LA and didn't feel like we had much support. We could either go to NJ to my family or Chicago with her family. I spoke with Drew's mom and she said I really can't help you if you stay in LA. Drew has a big family, her mom and dad and 4 sisters. It was a no brainer and we relocated to Chicago before Machai was born. I didn't have a chance to fully assume the "Dad" role as everything was moving fast. We were living under the same roof however Drew was making moves the way she programmed and without much involvement or opinion from my side. There were a few things that I didn't like entirely too much such as JoJo staying up until any time he wanted as if he was a little rockstar in a diaper and him sleeping in the same bed. Drew wasn't receptive to him staying up late and defended by saying she's an actress and her hours flucturate. To combat, I provided studies and reports on best practices for sleeping. I also provided a guidance for the tv staying on all night and she said her parents did it with them and everyone is okay so it's not that bad. I tried developing the "My House, My Rules" concept but it quickly fell on death ears as my concerns weren't enforced. Opposed to supporting, JoJo would cry and mom would come to the rescue. I began to see a common thread, where JoJo was also learning how to get his way and It then became an issue where it was Me vs. Them.

Boiling Point where I felt I couldn't parent

Due to JoJo not receiving adequate sleep, he struggled to get up for school in the morning. Being a man, I had my way of getting you to follow directions which was to place the fear of God in you because at the end of the day, I'm the parent. JoJo stood by the sink and didn't want to brush his teeth so I "acted" as if I was going to give him a pinch and he started crying, not because of pain but because of the act. His mother ran upstairs and grabbed JoJo, asking what happened. JoJo responded, daddy pinched me. Drew grabbed JoJo and reprimanded me saying I told you not to do that to him. I asked JoJo to demonstrate on his mother exactly how hard I pinched him and he barely touched

his mother. I walked out the room as I felt emasculated and min-imized below a child. I thought to myself if I wanted to stay in a relationship where I didn't have a parenting voice. Besides all that I've done and contributed, I should feel more respected. We ended up seeking out a marriage counselor that told us we're doing things all wrong. We didn't have a plan and it shows.

but she did ask for my thoughts to correct him sleeping in the bed.

Introduce Drew's mom, millinial

Support we had and lacked

Realistic / Unrealistic Expectations

It's either him or me

Village mindset, when JoJo's dad came home, Respect. Territorial. No this is my house.

Drew received a call from JoJo's biological dad that he came home from jail and wanted to see his son if possible. At the time Drew was still hurt by the lack of support and effort. Her per-spective was, if you haven't been around or made an effort all this time, why now. JoJo doesn't need you. Besides she had me in her life which "filled" the void of JoJo's lack of a father figure. Once Drew brought the conversation and intention to my atten-tion, I had a lot of thinking to do also. As a man or the other man in the situation, I had several thoughts run through my mind. As men, we can rightfully be territorial and protective of their castle. After I let my pride down, put myself in his shoes and think big picture, there were a few things I had to evaluate. Did JoJo's father approach the situation respectfully for my wife and also for me? Did he do anything to neglect the wellbeing and safety of JoJo? What is the intention? Is this relationship in the best interest for JoJo? I immediately thought of my father and our circumstances.

As a child, no one couldn't tell me that my father wasn't the best in the world and guess what, that's my perspective. If you measured or quantified the value of our relationship, there would be large gaps in his presence, missed games and events,

missed birthdays, missed growth and bonding opportunities. Yet, my father was still the best thing that could have ever happened to me. How could this be, the heart doesn't measure value in the way our minds do. Love is blind and that's what makes love beautiful, innocent and cherished. Without love, we would be robots, incapable of forgiving or giving someone an opportunity to succeed. If we were robotic in our heart, we would leave a baby that didn't learn to walk fast enough or talk. Sometimes the greatest lessons on earth is experiencing life.

Interesting enough, Initially I didn't speak with JoJo's biological father as Drew had to feel comfortable with the interaction first however I was always by her side supporting the process. Change is very hard especially on a child therefore she wanted to make sure he wanted to really be part of his life before introducing his Father and he deciding he didn't want that role. Consistency is important to know if you're in this for the long run or if it's a nice experience because you think you should do it. Drew put JoJo's father on a call schedule to slowly introduce JoJo to his Father. JoJo visited with him as a baby but it's been years since they spoke and as a child, they don't know what a father means. The first few interactions was awkward just as any person that walks into a child's life that doesn't have kids, there is a learning process.

Adoption Because JoJo's father wasn't around, people would ask if I would adopt him, which is a great question. These are my rules on adopting in a blended family:

The Father doesn't want to be in the child's life therefore the child is fatherless

The Father is deceased.

The child is in harm or danger, therefore it's an unfit home.

The child doesn't have parents

In the event the child's mother dies, custody can be established through court order.....Find out the process. I really don't know.

If I would have adopted Josiah.

JoJo will get to a point where he seeks information and understanding for himself and he would approach his father asking, why didn't he make an effort to be in his life. His Father would more than likely respond, your parents didn't allow me to be a part of your life and pushed me out. JoJo can possibly develop resentment due to our actions, even if we felt it was in his best interest.

This is a great segway into the definition of "Dad." Dads come in all different forms, types, relationships and can be interchangeable for almost anyone providing support that uplifts positive change and growth. When my father wasn't around, coaches became father figures to me including men in the community that taught me fundamentals of manhood. When my father wasn't around, men in the community would hire me and my brother to pickup leaves. It probably was one of the worst jobs I've ever experienced but it built character and work ethic that I wouldn't trade for the world. There is a village that becomes available to instill the lessons children need to learn and the role of "dad" can often be spread throughout the village to ensure children learn fundamentals of life. This concept also applies when the dad is around. Everyone is limited on the amount of information we know. If someone excels in a certain area, send the child to exceed your own understanding as the future depends on our children being smarter and more skilled than us.

Confidence I'm a firm believer that what's for me is for me and no one can take it away. If something isn't for me, then it was only supposed to be in my life for a season and I'm fine.

Being okay with JoJo's biological dad coming into the picture Studies show, 85% of blended familes are dysfunctional.

In our scenario, we got married extremely fast and Drew was pregnant 2mo after. We had a huge decision to make, where do we stay to raise the kids. At the time we were in LA and didn't feel like we had much support. We could either go to NJ to my family or Chicago with her family. I spoke with Drew's mom and she said I really can't help you if you stay in LA. Drew has a big family, her mom and dad and 4 sisters. It was a no brainer and we relocated to Chicago before Machai was born. I didn't have a chance to fully assume the "Dad" role as everything was moving fast. We were living under the same roof however Drew was making moves the way she programmed and without much involvement or opinion from my side. There were a few things that I didn't like entirely too much such as JoJo staying up until any time he wanted as if he was a little rockstar in a diaper and him sleeping in the same bed. Drew wasn't receptive to him staying up late and defended by saying she's an actress and her hours flucturate. To combat, I provided studies and reports on best practices for sleeping. I also provided a guidance for the tv staying on all night and she said her parents did it with them and everyone is okay so it's not that bad. I tried developing the "My House, My Rules" concept but it quickly fell on death ears as my concerns weren't enforced. Opposed to supporting, JoJo would cry and mom would come to the rescue. I began to see a common thread, where JoJo was also learning how to get his way and It then became an issue where it was Me vs. Them.

Boiling Point where I felt I couldn't parent

Due to JoJo not receiving adequate sleep, he struggled to get up for school in the morning. Being a man, I had my way of getting you to follow directions which was to place the fear of God in you because at the end of the day, I'm the parent. JoJo stood by the sink and didn't want to brush his teeth so I "acted" as if I was going to give him a pinch and he started crying, not because of pain but because of the act. His mother ran upstairs and grabbed JoJo, asking what happened. JoJo responded, daddy pinched me. Drew grabbed JoJo and repremanded me saying I told you not to do that to him. I asked JoJo to demonstrate on his mother exactly how hard I pinched him and he barely touched his mother. I walked out the room as I felt emasculated and minimized below a child. I thought to myself if I wanted to stay in a relationship where I didn't have a parenting voice. Besides all that I've done and contributed, I should feel more respected. We

ended up seeking out a marriage counselor that told us we're doing things all wrong. We didn't have a plan and it shows.

but she did ask for my thoughts to correct him sleeping in the bed.

Introduce Drew's mom, millinial

Support we had and lacked

Realistic / Unrealistic Expectations

It's either him or me

Village mindset, when JoJo's dad came home, Respect. Territorial. No this is my house.

Drew received a call from JoJo's biological dad that he came home from jail and wanted to see his son if possible. At the time Drew was still hurt by the lack of support and effort. Her perspective was, if you haven't been around or made an effort all this time, why now. JoJo doesn't need you. Besides she had me in her life which "filled" the void of JoJo's lack of a father figure. Once Drew brought the conversation and intention to my attention, I had a lot of thinking to do also. As a man or the other man in the situation, I had several thoughts run through my mind. As men, we can rightfully be territorial and protective of their castle. After I let my pride down, put myself in his shoes and think big picture, there were a few things I had to evaluate. Did JoJo's father approach the situation respectfully for my wife and also for me? Did he do anything to neglect the wellbeing and safety of JoJo? What is the intention? Is this relationship in the best interest for JoJo? I immediately thought of my father and our circumstances.

As a child, no one couldn't tell me that my father wasn't the best in the world and guess what, that's my perspective. If you measured or quantified the value of our relationship, there would be large gaps in his presence, missed games and events, missed birthdays, missed growth and bonding opportunities. Yet, my father was still the best thing that could have ever happened to me. How could this be, the heart doesn't measure value in the way our minds do. Love is blind and that's what makes

love beautiful, innocent and cherished. Without love, we would be robots, incapable of forgiving or giving someone an opportunity to succeed. If we were robotic in our heart, we would leave a baby that didn't learn to walk fast enough or talk. Sometimes the greatest lessons on earth is experiencing life.

Interesting enough, Initially I didn't speak with JoJo's biological father as Drew had to feel comfortable with the interaction first however I was always by her side supporting the process. Change is very hard especially on a child therefore she wanted to make sure he wanted to really be part of his life before introducing his Father and he deciding he didn't want that role. Consistency is important to know if you're in this for the long run or if it's a nice experience because you think you should do it. Drew put JoJo's father on a call schedule to slowly introduce JoJo to his Father. JoJo visited with him as a baby but it's been years since they spoke and as a child, they don't know what a father means. The first few interactions was awkward just as any person that walks into a child's life that doesn't have kids, there is a learning process.

Adoption Because JoJo's father wasn't around, people would ask if I would adopt him, which is a great question. These are my rules on adopting in a blended family:

The Father doesn't want to be in the child's life therefore the child is fatherless

The Father is deceased.

The child is in harm or danger, therefore it's an unfit home.

The child doesn't have parents

In the event the child's mother dies, custody can be established through court order.....Find out the process. I really don't know.

If I would have adopted Josiah.

JoJo will get to a point where he seeks information and understanding for himself and he would approach his father asking, why didn't he make an effort to be in his life. His Father would more than likely respond, your parents didn't allow me to be a part of your life and pushed me out. JoJo can possibly develop

resentment due to our actions, even if we felt it was in his best interest.

This is a great segway into the definition of "Dad." Dads come in all different forms, types, relationships and can be interchangeable for almost anyone providing support that uplifts positive change and growth. When my father wasn't around, coaches became father figures to me including men in the community that taught me fundamentals of manhood. When my father wasn't around, men in the community would hire me and my brother to pickup leaves. It probably was one of the worst jobs I've ever experienced but it built character and work ethic that I wouldn't trade for the world. There is a village that becomes available to instill the lessons children need to learn and the role of "dad" can often be spread throughout the village to ensure children learn fundamentals of life. This concept also applies when the dad is around. Everyone is limited on the amount of information we know. If someone excels in a certain area, send the child to exceed your own understanding as the future depends on our children being smarter and more skilled than us.

Confidence I'm a firm believer that what's for me is for me and no one can take it away. If something isn't for me, then it was only supposed to be in my life for a season and I'm fine.

Being okay with JoJo's biological dad coming into the picture Studies show, 85% of blended familes are dysfunctional. While Drew and I were dating, she was very intentional not to allow me to play the dad role. She didn't want to scare me off or put responsibility on me before we had a chance to know if our relationship would last. Her family also assisted in our dating process. Their goal was to help Drew find the man of her dreams and would take JoJo so she could go out on dates. Well, that strategy worked! Drew and I went on a date that lasted 12hrs. Her family wasn't very happy when I brought her home at 4am. To no despair, we stayed in contact and she became my wife. I would ask Drew if I could take JoJo for ice cream or take him to the park while she was working if I felt she needed a helping hand

so I could build a stronger bond with him. I knew if I married Drew, he would become my son. JoJo's biological father currently wasn't around and I knew JoJo needed a male influence to help him navigate the world, instill moral and values and grow into the man he would become. I had great expectations however I didn't know what a son or father figure meant from my wifes's eyes. My thought was once we were married, I would automatically take on the father role.

In our scenario, we got married extremely fast and Drew was pregnant 2mo after. We had a huge decision to make, where do we stay to raise the kids. At the time we were in LA and didn't feel like we had much support. We could either go to NJ to my family or Chicago with her family. I spoke with Drew's mom and she said I really can't help you if you stay in LA. Drew has a big family, her mom and dad and 4 sisters. It was a no brainer and we relocated to Chicago before Machai was born. I didn't have a chance to fully assume the "Dad" role as everything was moving fast. We were living under the same roof however Drew was making moves the way she programmed and without much involvement or opinion from my side. There were a few things that I didn't like entirely too much such as JoJo staying up until any time he wanted as if he was a little rockstar in a diaper and him sleeping in the same bed. Drew wasn't receptive to him staying up late and defended by saying she's an actress and her hours flucturate. To combat, I provided studies and reports on best practices for sleeping. I also provided a guidance for the tv staying on all night and she said her parents did it with them and everyone is okay so it's not that bad. I tried developing the "My House, My Rules" concept but it quickly fell on death ears as my concerns weren't enforced. Opposed to supporting, JoJo would cry and mom would come to the rescue. I began to see a common thread, where JoJo was also learning how to get his way and It then became an issue where it was Me vs. Them.

Boiling Point where I felt I couldn't parent

THE STEP IN PARENTING

Due to JoJo not receiving adequate sleep, he struggled to get up for school in the morning. Being a man, I had my way of getting you to follow directions which was to place the fear of God in you because at the end of the day, I'm the parent. JoJo stood by the sink and didn't want to brush his teeth so I "acted" as if I was going to give him a pinch and he started crying, not because of pain but because of the act. His mother ran upstairs and grabbed JoJo, asking what happened. JoJo responded, daddy pinched me. Drew grabbed JoJo and repremanded me saying I told you not to do that to him. I asked JoJo to demonstrate on his mother exactly how hard I pinched him and he barely touched his mother. I walked out the room as I felt emasculated and minimized below a child. I thought to myself if I wanted to stay in a relationship where I didn't have a parenting voice. Besides all that I've done and contributed, I should feel more respected. We ended up seeking out a marriage counselor that told us we're doing things all wrong. We didn't have a plan and it shows.

but she did ask for my thoughts to correct him sleeping in the bed.

Introduce Drew's mom, millinial

Support we had and lacked

Realistic / Unrealistic Expectations

It's either him or me

Village mindset, when JoJo's dad came home, Respect. Territorial. No this is my house.

Drew received a call from JoJo's biological dad that he came home from jail and wanted to see his son if possible. At the time Drew was still hurt by the lack of support and effort. Her perspective was, if you haven't been around or made an effort all this time, why now. JoJo doesn't need you. Besides she had me in her life which "filled" the void of JoJo's lack of a father figure. Once Drew brought the conversation and intention to my attention, I had a lot of thinking to do also. As a man or the other man in the situation, I had several thoughts run through my mind. As men, we can rightfully be territorial and protective of their

castle. After I let my pride down, put myself in his shoes and think big picture, there were a few things I had to evaluate. Did JoJo's father approach the situation respectfully for my wife and also for me? Did he do anything to neglect the wellbeing and safety of JoJo? What is the intention? Is this relationship in the best interest for JoJo? I immediately thought of my father and our circumstances.

As a child, no one couldn't tell me that my father wasn't the best in the world and guess what, that's my perspective. If you measured or quantified the value of our relationship, there would be large gaps in his presence, missed games and events, missed birthdays, missed growth and bonding opportunities. Yet, my father was still the best thing that could have ever happened to me. How could this be, the heart doesn't measure value in the way our minds do. Love is blind and that's what makes love beautiful, innocent and cherished. Without love, we would be robots, incapable of forgiving or giving someone an opportunity to succeed. If we were robotic in our heart, we would leave a baby that didn't learn to walk fast enough or talk. Sometimes the greatest lessons on earth is experiencing life.

Interesting enough, Initially I didn't speak with JoJo's biological father as Drew had to feel comfortable with the interaction first however I was always by her side supporting the process. Change is very hard especially on a child therefore she wanted to make sure he wanted to really be part of his life before introducing his Father and he deciding he didn't want that role. Consistency is important to know if you're in this for the long run or if it's a nice experience because you think you should do it. Drew put JoJo's father on a call schedule to slowly introduce JoJo to his Father. JoJo visited with him as a baby but it's been years since they spoke and as a child, they don't know what a father means. The first few interactions was awkward just as any person that walks into a child's life that doesn't have kids, there is a learning process.

Me vs. Them

JOJO WILL GET to a point where he seeks information and understanding for himself and he would approach his father asking, why didn't he make an effort to be in his life. His Father would more than likely respond, your parents didn't allow me to be a part of your life and pushed me out. JoJo can possibly develop resentment due to our actions, even if we felt it was in his best interest.

This is a great segway into the definition of "Dad." Dads come in all different forms, types, relationships and can be interchangeable for almost anyone providing support that uplifts positive change and growth. When my father wasn't around, coaches became father figures to me including men in the community that taught me fundamentals of manhood. When my father wasn't around, men in the community would hire me and my brother to pickup leaves. It probably was one of the worst jobs I've ever experienced but it built character and work ethic that I wouldn't trade for the world. There is a village that becomes available to instill the lessons children need to learn and the role of "dad" can often be spread throughout the village to ensure children learn fundamentals of life. This concept also applies when the dad is around. Everyone is limited on the amount of information we know. If someone excels in a certain area, send the child to exceed your own understanding as the future depends on our children being smarter and more skilled than us.

Confidence I'm a firm believer that what's for me is for me and no one can take it away. If something isn't for me, then it was only supposed to be in my life for a season and I'm fine.

Being okay with JoJo's biological dad coming into the picture Studies show, 85% of blended famiies are dysfunctional.

In our scenario, we got married extremely fast and Drew was pregnant 2mo after. We had a huge decision to make, where do we stay to raise the kids. At the time we were in LA and didn't feel like we had much support. We could either go to NJ to my family or Chicago with her family. I spoke with Drew's mom and she said I really can't help you if you stay in LA. Drew has a big family, her mom and dad and 4 sisters. It was a no brainer and we relocated to Chicago before Machai was born. I didn't have a chance to fully assume the "Dad" role as everything was moving fast. We were living under the same roof however Drew was making moves the way she programmed and without much involvement or opinion from my side. There were a few things that I didn't like entirely too much such as JoJo staying up until any time he wanted as if he was a little rockstar in a diaper and him sleeping in the same bed. Drew wasn't receptive to him staying up late and defended by saying she's an actress and her hours flucturate. To combat, I provided studies and reports on best practices for sleeping. I also provided a guidance for the tv staying on all night and she said her parents did it with them and everyone is okay so it's not that bad. I tried developing the "My House, My Rules" concept but it quickly fell on death ears as my concerns weren't enforced. Opposed to supporting, JoJo would cry and mom would come to the rescue. I began to see a common thread, where JoJo was also learning how to get his way and It then became an issue where it was Me vs. Them.

Boiling Point where I felt I couldn't parent

Due to JoJo not receiving adequate sleep, he struggled to get up for school in the morning. Being a man, I had my way of getting you to follow directions which was to place the fear of God in you because at the end of the day, I'm the parent. JoJo stood by the sink and didn't want to brush his teeth so I "acted" as if I was going to give him a pinch and he started crying, not because of pain but because of the act. His mother ran upstairs and grabbed JoJo, asking what happened. JoJo responded, daddy pinched me. Drew grabbed JoJo and repremanded me saying I told you not to do that to him. I asked JoJo to demonstrate on his mother exactly how hard I pinched him and he barely touched his mother. I walked out the room as I felt emasculated and minimized below a child. I thought to myself if I wanted to stay in a relationship where I didn't have a parenting voice. Besides all that I've done and contributed, I should feel more respected. We ended up seeking out a marriage counselor that told us we're doing things all wrong. We didn't have a plan and it shows.

but she did ask for my thoughts to correct him sleeping in the bed.

Introduce Drew's mom, millinial

Support we had and lacked

Realistic / Unrealistic Expectations

It's either him or me

Village mindset, when JoJo's dad came home, Respect. Territorial. No this is my house.

Drew received a call from JoJo's biological dad that he came home from jail and wanted to see his son if possible. At the time Drew was still hurt by the lack of support and effort. Her perspective was, if you haven't been around or made an effort all this time, why now. JoJo doesn't need you. Besides she had me in her life which "filled" the void of JoJo's lack of a father figure. Once Drew brought the conversation and intention to my attention, I had a lot of thinking to do also. As a man or the other man in the situation, I had several thoughts run through my mind. As men, we can rightfully be territorial and protective of their castle. After I let my pride down, put myself in his shoes and think big picture, there were a few things I had to evaluate. Did

JoJo's father approach the situation respectfully for my wife and also for me? Did he do anything to neglect the wellbeing and safety of JoJo? What is the intention? Is this relationship in the best interest for JoJo? I immediately thought of my father and our circumstances.

As a child, no one couldn't tell me that my father wasn't the best in the world and guess what, that's my perspective. If you measured or quantified the value of our relationship, there would be large gaps in his presence, missed games and events, missed birthdays, missed growth and bonding opportunities. Yet, my father was still the best thing that could have ever happened to me. How could this be, the heart doesn't measure value in the way our minds do. Love is blind and that's what makes love beautiful, innocent and cherished. Without love, we would be robots, incapable of forgiving or giving someone an opportunity to succeed. If we were robotic in our heart, we would leave a baby that didn't learn to walk fast enough or talk. Sometimes the greatest lessons on earth is experiencing life.

Interesting enough, Initially I didn't speak with JoJo's biological father as Drew had to feel comfortable with the interaction first however I was always by her side supporting the process. Change is very hard especially on a child therefore she wanted to make sure he wanted to really be part of his life before introducing his Father and he deciding he didn't want that role. Consistency is important to know if you're in this for the long run or if it's a nice experience because you think you should do it. Drew put JoJo's father on a call schedule to slowly introduce JoJo to his Father. JoJo visited with him as a baby but it's been years since they spoke and as a child, they don't know what a father means. The first few interactions was awkward just as any person that walks into a child's life that doesn't have kids, there is a learning process.

Adoption Because JoJo's father wasn't around, people would ask if I would adopt him, which is a great question. These are my rules on adopting in a blended family:

The Father doesn't want to be in the child's life therefore the child is fatherless

The Father is deceased.

The child is in harm or danger, therefore it's an unfit home.

The child doesn't have parents

In the event the child's mother dies, custody can be established through court order.....Find out the process. I really don't know.

If I would have adopted Josiah.

JoJo will get to a point where he seeks information and understanding for himself and he would approach his father asking, why didn't he make an effort to be in his life. His Father would more than likely respond, your parents didn't allow me to be a part of your life and pushed me out. JoJo can possibly develop resentment due to our actions, even if we felt it was in his best interest.

This is a great segway into the definition of "Dad." Dads come in all different forms, types, relationships and can be interchangeable for almost anyone providing support that uplifts positive change and growth. When my father wasn't around, coaches became father figures to me including men in the community that taught me fundamentals of manhood. When my father wasn't around, men in the community would hire me and my brother to pickup leaves. It probably was one of the worst jobs I've ever experienced but it built character and work ethic that I wouldn't trade for the world. There is a village that becomes available to instill the lessons children need to learn and the role of "dad" can often be spread throughout the village to ensure children learn fundamentals of life. This concept also applies when the dad is around. Everyone is limited on the amount of information we know. If someone excels in a certain area, send the child to exceed your own understanding as the future depends on our children being smarter and more skilled than us.

Confidence I'm a firm believer that what's for me is for me and no one can take it away. If something isn't for me, then it was only supposed to be in my life for a season and I'm fine.

Being okay with JoJo's biological dad coming into the picture Studies show, 85% of blended famlies are dysfunctional. While Drew and I were dating, she was very intentional not to allow me to play the dad role. She didn't want to scare me off or put responsibility on me before we had a chance to know if our relationship would last. Her family also assisted in our dating process. Their goal was to help Drew find the man of her dreams and would take JoJo so she could go out on dates. Well, that strategy worked! Drew and I went on a date that lasted 12hrs. Her family wasn't very happy when I brought her home at 4am. To no despair, we stayed in contact and she became my wife. I would ask Drew if I could take JoJo for ice cream or take him to the park while she was working if I felt she needed a helping hand so I could build a stronger bond with him. I knew if I married Drew, he would become my son. JoJo's biological father currently wasn't around and I knew JoJo needed a male influence to help him navigate the world, instill moral and values and grow into the man he would become. I had great expectations however I didn't know what a son or father figure meant from my wifes's eyes. My thought was once we were married, I would automatically take on the father role.

In our scenario, we got married extremely fast and Drew was pregnant 2mo after. We had a huge decision to make, where do we stay to raise the kids. At the time we were in LA and didn't feel like we had much support. We could either go to NJ to my family or Chicago with her family. I spoke with Drew's mom and she said I really can't help you if you stay in LA. Drew has a big family, her mom and dad and 4 sisters. It was a no brainer and we relocated to Chicago before Machai was born. I didn't have a chance to fully assume the "Dad" role as everything was moving fast. We were living under the same roof however Drew was making moves the way she programmed and without much involvement or opinion from my side. There were a few things that I didn't like entirely too much such as JoJo staying up until any time he wanted as if he was a little rockstar in a diaper and

him sleeping in the same bed. Drew wasn't receptive to him staying up late and defended by saying she's an actress and her hours flucturate. To combat, I provided studies and reports on best practices for sleeping. I also provided a guidance for the tv staying on all night and she said her parents did it with them and everyone is okay so it's not that bad. I tried developing the "My House, My Rules" concept but it quickly fell on death ears as my concerns weren't enforced. Opposed to supporting, JoJo would cry and mom would come to the rescue. I began to see a common thread, where JoJo was also learning how to get his way and It then became an issue where it was Me vs. Them.

Boiling Point where I felt I couldn't parent

Due to JoJo not receiving adequate sleep, he struggled to get up for school in the morning. Being a man, I had my way of getting you to follow directions which was to place the fear of God in you because at the end of the day, I'm the parent. JoJo stood by the sink and didn't want to brush his teeth so I "acted" as if I was going to give him a pinch and he started crying, not because of pain but because of the act. His mother ran upstairs and grabbed JoJo, asking what happened. JoJo responded, daddy pinched me. Drew grabbed JoJo and repremanded me saying I told you not to do that to him. I asked JoJo to demonstrate on his mother exactly how hard I pinched him and he barely touched his mother. I walked out the room as I felt emasculated and minimized below a child. I thought to myself if I wanted to stay in a relationship where I didn't have a parenting voice. Besides all that I've done and contributed, I should feel more respected. We ended up seeking out a marriage counselor that told us we're doing things all wrong. We didn't have a plan and it shows.

but she did ask for my thoughts to correct him sleeping in the bed.

Introduce Drew's mom, millinial
Support we had and lacked
Realistic / Unrealistic Expectations
It's either him or me

Village mindset, when JoJo's dad came home, Respect.
Territorial. No this is my house.

Drew received a call from JoJo's biological dad that he came
home from jail and wanted to see his son if possible. At the time
Drew was still hurt by the lack of support and effort. Her perspective was, if you haven't been around or made an effort all
this time, why now. JoJo doesn't need you. Besides she had me
in her life which "filled" the void of JoJo's lack of a father figure.
Once Drew brought the conversation and intention to my attention, I had a lot of thinking to do also. As a man or the other man
in the situation, I had several thoughts run through my mind.
As men, we can rightfully be territorial and protective of their
castle. After I let my pride down, put myself in his shoes and
think big picture, there were a few things I had to evaluate. Did
JoJo's father approach the situation respectfully for my wife and
also for me? Did he do anything to neglect the wellbeing and
safety of JoJo? What is the intention? Is this relationship in the
best interest for JoJo? I immediately thought of my father and
our circumstances.

As a child, no one couldn't tell me that my father wasn't the
best in the world and guess what, that's my perspective. If you
measured or quantified the value of our relationship, there
would be large gaps in his presence, missed games and events,
missed birthdays, missed growth and bonding opportunities.
Yet, my father was still the best thing that could have ever happened to me. How could this be, the heart doesn't measure value
in the way our minds do. Love is blind and that's what makes
love beautiful, innocent and cherished. Without love, we would
be robots, incapable of forgiving or giving someone an opportunity to succeed. If we were robotic in our heart, we would leave a
baby that didn't learn to walk fast enough or talk. Sometimes the
greatest lessons on earth is experiencing life.

Interesting enough, Initially I didn't speak with JoJo's biological father as Drew had to feel comfortable with the interaction
first however I was always by her side supporting the process.

Change is very hard especially on a child therefore she wanted to make sure he wanted to really be part of his life before introducing his Father and he deciding he didn't want that role. Consistency is important to know if you're in this for the long run or if it's a nice experience because you think you should do it. Drew put JoJo's father on a call schedule to slowly introduce JoJo to his Father. JoJo visited with him as a baby but it's been years since they spoke and as a child, they don't know what a father means. The first few interactions was awkward just as any person that walks into a child's life that doesn't have kids, there is a learning process.

Adoption Because JoJo's father wasn't around, people would ask if I would adopt him, which is a great question. These are my rules on adopting in a blended family:

The Father doesn't want to be in the child's life therefore the child is fatherless

The Father is deceased.

The child is in harm or danger, therefore it's an unfit home.

The child doesn't have parents

In the event the child's mother dies, custody can be established through court order.....Find out the process. I really don't know.

If I would have adopted Josiah.

JoJo will get to a point where he seeks information and understanding for himself and he would approach his father asking, why didn't he make an effort to be in his life. His Father would more than likely respond, your parents didn't allow me to be a part of your life and pushed me out. JoJo can possibly develop resentment due to our actions, even if we felt it was in his best interest.

This is a great segway into the definition of "Dad." Dads come in all different forms, types, relationships and can be interchangeable for almost anyone providing support that uplifts positive change and growth. When my father wasn't around, coaches became father figures to me including men in the community that taught me fundamentals of manhood. When my father wasn't

around, men in the community would hire me and my brother to pickup leaves. It probably was one of the worst jobs I've ever experienced but it built character and work ethic that I wouldn't trade for the world. There is a village that becomes available to instill the lessons children need to learn and the role of "dad" can often be spread throughout the village to ensure children learn fundamentals of life. This concept also applies when the dad is around. Everyone is limited on the amount of information we know. If someone excels in a certain area, send the child to exceed your own understanding as the future depends on our children being smarter and more skilled than us.

Confidence I'm a firm believer that what's for me is for me and no one can take it away. If something isn't for me, then it was only supposed to be in my life for a season and I'm fine.

Being okay with JoJo's biological dad coming into the picture Studies show, 85% of blended familes are dysfunctional.

In our scenario, we got married extremely fast and Drew was pregnant 2mo after. We had a huge decision to make, where do we stay to raise the kids. At the time we were in LA and didn't feel like we had much support. We could either go to NJ to my family or Chicago with her family. I spoke with Drew's mom and she said I really can't help you if you stay in LA. Drew has a big family, her mom and dad and 4 sisters. It was a no brainer and we relocated to Chicago before Machai was born. I didn't have a chance to fully assume the "Dad" role as everything was moving fast. We were living under the same roof however Drew was making moves the way she programmed and without much involvement or opinion from my side. There were a few things that I didn't like entirely too much such as JoJo staying up until any time he wanted as if he was a little rockstar in a diaper and him sleeping in the same bed. Drew wasn't receptive to him staying up late and defended by saying she's an actress and her hours flucturate. To combat, I provided studies and reports on best practices for sleeping. I also provided a guidance for the tv staying on all night and she said her parents did it with them and

everyone is okay so it's not that bad. I tried developing the "My House, My Rules" concept but it quickly fell on death ears as my concerns weren't enforced. Opposed to supporting, JoJo would cry and mom would come to the rescue. I began to see a common thread, where JoJo was also learning how to get his way and It then became an issue where it was Me vs. Them.

Boiling Point where I felt I couldn't parent

Due to JoJo not receiving adequate sleep, he struggled to get up for school in the morning. Being a man, I had my way of getting you to follow directions which was to place the fear of God in you because at the end of the day, I'm the parent. JoJo stood by the sink and didn't want to brush his teeth so I "acted" as if I was going to give him a pinch and he started crying, not because of pain but because of the act. His mother ran upstairs and grabbed JoJo, asking what happened. JoJo responded, daddy pinched me. Drew grabbed JoJo and repremanded me saying I told you not to do that to him. I asked JoJo to demonstrate on his mother exactly how hard I pinched him and he barely touched his mother. I walked out the room as I felt emasculated and minimized below a child. I thought to myself if I wanted to stay in a relationship where I didn't have a parenting voice. Besides all that I've done and contributed, I should feel more respected. We ended up seeking out a marriage counselor that told us we're doing things all wrong. We didn't have a plan and it shows.

but she did ask for my thoughts to correct him sleeping in the bed.

Introduce Drew's mom, millinial

Support we had and lacked

Realistic / Unrealistic Expectations

It's either him or me

Village mindset, when JoJo's dad came home, Respect. Territorial. No this is my house.

Drew received a call from JoJo's biological dad that he came home from jail and wanted to see his son if possible. At the time Drew was still hurt by the lack of support and effort. Her

perspective was, if you haven't been around or made an effort all this time, why now. JoJo doesn't need you. Besides she had me in her life which "filled" the void of JoJo's lack of a father figure. Once Drew brought the conversation and intention to my attention, I had a lot of thinking to do also. As a man or the other man in the situation, I had several thoughts run through my mind. As men, we can rightfully be territorial and protective of their castle. After I let my pride down, put myself in his shoes and think big picture, there were a few things I had to evaluate. Did JoJo's father approach the situation respectfully for my wife and also for me? Did he do anything to neglect the wellbeing and safety of JoJo? What is the intention? Is this relationship in the best interest for JoJo? I immediately thought of my father and our circumstances.

As a child, no one couldn't tell me that my father wasn't the best in the world and guess what, that's my perspective. If you measured or quantified the value of our relationship, there would be large gaps in his presence, missed games and events, missed birthdays, missed growth and bonding opportunities. Yet, my father was still the best thing that could have ever happened to me. How could this be, the heart doesn't measure value in the way our minds do. Love is blind and that's what makes love beautiful, innocent and cherished. Without love, we would be robots, incapable of forgiving or giving someone an opportunity to succeed. If we were robotic in our heart, we would leave a baby that didn't learn to walk fast enough or talk. Sometimes the greatest lessons on earth is experiencing life.

Interesting enough, Initially I didn't speak with JoJo's biological father as Drew had to feel comfortable with the interaction first however I was always by her side supporting the process. Change is very hard especially on a child therefore she wanted to make sure he wanted to really be part of his life before introducing his Father and he deciding he didn't want that role. Consistency is important to know if you're in this for the long run or if it's a nice experience because you think you should do

it. Drew put JoJo's father on a call schedule to slowly introduce JoJo to his Father. JoJo visited with him as a baby but it's been years since they spoke and as a child, they don't know what a father means. The first few interactions was awkward just as any person that walks into a child's life that doesn't have kids, there is a learning process.

Adoption Because JoJo's father wasn't around, people would ask if I would adopt him, which is a great question. These are my rules on adopting in a blended family:

The Father doesn't want to be in the child's life therefore the child is fatherless

The Father is deceased.

The child is in harm or danger, therefore it's an unfit home.

The child doesn't have parents

In the event the child's mother dies, custody can be established through court order.....Find out the process. I really don't know.

If I would have adopted Josiah.

JoJo will get to a point where he seeks information and understanding for himself and he would approach his father asking, why didn't he make an effort to be in his life. His Father would more than likely respond, your parents didn't allow me to be a part of your life and pushed me out. JoJo can possibly develop resentment due to our actions, even if we felt it was in his best interest.

This is a great segway into the definition of "Dad." Dads come in all different forms, types, relationships and can be interchangeable for almost anyone providing support that uplifts positive change and growth. When my father wasn't around, coaches became father figures to me including men in the community that taught me fundamentals of manhood. When my father wasn't around, men in the community would hire me and my brother to pickup leaves. It probably was one of the worst jobs I've ever experienced but it built character and work ethic that I wouldn't trade for the world. There is a village that becomes available to instill the lessons children need to learn and the role of "dad"

can often be spread throughout the village to ensure children learn fundamentals of life. This concept also applies when the dad is around. Everyone is limited on the amount of information we know. If someone excels in a certain area, send the child to exceed your own understanding as the future depends on our children being smarter and more skilled than us.

Confidence I'm a firm believer that what's for me is for me and no one can take it away. If something isn't for me, then it was only supposed to be in my life for a season and I'm fine.

Being okay with JoJo's biological dad coming into the picture Studies show, 85% of blended familes are dysfunctional. While Drew and I were dating, she was very intentional not to allow me to play the dad role. She didn't want to scare me off or put responsibility on me before we had a chance to know if our relationship would last. Her family also assisted in our dating process. Their goal was to help Drew find the man of her dreams and would take JoJo so she could go out on dates. Well, that strategy worked! Drew and I went on a date that lasted 12hrs. Her family wasn't very happy when I brought her home at 4am. To no despair, we stayed in contact and she became my wife. I would ask Drew if I could take JoJo for ice cream or take him to the park while she was working if I felt she needed a helping hand so I could build a stronger bond with him. I knew if I married Drew, he would become my son. JoJo's biological father currently wasn't around and I knew JoJo needed a male influence to help him navigate the world, instill moral and values and grow into the man he would become. I had great expectations however I didn't know what a son or father figure meant from my wifes's eyes. My thought was once we were married, I would automatically take on the father role.

In our scenario, we got married extremely fast and Drew was pregnant 2mo after. We had a huge decision to make, where do we stay to raise the kids. At the time we were in LA and didn't feel like we had much support. We could either go to NJ to my family or Chicago with her family. I spoke with Drew's mom

and she said I really can't help you if you stay in LA. Drew has a big family, her mom and dad and 4 sisters. It was a no brainer and we relocated to Chicago before Machai was born. I didn't have a chance to fully assume the "Dad" role as everything was moving fast. We were living under the same roof however Drew was making moves the way she programmed and without much involvement or opinion from my side. There were a few things that I didn't like entirely too much such as JoJo staying up until any time he wanted as if he was a little rockstar in a diaper and him sleeping in the same bed. Drew wasn't receptive to him staying up late and defended by saying she's an actress and her hours flucturate. To combat, I provided studies and reports on best practices for sleeping. I also provided a guidance for the tv staying on all night and she said her parents did it with them and everyone is okay so it's not that bad. I tried developing the "My House, My Rules" concept but it quickly fell on death ears as my concerns weren't enforced. Opposed to supporting, JoJo would cry and mom would come to the rescue. I began to see a common thread, where JoJo was also learning how to get his way and It then became an issue where it was Me vs. Them.

Boiling Point where I felt I couldn't parent

Due to JoJo not receiving adequate sleep, he struggled to get up for school in the morning. Being a man, I had my way of getting you to follow directions which was to place the fear of God in you because at the end of the day, I'm the parent. JoJo stood by the sink and didn't want to brush his teeth so I "acted" as if I was going to give him a pinch and he started crying, not because of pain but because of the act. His mother ran upstairs and grabbed JoJo, asking what happened. JoJo responded, daddy pinched me. Drew grabbed JoJo and repremanded me saying I told you not to do that to him. I asked JoJo to demonstrate on his mother exactly how hard I pinched him and he barely touched his mother. I walked out the room as I felt emasculated and minimized below a child. I thought to myself if I wanted to stay in a relationship where I didn't have a parenting voice. Besides all

that I've done and contributed, I should feel more respected. We ended up seeking out a marriage counselor that told us we're doing things all wrong. We didn't have a plan and it shows.

but she did ask for my thoughts to correct him sleeping in the bed.

Introduce Drew's mom, millinial

Support we had and lacked

Realistic / Unrealistic Expectations

It's either him or me

Village mindset, when JoJo's dad came home, Respect. Territorial. No this is my house.

Drew received a call from JoJo's biological dad that he came home from jail and wanted to see his son if possible. At the time Drew was still hurt by the lack of support and effort. Her perspective was, if you haven't been around or made an effort all this time, why now. JoJo doesn't need you. Besides she had me in her life which "filled" the void of JoJo's lack of a father figure. Once Drew brought the conversation and intention to my attention, I had a lot of thinking to do also. As a man or the other man in the situation, I had several thoughts run through my mind. As men, we can rightfully be territorial and protective of their castle. After I let my pride down, put myself in his shoes and think big picture, there were a few things I had to evaluate. Did JoJo's father approach the situation respectfully for my wife and also for me? Did he do anything to neglect the wellbeing and safety of JoJo? What is the intention? Is this relationship in the best interest for JoJo? I immediately thought of my father and our circumstances.

As a child, no one couldn't tell me that my father wasn't the best in the world and guess what, that's my perspective. If you measured or quantified the value of our relationship, there would be large gaps in his presence, missed games and events, missed birthdays, missed growth and bonding opportunities. Yet, my father was still the best thing that could have ever happened to me. How could this be, the heart doesn't measure value

in the way our minds do. Love is blind and that's what makes love beautiful, innocent and cherished. Without love, we would be robots, incapable of forgiving or giving someone an opportunity to succeed. If we were robotic in our heart, we would leave a baby that didn't learn to walk fast enough or talk. Sometimes the greatest lessons on earth is experiencing life.

Interesting enough, Initially I didn't speak with JoJo's biological father as Drew had to feel comfortable with the interaction first however I was always by her side supporting the process. Change is very hard especially on a child therefore she wanted to make sure he wanted to really be part of his life before introducing his Father and he deciding he didn't want that role. Consistency is important to know if you're in this for the long run or if it's a nice experience because you think you should do it. Drew put JoJo's father on a call schedule to slowly introduce JoJo to his Father. JoJo visited with him as a baby but it's been years since they spoke and as a child, they don't know what a father means. The first few interactions was awkward just as any person that walks into a child's life that doesn't have kids, there is a learning process.

Adoption Because JoJo's father wasn't around, people would ask if I would adopt him, which is a great question. These are my rules on adopting in a blended family:

The Father doesn't want to be in the child's life therefore the child is fatherless

The Father is deceased.

The child is in harm or danger, therefore it's an unfit home.

The child doesn't have parents

In the event the child's mother dies, custody can be established through court order.....Find out the process. I really don't know.

If I would have adopted Josiah.

JoJo will get to a point where he seeks information and understanding for himself and he would approach his father asking, why didn't he make an effort to be in his life. His Father would more than likely respond, your parents didn't allow me to be a

part of your life and pushed me out. JoJo can possibly develop resentment due to our actions, even if we felt it was in his best interest.

This is a great segway into the definition of "Dad." Dads come in all different forms, types, relationships and can be interchangeable for almost anyone providing support that uplifts positive change and growth. When my father wasn't around, coaches became father figures to me including men in the community that taught me fundamentals of manhood. When my father wasn't around, men in the community would hire me and my brother to pickup leaves. It probably was one of the worst jobs I've ever experienced but it built character and work ethic that I wouldn't trade for the world. There is a village that becomes available to instill the lessons children need to learn and the role of "dad" can often be spread throughout the village to ensure children learn fundamentals of life. This concept also applies when the dad is around. Everyone is limited on the amount of information we know. If someone excels in a certain area, send the child to exceed your own understanding as the future depends on our children being smarter and more skilled than us.

Confidence I'm a firm believer that what's for me is for me and no one can take it away. If something isn't for me, then it was only supposed to be in my life for a season and I'm fine.

Being okay with JoJo's biological dad coming into the picture Studies show, 85% of blended familes are dysfunctional.

In our scenario, we got married extremely fast and Drew was pregnant 2mo after. We had a huge decision to make, where do we stay to raise the kids. At the time we were in LA and didn't feel like we had much support. We could either go to NJ to my family or Chicago with her family. I spoke with Drew's mom and she said I really can't help you if you stay in LA. Drew has a big family, her mom and dad and 4 sisters. It was a no brainer and we relocated to Chicago before Machai was born. I didn't have a chance to fully assume the "Dad" role as everything was moving fast. We were living under the same roof however Drew was making moves the way she programmed and without much involvement or opinion from my side. There were a few things that I didn't like entirely too much such as JoJo staying up until any time he wanted as if he was a little rockstar in a diaper and him sleeping in the same bed. Drew wasn't receptive to him staying up late and defended by saying she's an actress and her hours flucturate. To combat, I provided studies and reports on best practices for sleeping. I also provided a guidance for the tv staying on all night and she said her parents did it with them and everyone is okay so it's not that bad. I tried developing the "My House, My Rules" concept but it quickly fell on death ears as my concerns weren't enforced. Opposed to supporting, JoJo would cry and mom would come to the rescue. I began to see a common thread, where JoJo was also learning how to get his way and It then became an issue where it was Me vs. Them.

Boiling Point where I felt I couldn't parent

Due to JoJo not receiving adequate sleep, he struggled to get up for school in the morning. Being a man, I had my way of getting you to follow directions which was to place the fear of God in you because at the end of the day, I'm the parent. JoJo stood by the sink and didn't want to brush his teeth so I "acted" as if I was going to give him a pinch and he started crying, not because of pain but because of the act. His mother ran upstairs and grabbed JoJo, asking what happened. JoJo responded, daddy pinched me. Drew grabbed JoJo and reprimanded me saying I told you not to do that to him. I asked JoJo to demonstrate on his mother exactly how hard I pinched him and he barely touched his mother. I walked out the room as I felt emasculated and minimized below a child. I thought to myself if I wanted to stay in a relationship where I didn't have a parenting voice. Besides all that I've done and contributed, I should feel more respected. We ended up seeking out a marriage counselor that told us we're doing things all wrong. We didn't have a plan and it shows.

but she did ask for my thoughts to correct him sleeping in the bed.

Introduce Drew's mom, millinial
Support we had and lacked
Realistic / Unrealistic Expectations
It's either him or me
Village mindset, when JoJo's dad came home, Respect. Territorial. No this is my house.

Drew received a call from JoJo's biological dad that he came home from jail and wanted to see his son if possible. At the time Drew was still hurt by the lack of support and effort. Her perspective was, if you haven't been around or made an effort all this time, why now. JoJo doesn't need you. Besides she had me in her life which "filled" the void of JoJo's lack of a father figure. Once Drew brought the conversation and intention to my attention, I had a lot of thinking to do also. As a man or the other man in the situation, I had several thoughts run through my mind. As men, we can rightfully be territorial and protective of their castle. After I let my pride down, put myself in his shoes and think big picture, there were a few things I had to evaluate. Did JoJo's father approach the situation respectfully for my wife and also for me? Did he do anything to neglect the wellbeing and safety of JoJo? What is the intention? Is this relationship in the best interest for JoJo? I immediately thought of my father and our circumstances.

As a child, no one couldn't tell me that my father wasn't the best in the world and guess what, that's my perspective. If you measured or quantified the value of our relationship, there would be large gaps in his presence, missed games and events, missed birthdays, missed growth and bonding opportunities. Yet, my father was still the best thing that could have ever happened to me. How could this be, the heart doesn't measure value in the way our minds do. Love is blind and that's what makes love beautiful, innocent and cherished. Without love, we would be robots, incapable of forgiving or giving someone an opportunity to succeed. If we were robotic in our heart, we would leave a baby that didn't learn to walk fast enough or talk. Sometimes the greatest lessons on earth is experiencing life.

Interesting enough, Initially I didn't speak with JoJo's biological father as Drew had to feel comfortable with the interaction first however I was always by her side supporting the process. Change is very hard especially on a child therefore she wanted to make sure he wanted to really be part of his life before introducing his Father and he deciding he didn't want that role. Consistency is important to know if you're in this for the long run or if it's a nice experience because you think you should do it. Drew put JoJo's father on a call schedule to slowly introduce JoJo to his Father. JoJo visited with him as a baby but it's been years since they spoke and as a child, they don't know what a father means. The first few interactions was awkward just as any person that walks into a child's life that doesn't have kids, there is a learning process.

Adoption Because JoJo's father wasn't around, people would ask if I would adopt him, which is a great question. These are my rules on adopting in a blended family:

The Father doesn't want to be in the child's life therefore the child is fatherless

The Father is deceased.

The child is in harm or danger, therefore it's an unfit home.

The child doesn't have parents

In the event the child's mother dies, custody can be established through court order.....Find out the process. I really don't know.

If I would have adopted Josiah.

JoJo will get to a point where he seeks information and understanding for himself and he would approach his father asking, why didn't he make an effort to be in his life. His Father would more than likely respond, your parents didn't allow me to be a part of your life and pushed me out. JoJo can possibly develop resentment due to our actions, even if we felt it was in his best interest.

This is a great segway into the definition of "Dad." Dads come in all different forms, types, relationships and can be interchangeable for almost anyone providing support that uplifts positive change and growth. When my father wasn't around, coaches became father figures to me including men in the community that taught me fundamentals of manhood. When my father wasn't around, men in the community would hire me and my brother to pickup leaves. It probably was one of the worst jobs I've ever experienced but it built character and work ethic that I wouldn't trade for the world. There is a village that becomes available to instill the lessons children need to learn and the role of "dad" can often be spread throughout the village to ensure children learn fundamentals of life. This concept also applies when the dad is around. Everyone is limited on the amount of information we know. If someone excels in a certain area, send the child to exceed your own understanding as the future depends on our children being smarter and more skilled than us.

Confidence I'm a firm believer that what's for me is for me and no one can take it away. If something isn't for me, then it was only supposed to be in my life for a season and I'm fine.

Being okay with JoJo's biological dad coming into the picture

Studies show, 85% of blended familes are dysfunctional. While Drew and I were dating, she was very intentional not to allow me to play the dad role. She didn't want to scare me off or put responsibility on me before we had a chance to know if our relationship would last. Her family also assisted in our dating process. Their goal was to help Drew find the man of her dreams and would take JoJo so she could go out on dates. Well, that strategy worked! Drew and I went on a date that lasted 12hrs. Her family wasn't very happy when I brought her home at 4am. To no despair, we stayed in contact and she became my wife. I would ask Drew if I could take JoJo for ice cream or take him to the park while she was working if I felt she needed a helping hand so I could build a stronger bond with him. I knew if I married Drew, he would become my son. JoJo's biological father currently

wasn't around and I knew JoJo needed a male influence to help him navigate the world, instill moral and values and grow into the man he would become. I had great expectations however I didn't know what a son or father figure meant from my wifes's eyes. My thought was once we were married, I would automatically take on the father role.

In our scenario, we got married extremely fast and Drew was pregnant 2mo after. We had a huge decision to make, where do we stay to raise the kids. At the time we were in LA and didn't feel like we had much support. We could either go to NJ to my family or Chicago with her family. I spoke with Drew's mom and she said I really can't help you if you stay in LA. Drew has a big family, her mom and dad and 4 sisters. It was a no brainer and we relocated to Chicago before Machai was born. I didn't have a chance to fully assume the "Dad" role as everything was moving fast. We were living under the same roof however Drew was making moves the way she programmed and without much involvement or opinion from my side. There were a few things that I didn't like entirely too much such as JoJo staying up until any time he wanted as if he was a little rockstar in a diaper and him sleeping in the same bed. Drew wasn't receptive to him staying up late and defended by saying she's an actress and her hours flucturate. To combat, I provided studies and reports on best practices for sleeping. I also provided a guidance for the tv staying on all night and she said her parents did it with them and everyone is okay so it's not that bad. I tried developing the "My House, My Rules" concept but it quickly fell on death ears as my concerns weren't enforced. Opposed to supporting, JoJo would cry and mom would come to the rescue. I began to see a common thread, where JoJo was also learning how to get his way and It then became an issue where it was Me vs. Them.

Boiling Point where I felt I couldn't parent

Due to JoJo not receiving adequate sleep, he struggled to get up for school in the morning. Being a man, I had my way of getting you to follow directions which was to place the fear of God

in you because at the end of the day, I'm the parent. JoJo stood by the sink and didn't want to brush his teeth so I "acted" as if I was going to give him a pinch and he started crying, not because of pain but because of the act. His mother ran upstairs and grabbed JoJo, asking what happened. JoJo responded, daddy pinched me. Drew grabbed JoJo and repremanded me saying I told you not to do that to him. I asked JoJo to demonstrate on his mother exactly how hard I pinched him and he barely touched his mother. I walked out the room as I felt emasculated and minimized below a child. I thought to myself if I wanted to stay in a relationship where I didn't have a parenting voice. Besides all that I've done and contributed, I should feel more respected. We ended up seeking out a marriage counselor that told us we're doing things all wrong. We didn't have a plan and it shows.

but she did ask for my thoughts to correct him sleeping in the bed.

Introduce Drew's mom, millinial

Support we had and lacked

Realistic / Unrealistic Expectations

It's either him or me

Village mindset, when JoJo's dad came home, Respect. Territorial. No this is my house.

Drew received a call from JoJo's biological dad that he came home from jail and wanted to see his son if possible. At the time Drew was still hurt by the lack of support and effort. Her perspective was, if you haven't been around or made an effort all this time, why now. JoJo doesn't need you. Besides she had me in her life which "filled" the void of JoJo's lack of a father figure. Once Drew brought the conversation and intention to my attention, I had a lot of thinking to do also. As a man or the other man in the situation, I had several thoughts run through my mind. As men, we can rightfully be territorial and protective of their castle. After I let my pride down, put myself in his shoes and think big picture, there were a few things I had to evaluate. Did JoJo's father approach the situation respectfully for my wife and

also for me? Did he do anything to neglect the wellbeing and safety of JoJo? What is the intention? Is this relationship in the best interest for JoJo? I immediately thought of my father and our circumstances.

As a child, no one couldn't tell me that my father wasn't the best in the world and guess what, that's my perspective. If you measured or quantified the value of our relationship, there would be large gaps in his presence, missed games and events, missed birthdays, missed growth and bonding opportunities. Yet, my father was still the best thing that could have ever happened to me. How could this be, the heart doesn't measure value in the way our minds do. Love is blind and that's what makes love beautiful, innocent and cherished. Without love, we would be robots, incapable of forgiving or giving someone an opportunity to succeed. If we were robotic in our heart, we would leave a baby that didn't learn to walk fast enough or talk. Sometimes the greatest lessons on earth is experiencing life.

Interesting enough, Initially I didn't speak with JoJo's biological father as Drew had to feel comfortable with the interaction first however I was always by her side supporting the process. Change is very hard especially on a child therefore she wanted to make sure he wanted to really be part of his life before introducing his Father and he deciding he didn't want that role. Consistency is important to know if you're in this for the long run or if it's a nice experience because you think you should do it. Drew put JoJo's father on a call schedule to slowly introduce JoJo to his Father. JoJo visited with him as a baby but it's been years since they spoke and as a child, they don't know what a father means. The first few interactions was awkward just as any person that walks into a child's life that doesn't have kids, there is a learning process.

Adoption Because JoJo's father wasn't around, people would ask if I would adopt him, which is a great question. These are my rules on adopting in a blended family:

The Father doesn't want to be in the child's life therefore the child is fatherless

The Father is deceased.

The child is in harm or danger, therefore it's an unfit home.

The child doesn't have parents

In the event the child's mother dies, custody can be established through court order......Find out the process. I really don't know.

If I would have adopted Josiah.

JoJo will get to a point where he seeks information and understanding for himself and he would approach his father asking, why didn't he make an effort to be in his life. His Father would more than likely respond, your parents didn't allow me to be a part of your life and pushed me out. JoJo can possibly develop resentment due to our actions, even if we felt it was in his best interest.

This is a great segway into the definition of "Dad." Dads come in all different forms, types, relationships and can be interchangeable for almost anyone providing support that uplifts positive change and growth. When my father wasn't around, coaches became father figures to me including men in the community that taught me fundamentals of manhood. When my father wasn't around, men in the community would hire me and my brother to pickup leaves. It probably was one of the worst jobs I've ever experienced but it built character and work ethic that I wouldn't trade for the world. There is a village that becomes available to instill the lessons children need to learn and the role of "dad" can often be spread throughout the village to ensure children learn fundamentals of life. This concept also applies when the dad is around. Everyone is limited on the amount of information we know. If someone excels in a certain area, send the child to exceed your own understanding as the future depends on our children being smarter and more skilled than us.

Confidence I'm a firm believer that what's for me is for me and no one can take it away. If something isn't for me, then it was only supposed to be in my life for a season and I'm fine.

Being okay with JoJo's biological dad coming into the picture
Studies show, 85% of blended familes are dysfunctional.

In our scenario, we got married extremely fast and Drew was
pregnant 2mo after. We had a huge decision to make, where do
we stay to raise the kids. At the time we were in LA and didn't
feel like we had much support. We could either go to NJ to my
family or Chicago with her family. I spoke with Drew's mom
and she said I really can't help you if you stay in LA. Drew has
a big family, her mom and dad and 4 sisters. It was a no brainer
and we relocated to Chicago before Machai was born. I didn't
have a chance to fully assume the "Dad" role as everything was
moving fast. We were living under the same roof however Drew
was making moves the way she programmed and without much
involvement or opinion from my side. There were a few things
that I didn't like entirely too much such as JoJo staying up until
any time he wanted as if he was a little rockstar in a diaper and
him sleeping in the same bed. Drew wasn't receptive to him
staying up late and defended by saying she's an actress and her
hours flucturate. To combat, I provided studies and reports on
best practices for sleeping. I also provided a guidance for the tv
staying on all night and she said her parents did it with them and
everyone is okay so it's not that bad. I tried developing the "My
House, My Rules" concept but it quickly fell on death ears as my
concerns weren't enforced. Opposed to supporting, JoJo would
cry and mom would come to the rescue. I began to see a common
thread, where JoJo was also learning how to get his way and It
then became an issue where it was Me vs. Them.

It's Either Him Or Me

VILLAGE MINDSET, WHEN JoJo's dad came home, Respect. Territorial. No this is my house.

Drew received a call from JoJo's biological dad that he came home from jail and wanted to see his son if possible. At the time Drew was still hurt by the lack of support and effort. Her perspective was, if you haven't been around or made an effort all this time, why now. JoJo doesn't need you. Besides she had me in her life which "filled" the void of JoJo's lack of a father figure. Once Drew brought the conversation and intention to my attention, I had a lot of thinking to do also. As a man or the other man in the situation, I had several thoughts run through my mind. As men, we can rightfully be territorial and protective of their castle. After I let my pride down, put myself in his shoes and think big picture, there were a few things I had to evaluate. Did JoJo's father approach the situation respectfully for my wife and also for me? Did he do anything to neglect the wellbeing and safety of JoJo? What is the intention? Is this relationship in the best interest for JoJo? I immediately thought of my father and our circumstances.

As a child, no one couldn't tell me that my father wasn't the best in the world and guess what, that's my perspective. If you measured or quantified the value of our relationship, there would be large gaps in his presence, missed games and events, missed birthdays, missed growth and bonding opportunities. Yet, my father was still the best thing that could have ever happened to me. How could this be, the heart doesn't measure value in the way our minds do. Love is blind and that's what makes love beautiful, innocent and cherished. Without love, we would be robots, incapable of forgiving or giving someone an opportunity to succeed. If we were robotic in our heart, we would leave a baby that didn't learn to walk fast enough or talk. Sometimes the greatest lessons on earth is experiencing life.

Interesting enough, Initially I didn't speak with JoJo's biological father as Drew had to feel comfortable with the interaction first however I was always by her side supporting the process. Change is very hard especially on a child therefore she wanted to make sure he wanted to really be part of his life before introducing his Father and he deciding he didn't want that role. Consistency is important to know if you're in this for the long run or if it's a nice experience because you think you should do it. Drew put JoJo's father on a call schedule to slowly introduce JoJo to his Father. JoJo visited with him as a baby but it's been years since they spoke and as a child, they don't know what a father means. The first few interactions was awkward just as any person that walks into a child's life that doesn't have kids, there is a learning process.

Adoption Because JoJo's father wasn't around, people would ask if I would adopt him, which is a great question. These are my rules on adopting in a blended family:

The Father doesn't want to be in the child's life therefore the child is fatherless

The Father is deceased.

The child is in harm or danger, therefore it's an unfit home.

The child doesn't have parents

In the event the child's mother dies, custody can be established through court order.....Find out the process. I really don't know.

If I would have adopted Josiah.

JoJo will get to a point where he seeks information and under-standing for himself and he would approach his father asking, why didn't he make an effort to be in his life. His Father would more than likely respond, your parents didn't allow me to be a part of your life and pushed me out. JoJo can possibly develop resentment due to our actions, even if we felt it was in his best interest.

This is a great segway into the definition of "Dad." Dads come in all different forms, types, relationships and can be interchange-able for almost anyone providing support that uplifts positive change and growth. When my father wasn't around, coaches became father figures to me including men in the community that taught me fundamentals of manhood. When my father wasn't around, men in the community would hire me and my brother to pickup leaves. It probably was one of the worst jobs I've ever experienced but it built character and work ethic that I wouldn't trade for the world. There is a village that becomes available to instill the lessons children need to learn and the role of "dad" can often be spread throughout the village to ensure children learn fundamentals of life. This concept also applies when the dad is around. Everyone is limited on the amount of information we know. If someone excels in a certain area, send the child to exceed your own understanding as the future depends on our children being smarter and more skilled than us.

Confidence I'm a firm believer that what's for me is for me and no one can take it away. If something isn't for me, then it was only supposed to be in my life for a season and I'm fine.

Being okay with JoJo's biological dad coming into the picture
Studies show, 85% of blended familes are dysfunctional. While Drew and I were dating, she was very intentional not to allow me to play the dad role. She didn't want to scare me off or put responsibility on me before we had a chance to know if our relationship would last. Her family also assisted in our dating process. Their goal was to help Drew find the man of her dreams and would take JoJo so she could go out on dates. Well, that

strategy worked! Drew and I went on a date that lasted 12hrs. Her family wasn't very happy when I brought her home at 4am. To no despair, we stayed in contact and she became my wife. I would ask Drew if I could take JoJo for ice cream or take him to the park while she was working if I felt she needed a helping hand so I could build a stronger bond with him. I knew if I married Drew, he would become my son. JoJo's biological father currently wasn't around and I knew JoJo needed a male influence to help him navigate the world, instill moral and values and grow into the man he would become. I had great expectations however I didn't know what a son or father figure meant from my wifes's eyes. My thought was once we were married, I would automatically take on the father role.

In our scenario, we got married extremely fast and Drew was pregnant 2mo after. We had a huge decision to make, where do we stay to raise the kids. At the time we were in LA and didn't feel like we had much support. We could either go to NJ to my family or Chicago with her family. I spoke with Drew's mom and she said I really can't help you if you stay in LA. Drew has a big family, her mom and dad and 4 sisters. It was a no brainer and we relocated to Chicago before Machai was born. I didn't have a chance to fully assume the "Dad" role as everything was moving fast. We were living under the same roof however Drew was making moves the way she programmed and without much involvement or opinion from my side. There were a few things that I didn't like entirely too much such as JoJo staying up until any time he wanted as if he was a little rockstar in a diaper and him sleeping in the same bed. Drew wasn't receptive to him staying up late and defended by saying she's an actress and her hours flucturate. To combat, I provided studies and reports on best practices for sleeping. I also provided a guidance for the tv staying on all night and she said her parents did it with them and everyone is okay so it's not that bad. I tried developing the "My House, My Rules" concept but it quickly fell on death ears as my concerns weren't enforced. Opposed to supporting, JoJo would

cry and mom would come to the rescue. I began to see a common thread, where JoJo was also learning how to get his way and It then became an issue where it was Me vs. Them.

Boiling Point where I felt I couldn't parent

Due to JoJo not receiving adequate sleep, he struggled to get up for school in the morning. Being a man, I had my way of getting you to follow directions which was to place the fear of God in you because at the end of the day, I'm the parent. JoJo stood by the sink and didn't want to brush his teeth so I "acted" as if I was going to give him a pinch and he started crying, not because of pain but because of the act. His mother ran upstairs and grabbed JoJo, asking what happened. JoJo responded, daddy pinched me. Drew grabbed JoJo and repremanded me saying I told you not to do that to him. I asked JoJo to demonstrate on his mother exactly how hard I pinched him and he barely touched his mother. I walked out the room as I felt emasculated and minimized below a child. I thought to myself if I wanted to stay in a relationship where I didn't have a parenting voice. Besides all that I've done and contributed, I should feel more respected. We ended up seeking out a marriage counselor that told us we're doing things all wrong. We didn't have a plan and it shows.

but she did ask for my thoughts to correct him sleeping in the bed.

Introduce Drew's mom, millinial

Support we had and lacked

Realistic / Unrealistic Expectations

It's either him or me

Village mindset, when JoJo's dad came home, Respect. Territorial. No this is my house.

Drew received a call from JoJo's biological dad that he came home from jail and wanted to see his son if possible. At the time Drew was still hurt by the lack of support and effort. Her perspective was, if you haven't been around or made an effort all this time, why now. JoJo doesn't need you. Besides she had me in her life which "filled" the void of JoJo's lack of a father figure.

Once Drew brought the conversation and intention to my attention, I had a lot of thinking to do also. As a man or the other man in the situation, I had several thoughts run through my mind. As men, we can rightfully be territorial and protective of their castle. After I let my pride down, put myself in his shoes and think big picture, there were a few things I had to evaluate. Did JoJo's father approach the situation respectfully for my wife and also for me? Did he do anything to neglect the wellbeing and safety of JoJo? What is the intention? Is this relationship in the best interest for JoJo? I immediately thought of my father and our circumstances.

As a child, no one couldn't tell me that my father wasn't the best in the world and guess what, that's my perspective. If you measured or quantified the value of our relationship, there would be large gaps in his presence, missed games and events, missed birthdays, missed growth and bonding opportunities. Yet, my father was still the best thing that could have ever happened to me. How could this be, the heart doesn't measure value in the way our minds do. Love is blind and that's what makes love beautiful, innocent and cherished. Without love, we would be robots, incapable of forgiving or giving someone an opportunity to succeed. If we were robotic in our heart, we would leave a baby that didn't learn to walk fast enough or talk. Sometimes the greatest lessons on earth is experiencing life.

Interesting enough, Initially I didn't speak with JoJo's biological father as Drew had to feel comfortable with the interaction first however I was always by her side supporting the process. Change is very hard especially on a child therefore she wanted to make sure he wanted to really be part of his life before introducing his Father and he deciding he didn't want that role. Consistency is important to know if you're in this for the long run or if it's a nice experience because you think you should do it. Drew put JoJo's father on a call schedule to slowly introduce JoJo to his Father. JoJo visited with him as a baby but it's been years since they spoke and as a child, they don't know what a

father means. The first few interactions was awkward just as any person that walks into a child's life that doesn't have kids, there is a learning process.

Adoption Because JoJo's father wasn't around, people would ask if I would adopt him, which is a great question. These are my rules on adopting in a blended family:

The Father doesn't want to be in the child's life therefore the child is fatherless

The Father is deceased.

The child is in harm or danger, therefore it's an unfit home.

The child doesn't have parents

In the event the child's mother dies, custody can be established through court order.....Find out the process. I really don't know.

If I would have adopted Josiah.

JoJo will get to a point where he seeks information and understanding for himself and he would approach his father asking, why didn't he make an effort to be in his life. His Father would more than likely respond, your parents didn't allow me to be a part of your life and pushed me out. JoJo can possibly develop resentment due to our actions, even if we felt it was in his best interest.

This is a great segway into the definition of "Dad." Dads come in all different forms, types, relationships and can be interchangeable for almost anyone providing support that uplifts positive change and growth. When my father wasn't around, coaches became father figures to me including men in the community that taught me fundamentals of manhood. When my father wasn't around, men in the community would hire me and my brother to pickup leaves. It probably was one of the worst jobs I've ever experienced but it built character and work ethic that I wouldn't trade for the world. There is a village that becomes available to instill the lessons children need to learn and the role of "dad" can often be spread throughout the village to ensure children learn fundamentals of life. This concept also applies when the dad is around. Everyone is limited on the amount of information

we know. If someone excels in a certain area, send the child to exceed your own understanding as the future depends on our children being smarter and more skilled than us.

Confidence I'm a firm believer that what's for me is for me and no one can take it away. If something isn't for me, then it was only supposed to be in my life for a season and I'm fine.

Being okay with JoJo's biological dad coming into the picture Studies show, 85% of blended familes are dysfunctional.

In our scenario, we got married extremely fast and Drew was pregnant 2mo after. We had a huge decision to make, where do we stay to raise the kids. At the time we were in LA and didn't feel like we had much support. We could either go to NJ to my family or Chicago with her family. I spoke with Drew's mom and she said I really can't help you if you stay in LA. Drew has a big family, her mom and dad and 4 sisters. It was a no brainer and we relocated to Chicago before Machai was born. I didn't have a chance to fully assume the "Dad" role as everything was moving fast. We were living under the same roof however Drew was making moves the way she programmed and without much involvement or opinion from my side. There were a few things that I didn't like entirely too much such as JoJo staying up until any time he wanted as if he was a little rockstar in a diaper and him sleeping in the same bed. Drew wasn't receptive to him staying up late and defended by saying she's an actress and her hours flucturate. To combat, I provided studies and reports on best practices for sleeping. I also provided a guidance for the tv staying on all night and she said her parents did it with them and everyone is okay so it's not that bad. I tried developing the "My House, My Rules" concept but it quickly fell on death ears as my concerns weren't enforced. Opposed to supporting, JoJo would cry and mom would come to the rescue. I began to see a common thread, where JoJo was also learning how to get his way and It then became an issue where it was Me vs. Them.

Boiling Point where I felt I couldn't parent

Due to JoJo not receiving adequate sleep, he struggled to get up for school in the morning. Being a man, I had my way of getting you to follow directions which was to place the fear of God in you because at the end of the day, I'm the parent. JoJo stood by the sink and didn't want to brush his teeth so I "acted" as if I was going to give him a pinch and he started crying, not because of pain but because of the act. His mother ran upstairs and grabbed JoJo, asking what happened. JoJo responded, daddy pinched me. Drew grabbed JoJo and repremanded me saying I told you not to do that to him. I asked JoJo to demonstrate on his mother exactly how hard I pinched him and he barely touched his mother. I walked out the room as I felt emasculated and minimized below a child. I thought to myself if I wanted to stay in a relationship where I didn't have a parenting voice. Besides all that I've done and contributed, I should feel more respected. We ended up seeking out a marriage counselor that told us we're doing things all wrong. We didn't have a plan and it shows.

but she did ask for my thoughts to correct him sleeping in the bed.

Introduce Drew's mom, millinial

Support we had and lacked

Realistic / Unrealistic Expectations

It's either him or me

Village mindset, when JoJo's dad came home, Respect. Territorial. No this is my house.

Drew received a call from JoJo's biological dad that he came home from jail and wanted to see his son if possible. At the time Drew was still hurt by the lack of support and effort. Her perspective was, if you haven't been around or made an effort all this time, why now. JoJo doesn't need you. Besides she had me in her life which "filled" the void of JoJo's lack of a father figure. Once Drew brought the conversation and intention to my attention, I had a lot of thinking to do also. As a man or the other man in the situation, I had several thoughts run through my mind. As men, we can rightfully be territorial and protective of their

castle. After I let my pride down, put myself in his shoes and think big picture, there were a few things I had to evaluate. Did JoJo's father approach the situation respectfully for my wife and also for me? Did he do anything to neglect the wellbeing and safety of JoJo? What is the intention? Is this relationship in the best interest for JoJo? I immediately thought of my father and our circumstances.

As a child, no one couldn't tell me that my father wasn't the best in the world and guess what, that's my perspective. If you measured or quantified the value of our relationship, there would be large gaps in his presence, missed games and events, missed birthdays, missed growth and bonding opportunities. Yet, my father was still the best thing that could have ever happened to me. How could this be, the heart doesn't measure value in the way our minds do. Love is blind and that's what makes love beautiful, innocent and cherished. Without love, we would be robots, incapable of forgiving or giving someone an opportunity to succeed. If we were robotic in our heart, we would leave a baby that didn't learn to walk fast enough or talk. Sometimes the greatest lessons on earth is experiencing life.

Interesting enough, Initially I didn't speak with JoJo's biological father as Drew had to feel comfortable with the interaction first however I was always by her side supporting the process. Change is very hard especially on a child therefore she wanted to make sure he wanted to really be part of his life before introducing his Father and he deciding he didn't want that role. Consistency is important to know if you're in this for the long run or if it's a nice experience because you think you should do it. Drew put JoJo's father on a call schedule to slowly introduce JoJo to his Father. JoJo visited with him as a baby but it's been years since they spoke and as a child, they don't know what a father means. The first few interactions was awkward just as any person that walks into a child's life that doesn't have kids, there is a learning process.

Adoption Because JoJo's father wasn't around, people would ask if I would adopt him, which is a great question. These are my rules on adopting in a blended family:

The Father doesn't want to be in the child's life therefore the child is fatherless

The Father is deceased.

The child is in harm or danger, therefore it's an unfit home.

The child doesn't have parents

In the event the child's mother dies, custody can be established through court order.....Find out the process. I really don't know.

If I would have adopted Josiah.

JoJo will get to a point where he seeks information and understanding for himself and he would approach his father asking, why didn't he make an effort to be in his life. His Father would more than likely respond, your parents didn't allow me to be a part of your life and pushed me out. JoJo can possibly develop resentment due to our actions, even if we felt it was in his best interest.

This is a great segway into the definition of "Dad." Dads come in all different forms, types, relationships and can be interchangeable for almost anyone providing support that uplifts positive change and growth. When my father wasn't around, coaches became father figures to me including men in the community that taught me fundamentals of manhood. When my father wasn't around, men in the community would hire me and my brother to pickup leaves. It probably was one of the worst jobs I've ever experienced but it built character and work ethic that I wouldn't trade for the world. There is a village that becomes available to instill the lessons children need to learn and the role of "dad" can often be spread throughout the village to ensure children learn fundamentals of life. This concept also applies when the dad is around. Everyone is limited on the amount of information we know. If someone excels in a certain area, send the child to exceed your own understanding as the future depends on our children being smarter and more skilled than us.

Confidence I'm a firm believer that what's for me is for me and no one can take it away. If something isn't for me, then it was only supposed to be in my life for a season and I'm fine.

Being okay with JoJo's biological dad coming into the picture Studies show, 85% of blended familes are dysfunctional. While Drew and I were dating, she was very intentional not to allow me to play the dad role. She didn't want to scare me off or put responsibility on me before we had a chance to know if our relationship would last. Her family also assisted in our dating process. Their goal was to help Drew find the man of her dreams and would take JoJo so she could go out on dates. Well, that strategy worked! Drew and I went on a date that lasted 12hrs. Her family wasn't very happy when I brought her home at 4am. To no despair, we stayed in contact and she became my wife. I would ask Drew if I could take JoJo for ice cream or take him to the park while she was working if I felt she needed a helping hand so I could build a stronger bond with him. I knew if I married Drew, he would become my son. JoJo's biological father currently wasn't around and I knew JoJo needed a male influence to help him navigate the world, instill moral and values and grow into the man he would become. I had great expectations however I didn't know what a son or father figure meant from my wifes's eyes. My thought was once we were married, I would automatically take on the father role.

In our scenario, we got married extremely fast and Drew was pregnant 2mo after. We had a huge decision to make, where do we stay to raise the kids. At the time we were in LA and didn't feel like we had much support. We could either go to NJ to my family or Chicago with her family. I spoke with Drew's mom and she said I really can't help you if you stay in LA. Drew has a big family, her mom and dad and 4 sisters. It was a no brainer and we relocated to Chicago before Machai was born. I didn't have a chance to fully assume the "Dad" role as everything was moving fast. We were living under the same roof however Drew was making moves the way she programmed and without much

involvement or opinion from my side. There were a few things that I didn't like entirely too much such as JoJo staying up until any time he wanted as if he was a little rockstar in a diaper and him sleeping in the same bed. Drew wasn't receptive to him staying up late and defended by saying she's an actress and her hours flucturate. To combat, I provided studies and reports on best practices for sleeping. I also provided a guidance for the tv staying on all night and she said her parents did it with them and everyone is okay so it's not that bad. I tried developing the "My House, My Rules" concept but it quickly fell on death ears as my concerns weren't enforced. Opposed to supporting, JoJo would cry and mom would come to the rescue. I began to see a common thread, where JoJo was also learning how to get his way and It then became an issue where it was Me vs. Them.

Boiling Point where I felt I couldn't parent

Due to JoJo not receiving adequate sleep, he struggled to get up for school in the morning. Being a man, I had my way of getting you to follow directions which was to place the fear of God in you because at the end of the day, I'm the parent. JoJo stood by the sink and didn't want to brush his teeth so I "acted" as if I was going to give him a pinch and he started crying, not because of pain but because of the act. His mother ran upstairs and grabbed JoJo, asking what happened. JoJo responded, daddy pinched me. Drew grabbed JoJo and repremanded me saying I told you not to do that to him. I asked JoJo to demonstrate on his mother exactly how hard I pinched him and he barely touched his mother. I walked out the room as I felt emasculated and minimized below a child. I thought to myself if I wanted to stay in a relationship where I didn't have a parenting voice. Besides all that I've done and contributed, I should feel more respected. We ended up seeking out a marriage counselor that told us we're doing things all wrong. We didn't have a plan and it shows.

but she did ask for my thoughts to correct him sleeping in the bed.

Introduce Drew's mom, millinial

Support we had and lacked
Realistic / Unrealistic Expectations
It's either him or me
Village mindset, when JoJo's dad came home, Respect. Territorial. No this is my house.

Drew received a call from JoJo's biological dad that he came home from jail and wanted to see his son if possible. At the time Drew was still hurt by the lack of support and effort. Her perspective was, if you haven't been around or made an effort all this time, why now. JoJo doesn't need you. Besides she had me in her life which "filled" the void of JoJo's lack of a father figure. Once Drew brought the conversation and intention to my attention, I had a lot of thinking to do also. As a man or the other man in the situation, I had several thoughts run through my mind. As men, we can rightfully be territorial and protective of their castle. After I let my pride down, put myself in his shoes and think big picture, there were a few things I had to evaluate. Did JoJo's father approach the situation respectfully for my wife and also for me? Did he do anything to neglect the wellbeing and safety of JoJo? What is the intention? Is this relationship in the best interest for JoJo? I immediately thought of my father and our circumstances.

As a child, no one couldn't tell me that my father wasn't the best in the world and guess what, that's my perspective. If you measured or quantified the value of our relationship, there would be large gaps in his presence, missed games and events, missed birthdays, missed growth and bonding opportunities. Yet, my father was still the best thing that could have ever happened to me. How could this be, the heart doesn't measure value in the way our minds do. Love is blind and that's what makes love beautiful, innocent and cherished. Without love, we would be robots, incapable of forgiving or giving someone an opportunity to succeed. If we were robotic in our heart, we would leave a baby that didn't learn to walk fast enough or talk. Sometimes the greatest lessons on earth is experiencing life.

Interesting enough, Initially I didn't speak with JoJo's biological father as Drew had to feel comfortable with the interaction first however I was always by her side supporting the process. Change is very hard especially on a child therefore she wanted to make sure he wanted to really be part of his life before introducing his Father and he deciding he didn't want that role. Consistency is important to know if you're in this for the long run or if it's a nice experience because you think you should do it. Drew put JoJo's father on a call schedule to slowly introduce JoJo to his Father. JoJo visited with him as a baby but it's been years since they spoke and as a child, they don't know what a father means. The first few interactions was awkward just as any person that walks into a child's life that doesn't have kids, there is a learning process.

Adoption Because JoJo's father wasn't around, people would ask if I would adopt him, which is a great question. These are my rules on adopting in a blended family:

The Father doesn't want to be in the child's life therefore the child is fatherless

The Father is deceased.

The child is in harm or danger, therefore it's an unfit home.

The child doesn't have parents

In the event the child's mother dies, custody can be established through court order.....Find out the process. I really don't know.

If I would have adopted Josiah.

JoJo will get to a point where he seeks information and understanding for himself and he would approach his father asking, why didn't he make an effort to be in his life. His Father would more than likely respond, your parents didn't allow me to be a part of your life and pushed me out. JoJo can possibly develop resentment due to our actions, even if we felt it was in his best interest.

This is a great segway into the definition of "Dad." Dads come in all different forms, types, relationships and can be interchangeable for almost anyone providing support that uplifts positive

change and growth. When my father wasn't around, coaches became father figures to me including men in the community that taught me fundamentals of manhood. When my father wasn't around, men in the community would hire me and my brother to pickup leaves. It probably was one of the worst jobs I've ever experienced but it built character and work ethic that I wouldn't trade for the world. There is a village that becomes available to instill the lessons children need to learn and the role of "dad" can often be spread throughout the village to ensure children learn fundamentals of life. This concept also applies when the dad is around. Everyone is limited on the amount of information we know. If someone excels in a certain area, send the child to exceed your own understanding as the future depends on our children being smarter and more skilled than us.

Confidence I'm a firm believer that what's for me is for me and no one can take it away. If something isn't for me, then it was only supposed to be in my life for a season and I'm fine.

Being okay with JoJo's biological dad coming into the picture Studies show, 85% of blended familes are dysfunctional.

In our scenario, we got married extremely fast and Drew was pregnant 2mo after. We had a huge decision to make, where do we stay to raise the kids. At the time we were in LA and didn't feel like we had much support. We could either go to NJ to my family or Chicago with her family. I spoke with Drew's mom and she said I really can't help you if you stay in LA. Drew has a big family, her mom and dad and 4 sisters. It was a no brainer and we relocated to Chicago before Machai was born. I didn't have a chance to fully assume the "Dad" role as everything was moving fast. We were living under the same roof however Drew was making moves the way she programmed and without much involvement or opinion from my side. There were a few things that I didn't like entirely too much such as JoJo staying up until any time he wanted as if he was a little rockstar in a diaper and him sleeping in the same bed. Drew wasn't receptive to him staying up late and defended by saying she's an actress and her hours flucturate. To combat, I provided studies and reports on best practices for sleeping. I also provided a guidance for the tv staying on all night and she said her parents did it with them and everyone is okay so it's not that bad. I tried developing the "My House, My Rules" concept but it quickly fell on death ears as my concerns weren't enforced. Opposed to supporting, JoJo would cry and mom would come to the rescue. I began to see a common thread, where JoJo was also learning how to get his way and It then became an issue where it was Me vs. Them.

Boiling Point where I felt I couldn't parent

Due to JoJo not receiving adequate sleep, he struggled to get up for school in the morning. Being a man, I had my way of getting you to follow directions which was to place the fear of God in you because at the end of the day, I'm the parent. JoJo stood by the sink and didn't want to brush his teeth so I "acted" as if I was going to give him a pinch and he started crying, not because of pain but because of the act. His mother ran upstairs and grabbed JoJo, asking what happened. JoJo responded, daddy pinched me. Drew grabbed JoJo and repremanded me saying I told you not to do that to him. I asked JoJo to demonstrate on his mother exactly how hard I pinched him and he barely touched his mother. I walked out the room as I felt emasculated and minimized below a child. I thought to myself if I wanted to stay in a relationship where I didn't have a parenting voice. Besides all that I've done and contributed, I should feel more respected. We ended up seeking out a marriage counselor that told us we're doing things all wrong. We didn't have a plan and it shows.

but she did ask for my thoughts to correct him sleeping in the bed.

Introduce Drew's mom, millinial

Support we had and lacked

Realistic / Unrealistic Expectations

It's either him or me

Village mindset, when JoJo's dad came home, Respect. Territorial. No this is my house.

Drew received a call from JoJo's biological dad that he came home from jail and wanted to see his son if possible. At the time Drew was still hurt by the lack of support and effort. Her perspective was, if you haven't been around or made an effort all this time, why now. JoJo doesn't need you. Besides she had me in her life which "filled" the void of JoJo's lack of a father figure. Once Drew brought the conversation and intention to my attention, I had a lot of thinking to do also. As a man or the other man in the situation, I had several thoughts run through my mind. As men, we can rightfully be territorial and protective of their castle. After I let my pride down, put myself in his shoes and think big picture, there were a few things I had to evaluate. Did JoJo's father approach the situation respectfully for my wife and also for me? Did he do anything to neglect the wellbeing and safety of JoJo? What is the intention? Is this relationship in the best interest for JoJo? I immediately thought of my father and our circumstances.

As a child, no one couldn't tell me that my father wasn't the best in the world and guess what, that's my perspective. If you measured or quantified the value of our relationship, there would be large gaps in his presence, missed games and events, missed birthdays, missed growth and bonding opportunities. Yet, my father was still the best thing that could have ever happened to me. How could this be, the heart doesn't measure value in the way our minds do. Love is blind and that's what makes love beautiful, innocent and cherished. Without love, we would be robots, incapable of forgiving or giving someone an opportunity to succeed. If we were robotic in our heart, we would leave a baby that didn't learn to walk fast enough or talk. Sometimes the greatest lessons on earth is experiencing life.

Interesting enough, Initially I didn't speak with JoJo's biological father as Drew had to feel comfortable with the interaction first however I was always by her side supporting the process. Change is very hard especially on a child therefore she wanted to make sure he wanted to really be part of his life before

introducing his Father and he deciding he didn't want that role. Consistency is important to know if you're in this for the long run or if it's a nice experience because you think you should do it. Drew put JoJo's father on a call schedule to slowly introduce JoJo to his Father. JoJo visited with him as a baby but it's been years since they spoke and as a child, they don't know what a father means. The first few interactions was awkward just as any person that walks into a child's life that doesn't have kids, there is a learning process.

Adoption Because JoJo's father wasn't around, people would ask if I would adopt him, which is a great question. These are my rules on adopting in a blended family:

The Father doesn't want to be in the child's life therefore the child is fatherless

The Father is deceased.

The child is in harm or danger, therefore it's an unfit home.

The child doesn't have parents

In the event the child's mother dies, custody can be established through court order.....Find out the process. I really don't know.

If I would have adopted Josiah.

JoJo will get to a point where he seeks information and understanding for himself and he would approach his father asking, why didn't he make an effort to be in his life. His Father would more than likely respond, your parents didn't allow me to be a part of your life and pushed me out. JoJo can possibly develop resentment due to our actions, even if we felt it was in his best interest.

This is a great segway into the definition of "Dad." Dads come in all different forms, types, relationships and can be interchangeable for almost anyone providing support that uplifts positive change and growth. When my father wasn't around, coaches became father figures to me including men in the community that taught me fundamentals of manhood. When my father wasn't around, men in the community would hire me and my brother to pickup leaves. It probably was one of the worst jobs I've ever

experienced but it built character and work ethic that I wouldn't trade for the world. There is a village that becomes available to instill the lessons children need to learn and the role of "dad" can often be spread throughout the village to ensure children learn fundamentals of life. This concept also applies when the dad is around. Everyone is limited on the amount of information we know. If someone excels in a certain area, send the child to exceed your own understanding as the future depends on our children being smarter and more skilled than us.

Confidence I'm a firm believer that what's for me is for me and no one can take it away. If something isn't for me, then it was only supposed to be in my life for a season and I'm fine.

Being okay with JoJo's biological dad coming into the picture Studies show, 85% of blended familes are dysfunctional. While Drew and I were dating, she was very intentional not to allow me to play the dad role. She didn't want to scare me off or put responsibility on me before we had a chance to know if our relationship would last. Her family also assisted in our dating process. Their goal was to help Drew find the man of her dreams and would take JoJo so she could go out on dates. Well, that strategy worked! Drew and I went on a date that lasted 12hrs. Her family wasn't very happy when I brought her home at 4am. To no despair, we stayed in contact and she became my wife. I would ask Drew if I could take JoJo for ice cream or take him to the park while she was working if I felt she needed a helping hand so I could build a stronger bond with him. I knew if I married Drew, he would become my son. JoJo's biological father currently wasn't around and I knew JoJo needed a male influence to help him navigate the world, instill moral and values and grow into the man he would become. I had great expectations however I didn't know what a son or father figure meant from my wifes's eyes. My thought was once we were married, I would automatically take on the father role.

In our scenario, we got married extremely fast and Drew was pregnant 2mo after. We had a huge decision to make, where do

314

we stay to raise the kids. At the time we were in LA and didn't feel like we had much support. We could either go to NJ to my family or Chicago with her family. I spoke with Drew's mom and she said I really can't help you if you stay in LA. Drew has a big family, her mom and dad and 4 sisters. It was a no brainer and we relocated to Chicago before Machai was born. I didn't have a chance to fully assume the "Dad" role as everything was moving fast. We were living under the same roof however Drew was making moves the way she programmed and without much involvement or opinion from my side. There were a few things that I didn't like entirely too much such as JoJo staying up until any time he wanted as if he was a little rockstar in a diaper and him sleeping in the same bed. Drew wasn't receptive to him staying up late and defended by saying she's an actress and her hours flucturate. To combat, I provided studies and reports on best practices for sleeping. I also provided a guidance for the tv staying on all night and she said her parents did it with them and everyone is okay so it's not that bad. I tried developing the "My House, My Rules" concept but it quickly fell on death ears as my concerns weren't enforced. Opposed to supporting, JoJo would cry and mom would come to the rescue. I began to see a common thread, where JoJo was also learning how to get his way and It then became an issue where it was Me vs. Them.

Boiling Point where I felt I couldn't parent

Due to JoJo not receiving adequate sleep, he struggled to get up for school in the morning. Being a man, I had my way of getting you to follow directions which was to place the fear of God in you because at the end of the day, I'm the parent. JoJo stood by the sink and didn't want to brush his teeth so I "acted" as if I was going to give him a pinch and he started crying, not because of pain but because of the act. His mother ran upstairs and grabbed JoJo, asking what happened. JoJo responded, daddy pinched me. Drew grabbed JoJo and repremanded me saying I told you not to do that to him. I asked JoJo to demonstrate on his mother exactly how hard I pinched him and he barely touched

his mother. I walked out the room as I felt emasculated and minimized below a child. I thought to myself if I wanted to stay in a relationship where I didn't have a parenting voice. Besides all that I've done and contributed, I should feel more respected. We ended up seeking out a marriage counselor that told us we're doing things all wrong. We didn't have a plan and it shows.

JoJo will get to a point where he seeks information and understanding for himself and he would approach his father asking, why didn't he make an effort to be in his life. His Father would more than likely respond, your parents didn't allow me to be a part of your life and pushed me out. JoJo can possibly develop resentment due to our actions, even if we felt it was in his best interest.

This is a great segway into the definition of "Dad." Dads come in all different forms, types, relationships and can be interchangeable for almost anyone providing support that uplifts positive change and growth. When my father wasn't around, coaches became father figures to me including men in the community that taught me fundamentals of manhood. When my father wasn't around, men in the community would hire me and my brother to pickup leaves. It probably was one of the worst jobs I've ever experienced but it built character and work ethic that I wouldn't trade for the world. There is a village that becomes available to instill the lessons children need to learn and the role of "dad" can often be spread throughout the village to ensure children learn fundamentals of life. This concept also applies when the dad is around. Everyone is limited on the amount of information we know. If someone excels in a certain area, send the child to exceed your own understanding as the future depends on our children being smarter and more skilled than us.

Confidence I'm a firm believer that what's for me is for me and no one can take it away. If something isn't for me, then it was only supposed to be in my life for a season and I'm fine.

Being okay with JoJo's biological dad coming into the picture

Studies show, 85% of blended families are dysfunctional. While Drew and I were dating, she was very intentional not to allow me to play the dad role. She didn't want to scare me off or put responsibility on me before we had a chance to know if our relationship would last. Her family also assisted in our dating process. Their goal was to help Drew find the man of her dreams and would take JoJo so she could go out on dates. Well, that strategy worked! Drew and I went on a date that lasted 12hrs. Her family wasn't very happy when I brought her home at 4am. To no despair, we stayed in contact and she became my wife. I would ask Drew if I could take JoJo for ice cream or take him to the park while she was working if I felt she needed a helping hand so I could build a stronger bond with him. I knew if I married Drew, he would become my son. JoJo's biological father currently wasn't around and I knew JoJo needed a male influence to help him navigate the world, instill moral and values and grow into the man he would become. I had great expectations however I didn't know what a son or father figure meant from my wifes's eyes. My thought was once we were married, I would automatically take on the father role.

In our scenario, we got married extremely fast and Drew was pregnant 2mo after. We had a huge decision to make, where do we stay to raise the kids. At the time we were in LA and didn't feel like we had much support. We could either go to NJ to my family or Chicago with her family. I spoke with Drew's mom and she said I really can't help you if you stay in LA. Drew has a big family, her mom and dad and 4 sisters. It was a no brainer and we relocated to Chicago before Machai was born. I didn't have a chance to fully assume the "Dad" role as everything was moving fast. We were living under the same roof however Drew was making moves the way she programmed and without much involvement or opinion from my side. There were a few things that I didn't like entirely too much such as JoJo staying up until any time he wanted as if he was a little rockstar in a diaper and him sleeping in the same bed. Drew wasn't receptive to him staying up late and defended by saying she's an actress and her hours flucturate. To combat, I provided studies and reports on best practices for sleeping. I also provided a guidance for the tv staying on all night and she said her parents did it with them and everyone is okay so it's not that bad. I tried developing the "My House, My Rules" concept but it quickly fell on death ears as my concerns weren't enforced. Opposed to supporting, JoJo would cry and mom would come to the rescue. I began to see a common thread, where JoJo was also learning how to get his way and It then became an issue where it was Me vs. Them. but she did ask for my thoughts to correct him sleeping in the bed.

Introduce Drew's mom, millinial

Support we had and lacked

Realistic / Unrealistic Expectations

It's either him or me

Village mindset, when JoJo's dad came home, Respect. Territorial. No this is my house.

Drew received a call from JoJo's biological dad that he came home from jail and wanted to see his son if possible. At the time Drew was still hurt by the lack of support and effort. Her perspective was, if you haven't been around or made an effort all this time, why now. JoJo doesn't need you. Besides she had me in her life which "filled" the void of JoJo's lack of a father figure. Once Drew brought the conversation and intention to my attention, I had a lot of thinking to do also. As a man or the other man in the situation, I had several thoughts run through my mind. As men, we can rightfully be territorial and protective of their castle. After I let my pride down, put myself in his shoes and think big picture, there were a few things I had to evaluate. Did JoJo's father approach the situation respectfully for my wife and also for me? Did he do anything to neglect the wellbeing and safety of JoJo? What is the intention? Is this relationship in the best interest for JoJo? I immediately thought of my father and our circumstances.

As a child, no one couldn't tell me that my father wasn't the best in the world and guess what, that's my perspective. If you measured or quantified the value of our relationship, there would be large gaps in his presence, missed games and events, missed birthdays, missed growth and bonding opportunities. Yet, my father was still the best thing that could have ever happened to me. How could this be, the heart doesn't measure value in the way our minds do. Love is blind and that's what makes love beautiful, innocent and cherished. Without love, we would be robots, incapable of forgiving or giving someone an opportunity to succeed. If we were robotic in our heart, we would leave a baby that didn't learn to walk fast enough or talk. Sometimes the greatest lessons on earth is experiencing life.

Interesting enough, Initially I didn't speak with JoJo's biological father as Drew had to feel comfortable with the interaction first however I was always by her side supporting the process. Change is very hard especially on a child therefore she wanted to make sure he wanted to really be part of his life before introducing his Father and he deciding he didn't want that role. Consistency is important to know if you're in this for the long run or if it's a nice experience because you think you should do it. Drew put JoJo's father on a call schedule to slowly introduce JoJo to his Father. JoJo visited with him as a baby but it's been years since they spoke and as a child, they don't know what a father means. The first few interactions was awkward just as any person that walks into a child's life that doesn't have kids, there is a learning process.

Adoption Because JoJo's father wasn't around, people would ask if I would adopt him, which is a great question. These are my rules on adopting in a blended family:

The Father doesn't want to be in the child's life therefore the child is fatherless

The Father is deceased.

The child is in harm or danger, therefore it's an unfit home.

The child doesn't have parents

In the event the child's mother dies, custody can be established through court order.....Find out the process. I really don't know.

If I would have adopted Josiah.

JoJo will get to a point where he seeks information and understanding for himself and he would approach his father asking, why didn't he make an effort to be in his life. His Father would more than likely respond, your parents didn't allow me to be a part of your life and pushed me out. JoJo can possibly develop resentment due to our actions, even if we felt it was in his best interest.

Love Is Beautiful

THIS IS A great segway into the definition of "Dad." Dads come in all different forms, types, relationships and can be interchangeable for almost anyone providing support that uplifts positive change and growth. When my father wasn't around, coaches became father figures to me including men in the community that taught me fundamentals of manhood. When my father wasn't around, men in the community would hire me and my brother to pickup leaves. It probably was one of the worst jobs I've ever experienced but it built character and work ethic that I wouldn't trade for the world. There is a village that becomes available to instill the lessons children need to learn and the role of "dad" can often be spread throughout the village to ensure children learn fundamentals of life. This concept also applies when the dad is around. Everyone is limited on the amount of information we know. If someone excels in a certain area, send the child to exceed your own understanding as the future depends on our children being smarter and more skilled than us.

Confidence I'm a firm believer that what's for me is for me and no one can take it away. If something isn't for me, then it was only supposed to be in my life for a season and I'm fine.

Being okay with JoJo's biological dad coming into the picture

Studies show, 85% of blended familes are dysfunctional.

In our scenario, we got married extremely fast and Drew was pregnant 2mo after. We had a huge decision to make, where do we stay to raise the kids. At the time we were in LA and didn't feel like we had much support. We could either go to NJ to my family or Chicago with her family. I spoke with Drew's mom and she said I really can't help you if you stay in LA. Drew has a big family, her mom and dad and 4 sisters. It was a no brainer and we relocated to Chicago before Machai was born. I didn't have a chance to fully assume the "Dad" role as everything was moving fast. We were living under the same roof however Drew was making moves the way she programmed and without much involvement or opinion from my side. There were a few things that I didn't like entirely too much such as JoJo staying up until any time he wanted as if he was a little rockstar in a diaper and him sleeping in the same bed. Drew wasn't receptive to him staying up late and defended by saying she's an actress and her hours flucturate. To combat, I provided studies and reports on best practices for sleeping. I also provided a guidance for the tv staying on all night and she said her parents did it with them and everyone is okay so it's not that bad. I tried developing the "My House, My Rules" concept but it quickly fell on death ears as my concerns weren't enforced. Opposed to supporting, JoJo would cry and mom would come to the rescue. I began to see a common thread, where JoJo was also learning how to get his way and It then became an issue where it was Me vs. Them.

Boiling Point where I felt I couldn't parent

Due to JoJo not receiving adequate sleep, he struggled to get up for school in the morning. Being a man, I had my way of getting you to follow directions which was to place the fear of God in you because at the end of the day, I'm the parent. JoJo stood by the sink and didn't want to brush his teeth so I "acted" as if I was going to give him a pinch and he started crying, not because of pain but because of the act. His mother ran upstairs and grabbed JoJo, asking what happened. JoJo responded, daddy pinched me. Drew grabbed JoJo and repremanded me saying I told you not to do that to him. I asked JoJo to demonstrate on his mother exactly how hard I pinched him and he barely touched his mother. I walked out the room as I felt emasculated and minimized below a child. I thought to myself if I wanted to stay in a relationship where I didn't have a parenting voice. Besides all that I've done and contributed, I should feel more respected. We ended up seeking out a marriage counselor that told us we're doing things all wrong. We didn't have a plan and it shows.

but she did ask for my thoughts to correct him sleeping in the bed.

Introduce Drew's mom, millinial

Support we had and lacked

Realistic / Unrealistic Expectations

It's either him or me

Village mindset, when JoJo's dad came home, Respect. Territorial. No this is my house.

Drew received a call from JoJo's biological dad that he came home from jail and wanted to see his son if possible. At the time Drew was still hurt by the lack of support and effort. Her perspective was, if you haven't been around or made an effort all this time, why now. JoJo doesn't need you. Besides she had me in her life which "filled" the void of JoJo's lack of a father figure. Once Drew brought the conversation and intention to my attention, I had a lot of thinking to do also. As a man or the other man in the situation, I had several thoughts run through my mind. As men, we can rightfully be territorial and protective of their castle. After I let my pride down, put myself in his shoes and think big picture, there were a few things I had to evaluate. Did JoJo's father approach the situation respectfully for my wife and also for me? Did he do anything to neglect the wellbeing and safety of JoJo? What is the intention? Is this relationship in the best interest for JoJo? I immediately thought of my father and our circumstances.

As a child, no one couldn't tell me that my father wasn't the best in the world and guess what, that's my perspective. If you measured or quantified the value of our relationship, there would be large gaps in his presence, missed games and events, missed birthdays, missed growth and bonding opportunities. Yet, my father was still the best thing that could have ever happened to me. How could this be, the heart doesn't measure value in the way our minds do. Love is blind and that's what makes love beautiful, innocent and cherished. Without love, we would be robots, incapable of forgiving or giving someone an opportunity to succeed. If we were robotic in our heart, we would leave a baby that didn't learn to walk fast enough or talk. Sometimes the greatest lessons on earth is experiencing life.

Interesting enough, Initially I didn't speak with JoJo's biological father as Drew had to feel comfortable with the interaction first however I was always by her side supporting the process. Change is very hard especially on a child therefore she wanted to make sure he wanted to really be part of his life before introducing his Father and he deciding he didn't want that role. Consistency is important to know if you're in this for the long run or if it's a nice experience because you think you should do it. Drew put JoJo's father on a call schedule to slowly introduce JoJo to his Father. JoJo visited with him as a baby but it's been years since they spoke and as a child, they don't know what a father means. The first few interactions was awkward just as any person that walks into a child's life that doesn't have kids, there is a learning process.

Adoption Because JoJo's father wasn't around, people would ask if I would adopt him, which is a great question. These are my rules on adopting in a blended family:

The Father doesn't want to be in the child's life therefore the child is fatherless

The Father is deceased.

The child is in harm or danger, therefore it's an unfit home.

The child doesn't have parents

In the event the child's mother dies, custody can be established through court order.....Find out the process. I really don't know.

If I would have adopted Josiah.

JoJo will get to a point where he seeks information and understanding for himself and he would approach his father asking, why didn't he make an effort to be in his life. His Father would more than likely respond, your parents didn't allow me to be a part of your life and pushed me out. JoJo can possibly develop resentment due to our actions, even if we felt it was in his best interest.

This is a great segway into the definition of "Dad." Dads come in all different forms, types, relationships and can be interchangeable for almost anyone providing support that uplifts positive change and growth. When my father wasn't around, coaches became father figures to me including men in the community that taught me fundamentals of manhood. When my father wasn't around, men in the community would hire me and my brother to pickup leaves. It probably was one of the worst jobs I've ever experienced but it built character and work ethic that I wouldn't trade for the world. There is a village that becomes available to instill the lessons children need to learn and the role of "dad" can often be spread throughout the village to ensure children learn fundamentals of life. This concept also applies when the dad is around. Everyone is limited on the amount of information we know. If someone excels in a certain area, send the child to exceed your own understanding as the future depends on our children being smarter and more skilled than us.

Confidence I'm a firm believer that what's for me is for me and no one can take it away. If something isn't for me, then it was only supposed to be in my life for a season and I'm fine.

Being okay with JoJo's biological dad coming into the picture Studies show, 85% of blended familes are dysfunctional. While Drew and I were dating, she was very intentional not to allow me to play the dad role. She didn't want to scare me off or put responsibility on me before we had a chance to know if

our relationship would last. Her family also assisted in our dating process. Their goal was to help Drew find the man of her dreams and would take JoJo so she could go out on dates. Well, that strategy worked! Drew and I went on a date that lasted 12hrs. Her family wasn't very happy when I brought her home at 4am. To no despair, we stayed in contact and she became my wife. I would ask Drew if I could take JoJo for ice cream or take him to the park while she was working if I felt she needed a helping hand so I could build a stronger bond with him. I knew if I married Drew, he would become my son. JoJo's biological father currently wasn't around and I knew JoJo needed a male influence to help him navigate the world, instill moral and values and grow into the man he would become. I had great expectations however I didn't know what a son or father figure meant from my wifes's eyes. My thought was once we were married, I would automatically take on the father role.

In our scenario, we got married extremely fast and Drew was pregnant 2mo after. We had a huge decision to make, where do we stay to raise the kids. At the time we were in LA and didn't feel like we had much support. We could either go to NJ to my family or Chicago with her family. I spoke with Drew's mom and she said I really can't help you if you stay in LA. Drew has a big family, her mom and dad and 4 sisters. It was a no brainer and we relocated to Chicago before Machai was born. I didn't have a chance to fully assume the "Dad" role as everything was moving fast. We were living under the same roof however Drew was making moves the way she programmed and without much involvement or opinion from my side. There were a few things that I didn't like entirely too much such as JoJo staying up until any time he wanted as if he was a little rockstar in a diaper and him sleeping in the same bed. Drew wasn't receptive to him staying up late and defended by saying she's an actress and her hours flucturate. To combat, I provided studies and reports on best practices for sleeping. I also provided a guidance for the tv staying on all night and she said her parents did it with them and

everyone is okay so it's not that bad. I tried developing the "My House, My Rules" concept but it quickly fell on death ears as my concerns weren't enforced. Opposed to supporting, JoJo would cry and mom would come to the rescue. I began to see a common thread, where JoJo was also learning how to get his way and It then became an issue where it was Me vs. Them.

Boiling Point where I felt I couldn't parent

Due to JoJo not receiving adequate sleep, he struggled to get up for school in the morning. Being a man, I had my way of getting you to follow directions which was to place the fear of God in you because at the end of the day, I'm the parent. JoJo stood by the sink and didn't want to brush his teeth so I "acted" as if I was going to give him a pinch and he started crying, not because of pain but because of the act. His mother ran upstairs and grabbed JoJo, asking what happened. JoJo responded, daddy pinched me. Drew grabbed JoJo and repremanded me saying I told you not to do that to him. I asked JoJo to demonstrate on his mother exactly how hard I pinched him and he barely touched his mother. I walked out the room as I felt emasculated and minimized below a child. I thought to myself if I wanted to stay in a relationship where I didn't have a parenting voice. Besides all that I've done and contributed, I should feel more respected. We ended up seeking out a marriage counselor that told us we're doing things all wrong. We didn't have a plan and it shows.

but she did ask for my thoughts to correct him sleeping in the bed.

Introduce Drew's mom, millinial

Support we had and lacked

Realistic / Unrealistic Expectations

It's either him or me

Village mindset, when JoJo's dad came home, Respect. Territorial. No this is my house.

Drew received a call from JoJo's biological dad that he came home from jail and wanted to see his son if possible. At the time Drew was still hurt by the lack of support and effort. Her

perspective was, if you haven't been around or made an effort all this time, why now. JoJo doesn't need you. Besides she had me in her life which "filled" the void of JoJo's lack of a father figure. Once Drew brought the conversation and intention to my attention, I had a lot of thinking to do also. As a man or the other man in the situation, I had several thoughts run through my mind. As men, we can rightfully be territorial and protective of their castle. After I let my pride down, put myself in his shoes and think big picture, there were a few things I had to evaluate. Did JoJo's father approach the situation respectfully for my wife and also for me? Did he do anything to neglect the wellbeing and safety of JoJo? What is the intention? Is this relationship in the best interest for JoJo? I immediately thought of my father and our circumstances.

As a child, no one couldn't tell me that my father wasn't the best in the world and guess what, that's my perspective. If you measured or quantified the value of our relationship, there would be large gaps in his presence, missed games and events, missed birthdays, missed growth and bonding opportunities. Yet, my father was still the best thing that could have ever happened to me. How could this be, the heart doesn't measure value in the way our minds do. Love is blind and that's what makes love beautiful, innocent and cherished. Without love, we would be robots, incapable of forgiving or giving someone an opportunity to succeed. If we were robotic in our heart, we would leave a baby that didn't learn to walk fast enough or talk. Sometimes the greatest lessons on earth is experiencing life.

JoJo will get to a point where he seeks information and understanding for himself and he would approach his father asking, why didn't he make an effort to be in his life. His Father would more than likely respond, your parents didn't allow me to be a part of your life and pushed me out. JoJo can possibly develop resentment due to our actions, even if we felt it was in his best interest.

JoJo will get to a point where he seeks information and understanding for himself and he would approach his father asking, why didn't he make an effort to be in his life. His Father would more than likely respond, your parents didn't allow me to be a part of your life and pushed me out. JoJo can possibly develop resentment due to our actions, even if we felt it was in his best interest.

This is a great segway into the definition of "Dad." Dads come in all different forms, types, relationships and can be interchangeable for almost anyone providing support that uplifts positive change and growth. When my father wasn't around, coaches became father figures to me including men in the community that taught me fundamentals of manhood. When my father wasn't around, men in the community would hire me and my brother to pickup leaves. It probably was one of the worst jobs I've ever experienced but it built character and work ethic that I wouldn't trade for the world. There is a village that becomes available to instill the lessons children need to learn and the role of "dad" can often be spread throughout the village to ensure children learn fundamentals of life. This concept also applies when the dad is around. Everyone is limited on the amount of information we know. If someone excels in a certain area, send the child to exceed your own understanding as the future depends on our children being smarter and more skilled than us.

Confidence I'm a firm believer that what's for me is for me and no one can take it away. If something isn't for me, then it was only supposed to be in my life for a season and I'm fine.

This is a great segway into the definition of "Dad." Dads come in all different forms, types, relationships and can be interchangeable for almost anyone providing support that uplifts positive change and growth. When my father wasn't around, coaches became father figures to me including men in the community that taught me fundamentals of manhood. When my father wasn't around, men in the community would hire me and my brother to pickup leaves. It probably was one of the worst jobs I've ever

experienced but it built character and work ethic that I wouldn't trade for the world. There is a village that becomes available to instill the lessons children need to learn and the role of "dad" can often be spread throughout the village to ensure children learn fundamentals of life. This concept also applies when the dad is around. Everyone is limited on the amount of information we know. If someone excels in a certain area, send the child to exceed your own understanding as the future depends on our children being smarter and more skilled than us.

Confidence I'm a firm believer that what's for me is for me and no one can take it away. If something isn't for me, then it was only supposed to be in my life for a season and I'm fine.

Interesting enough, Initially I didn't speak with JoJo's biological father as Drew had to feel comfortable with the interaction first however I was always by her side supporting the process. Change is very hard especially on a child therefore she wanted to make sure he wanted to really be part of his life before introducing his Father and he deciding he didn't want that role. Consistency is important to know if you're in this for the long run or if it's a nice experience because you think you should do it. Drew put JoJo's father on a call schedule to slowly introduce JoJo to his Father. JoJo visited with him as a baby but it's been years since they spoke and as a child, they don't know what a father means. The first few interactions was awkward just as any person that walks into a child's life that doesn't have kids, there is a learning process.

Adoption Because JoJo's father wasn't around, people would ask if I would adopt him, which is a great question. These are my rules on adopting in a blended family:

The Father doesn't want to be in the child's life therefore the child is fatherless

The Father is deceased.

The child is in harm or danger, therefore it's an unfit home.

The child doesn't have parents

In the event the child's mother dies, custody can be established through court order......Find out the process. I really don't know.

If I would have adopted Josiah.

JoJo will get to a point where he seeks information and understanding for himself and he would approach his father asking, why didn't he make an effort to be in his life. His Father would more than likely respond, your parents didn't allow me to be a part of your life and pushed me out. JoJo can possibly develop resentment due to our actions, even if we felt it was in his best interest.

This is a great segway into the definition of "Dad." Dads come in all different forms, types, relationships and can be interchangeable for almost anyone providing support that uplifts positive change and growth. When my father wasn't around, coaches became father figures to me including men in the community that taught me fundamentals of manhood. When my father wasn't around, men in the community would hire me and my brother to pickup leaves. It probably was one of the worst jobs I've ever experienced but it built character and work ethic that I wouldn't trade for the world. There is a village that becomes available to instill the lessons children need to learn and the role of "dad" can often be spread throughout the village to ensure children learn fundamentals of life. This concept also applies when the dad is around. Everyone is limited on the amount of information we know. If someone excels in a certain area, send the child to exceed your own understanding as the future depends on our children being smarter and more skilled than us.

Confidence I'm a firm believer that what's for me is for me and no one can take it away. If something isn't for me, then it was only supposed to be in my life for a season and I'm fine.

Being okay with JoJo's biological dad coming into the picture Studies show, 85% of blended familes are dysfunctional.

As a child, no one couldn't tell me that my father wasn't the best in the world and guess what, that's my perspective. If you measured or quantified the value of our relationship, there would be large gaps in his presence, missed games and events, missed birthdays, missed growth and bonding opportunities. Yet, my father was still the best thing that could have ever happened to me. How could this be, the heart doesn't measure value in the way our minds do. Love is blind and that's what makes love beautiful, innocent and cherished. Without love, we would be robots, incapable of forgiving or giving someone an opportunity to succeed. If we were robotic in our heart, we would leave a baby that didn't learn to walk fast enough or talk. Sometimes the greatest lessons on earth is experiencing life.

JoJo will get to a point where he seeks information and understanding for himself and he would approach his father asking, why didn't he make an effort to be in his life. His Father would more than likely respond, your parents didn't allow me to be a part of your life and pushed me out. JoJo can possibly develop resentment due to our actions, even if we felt it was in his best interest.

JoJo will get to a point where he seeks information and understanding for himself and he would approach his father asking, why didn't he make an effort to be in his life. His Father would more than likely respond, your parents didn't allow me to be a part of your life and pushed me out. JoJo can possibly develop resentment due to our actions, even if we felt it was in his best interest.

This is a great segway into the definition of "Dad." Dads come in all different forms, types, relationships and can be interchangeable for almost anyone providing support that uplifts positive change and growth. When my father wasn't around, coaches became father figures to me including men in the community that taught me fundamentals of manhood. When my father wasn't around, men in the community would hire me and my brother to pickup leaves. It probably was one of the worst jobs I've ever experienced but it built character and work ethic that I wouldn't trade for the world. There is a village that becomes available to instill the lessons children need to learn and the role of "dad"

can often be spread throughout the village to ensure children learn fundamentals of life. This concept also applies when the dad is around. Everyone is limited on the amount of information we know. If someone excels in a certain area, send the child to exceed your own understanding as the future depends on our children being smarter and more skilled than us.

As a child, no one couldn't tell me that my father wasn't the best in the world and guess what, that's my perspective. If you measured or quantified the value of our relationship, there would be large gaps in his presence, missed games and events, missed birthdays, missed growth and bonding opportunities. Yet, my father was still the best thing that could have ever happened to me. How could this be, the heart doesn't measure value in the way our minds do. Love is blind and that's what makes love beautiful, innocent and cherished. Without love, we would be robots, incapable of forgiving or giving someone an opportunity to succeed. If we were robotic in our heart, we would leave a baby that didn't learn to walk fast enough or talk. Sometimes the greatest lessons on earth is experiencing life.

JoJo will get to a point where he seeks information and understanding for himself and he would approach his father asking, why didn't he make an effort to be in his life. His Father would more than likely respond, your parents didn't allow me to be a part of your life and pushed me out. JoJo can possibly develop resentment due to our actions, even if we felt it was in his best interest.

JoJo will get to a point where he seeks information and understanding for himself and he would approach his father asking, why didn't he make an effort to be in his life. His Father would more than likely respond, your parents didn't allow me to be a part of your life and pushed me out. JoJo can possibly develop resentment due to our actions, even if we felt it was in his best interest.

This is a great segway into the definition of "Dad." Dads come in all different forms, types, relationships and can be interchangeable for almost anyone providing support that uplifts positive change and growth. When my father wasn't around, coaches became father figures to me including men in the community that taught me fundamentals of manhood. When my father wasn't around, men in the community would hire me and my brother to pickup leaves. It probably was one of the worst jobs I've ever experienced but it built character and work ethic that I wouldn't trade for the world. There is a village that becomes available to instill the lessons children need to learn and the role of "dad" can often be spread throughout the village to ensure children learn fundamentals of life. This concept also applies when the dad is around. Everyone is limited on the amount of information we know. If someone excels in a certain area, send the child to exceed your own understanding as the future depends on our children being smarter and more skilled than us.

As a child, no one couldn't tell me that my father wasn't the best in the world and guess what, that's my perspective. If you measured or quantified the value of our relationship, there would be large gaps in his presence, missed games and events, missed birthdays, missed growth and bonding opportunities. Yet, my father was still the best thing that could have ever happened to me. How could this be, the heart doesn't measure value in the way our minds do. Love is blind and that's what makes love beautiful, innocent and cherished. Without love, we would be robots, incapable of forgiving or giving someone an opportunity to succeed. If we were robotic in our heart, we would leave a baby that didn't learn to walk fast enough or talk. Sometimes the greatest lessons on earth is experiencing life.

JoJo will get to a point where he seeks information and understanding for himself and he would approach his father asking, why didn't he make an effort to be in his life. His Father would more than likely respond, your parents didn't allow me to be a part of your life and pushed me out. JoJo can possibly develop

resentment due to our actions, even if we felt it was in his best interest.

JoJo will get to a point where he seeks information and understanding for himself and he would approach his father asking, why didn't he make an effort to be in his life. His Father would more than likely respond, your parents didn't allow me to be a part of your life and pushed me out. JoJo can possibly develop resentment due to our actions, even if we felt it was in his best interest.

This is a great segway into the definition of "Dad." Dads come in all different forms, types, relationships and can be interchangeable for almost anyone providing support that uplifts positive change and growth. When my father wasn't around, coaches became father figures to me including men in the community that taught me fundamentals of manhood. When my father wasn't around, men in the community would hire me and my brother to pickup leaves. It probably was one of the worst jobs I've ever experienced but it built character and work ethic that I wouldn't trade for the world. There is a village that becomes available to instill the lessons children need to learn and the role of "dad" can often be spread throughout the village to ensure children learn fundamentals of life. This concept also applies when the dad is around. Everyone is limited on the amount of information we know. If someone excels in a certain area, send the child to exceed your own understanding as the future depends on our children being smarter and more skilled than us.

As a child, no one couldn't tell me that my father wasn't the best in the world and guess what, that's my perspective. If you measured or quantified the value of our relationship, there would be large gaps in his presence, missed games and events, missed birthdays, missed growth and bonding opportunities. Yet, my father was still the best thing that could have ever happened to me. How could this be, the heart doesn't measure value in the way our minds do. Love is blind and that's what makes love beautiful, innocent and cherished. Without love, we would be robots, incapable of forgiving or giving someone an opportunity to succeed. If we were robotic in our heart, we would leave a baby that didn't learn to walk fast enough or talk. Sometimes the greatest lessons on earth is experiencing life.

JoJo will get to a point where he seeks information and understanding for himself and he would approach his father asking, why didn't he make an effort to be in his life. His Father would more than likely respond, your parents didn't allow me to be a part of your life and pushed me out. JoJo can possibly develop resentment due to our actions, even if we felt it was in his best interest.

JoJo will get to a point where he seeks information and understanding for himself and he would approach his father asking, why didn't he make an effort to be in his life. His Father would more than likely respond, your parents didn't allow me to be a part of your life and pushed me out. JoJo can possibly develop resentment due to our actions, even if we felt it was in his best interest.

This is a great segway into the definition of "Dad." Dads come in all different forms, types, relationships and can be interchangeable for almost anyone providing support that uplifts positive change and growth. When my father wasn't around, coaches became father figures to me including men in the community that taught me fundamentals of manhood. When my father wasn't around, men in the community would hire me and my brother to pickup leaves. It probably was one of the worst jobs I've ever experienced but it built character and work ethic that I wouldn't trade for the world. There is a village that becomes available to instill the lessons children need to learn and the role of "dad" can often be spread throughout the village to ensure children learn fundamentals of life. This concept also applies when the dad is around. Everyone is limited on the amount of information we know. If someone excels in a certain area, send the child to exceed your own understanding as the future depends on our children being smarter and more skilled than us.

As a child, no one couldn't tell me that my father wasn't the best in the world and guess what, that's my perspective. If you measured or quantified the value of our relationship, there would be large gaps in his presence, missed games and events, missed birthdays, missed growth and bonding opportunities. Yet, my father was still the best thing that could have ever happened to me. How could this be, the heart doesn't measure value in the way our minds do. Love is blind and that's what makes love beautiful, innocent and cherished. Without love, we would be robots, incapable of forgiving or giving someone an opportunity to succeed. If we were robotic in our heart, we would leave a baby that didn't learn to walk fast enough or talk. Sometimes the greatest lessons on earth is experiencing life.

JoJo will get to a point where he seeks information and understanding for himself and he would approach his father asking, why didn't he make an effort to be in his life. His Father would more than likely respond, your parents didn't allow me to be a part of your life and pushed me out. JoJo can possibly develop resentment due to our actions, even if we felt it was in his best interest.

JoJo will get to a point where he seeks information and understanding for himself and he would approach his father asking, why didn't he make an effort to be in his life. His Father would more than likely respond, your parents didn't allow me to be a part of your life and pushed me out. JoJo can possibly develop resentment due to our actions, even if we felt it was in his best interest.

This is a great segway into the definition of "Dad." Dads come in all different forms, types, relationships and can be interchangeable for almost anyone providing support that uplifts positive change and growth. When my father wasn't around, coaches became father figures to me including men in the community that taught me fundamentals of manhood. When my father wasn't around, men in the community would hire me and my brother to pickup leaves. It probably was one of the worst jobs I've ever

experienced but it built character and work ethic that I wouldn't trade for the world. There is a village that becomes available to instill the lessons children need to learn and the role of "dad" can often be spread throughout the village to ensure children learn fundamentals of life. This concept also applies when the dad is around. Everyone is limited on the amount of information we know. If someone excels in a certain area, send the child to exceed your own understanding as the future depends on our children being smarter and more skilled than us.

This is a great segway into the definition of "Dad." Dads come in all different forms, types, relationships and can be interchangeable for almost anyone providing support that uplifts positive change and growth. When my father wasn't around, coaches became father figures to me including men in the community that taught me fundamentals of manhood. When my father wasn't around, men in the community would hire me and my brother to pickup leaves. It probably was one of the worst jobs I've ever experienced but it built character and work ethic that I wouldn't trade for the world. There is a village that becomes available to instill the lessons children need to learn and the role of "dad" can often be spread throughout the village to ensure children learn fundamentals of life. This concept also applies when the dad is around. Everyone is limited on the amount of information we know. If someone excels in a certain area, send the child to exceed your own understanding as the future depends on our children being smarter and more skilled than us.

As a child, no one couldn't tell me that my father wasn't the best in the world and guess what, that's my perspective. If you measured or quantified the value of our relationship, there would be large gaps in his presence, missed games and events, missed birthdays, missed growth and bonding opportunities. Yet, my father was still the best thing that could have ever happened to me. How could this be, the heart doesn't measure value in the way our minds do. Love is blind and that's what makes love beautiful, innocent and cherished. Without love, we would be robots, incapable of forgiving or giving someone an opportunity to succeed. If we were robotic in our heart, we would leave a baby that didn't learn to walk fast enough or talk. Sometimes the greatest lessons on earth is experiencing life.

JoJo will get to a point where he seeks information and understanding for himself and he would approach his father asking, why didn't he make an effort to be in his life. His Father would more than likely respond, your parents didn't allow me to be a part of your life and pushed me out. JoJo can possibly develop resentment due to our actions, even if we felt it was in his best interest.